# Weekly Assessments

Mc
Graw
Hill
Education

**www.mheonline.com/readingwonders**

Send all inquiries to:
McGraw-Hill Education
Two Penn Plaza
New York, New York 10121

ISBN: 978-0-07-679530-7
MHID: 0-07-679530-6

Printed in the United States of America.

1 2 3 4 5 6 7 8 9 RHR 20 19 18 17 16 15
A

# Table of Contents

# Table of Contents– Cont'd.

# Teacher Introduction

# Weekly Assessments

The *Weekly Assessments* component is an integral part of the complete assessment program aligned with *Reading Wonders* and state standards.

## Purpose of *Weekly Assessments*

*Weekly Assessments* offers the opportunity to monitor student progress in a steady and structured manner while providing formative assessment data. As students complete each week of the reading program, they will be assessed on their understanding of key instructional content. The results of the assessments can be used to inform subsequent instruction.

The results of *Weekly Assessments* provide a status of current achievement in relation to student progress through the curriculum.

## Focus of *Weekly Assessments*

The focus of *Weekly Assessments* is on two key areas of English Language Arts—Reading and Language. Students will read two selections each week and respond to items focusing on Comprehension Skills and Vocabulary Strategies. These items assess the ability to access meaning from the text and demonstrate understanding of unknown and multiple-meaning words and phrases.

## Administering *Weekly Assessments*

Each weekly assessment should be administered once the instruction for the specific week is completed. Make copies of the weekly assessment for the class. You will need one copy of the Answer Key page for each student taking the assessment. The scoring table at the bottom of the Answer Key provides a place to list student scores. The accumulated data from each weekly assessment charts student progress and underscores strengths and weaknesses.

After each student has a copy of the assessment, provide a version of the following directions: **Say:** *Write your name and the date on the question pages for this assessment.* (When students are finished, continue with the directions.) *You will read two selections and answer questions about them. Read each selection and the questions that follow it carefully. For the multiple-choice items, completely fill in the circle next to the correct answer. For items that require a written response, write that response clearly in the space provided. For the constructed response item, write your response on the lines provided. When you have completed the assessment, put your pencil down and turn the pages over. You may begin now.*

Answer procedural questions during the assessment, but do not provide any assistance on the items or selections. After the class has completed the assessment, ask students to verify that their names and the date are written on the necessary pages.

# Teacher Introduction

# Overview of *Weekly Assessments*

Each weekly assessment is comprised of the following

- 2 "Cold Read" selections
- 10 items assessing Comprehension Skills and Vocabulary Strategies
- 1 constructed response item assessing Comprehension and the ability to write across texts

## Reading Selections

Each weekly assessment features two selections on which the assessment items are based. (In instances where poetry is used, multiple poems may be set as a selection.) The selections reflect the unit theme and/or weekly Essential Question to support the focus of the classroom instruction. Because the weekly assessments have been composed to assess student application of the skills rather than genre or genre knowledge, selections are not always the same genre as the reading selections in the Literature Anthology or RWW.

Selections increase in complexity as the school year progresses to mirror the rigor of reading materials students encounter in the classroom. The Lexile goal by unit is as follows— Unit 1: 830L; Unit 2: 866L; Unit 3: 902L; Unit 4: 938L; Unit 5: 974L; and Unit 6: 1010L.

## Assessment Items

Weekly assessments feature the following item types—selected response (SR), multiple selected response (MSR), evidence-based selected response (EBSR), constructed response (CR), technology-enhanced constructed response (TECR), and extended constructed response (ECR). (Please note that the print versions of TECR items are available in this component; the full functionality of the items is available only through the online assessment.) This variety of item types provides multiple methods of assessing student understanding, allows for deeper investigation into skills and strategies, and provides students an opportunity to become familiar with the kinds of questions they will encounter in next generation assessments, both consortia-related and state-mandated.

## Comprehension Items

Each selection is followed by items that assess student understanding of the text through the use of Comprehension Skills—both that week's Comprehension Skill focus and a review Comprehension Skill. The review skill is taken from a week as near as possible to the current week and aligns with the instruction.

## Vocabulary Items

Each selection is followed by items that ask students to demonstrate the ability to uncover the meanings of unknown and multiple-meaning words and phrases using Vocabulary Strategies.

## Comprehension—Extended Constructed Response

At the close of each weekly assessment is a constructed response item that provides students the opportunity to craft a written response that shows their critical thinking skills and allows them to support an opinion/position by using text evidence from one or both selections.

**NOTE:** Please consider this item as an optional assessment that allows students to show comprehension of a text in a more in-depth manner as they make connections between and within texts.

**Weekly Assessment** · Teacher Introduction

# Teacher Introduction

# Scoring *Weekly Assessments*

Items 1–10 are each worth two points, for a twenty-point assessment. Each part of a EBSR is worth 1 point; MSR and TECR items should be answered correctly in full, though you may choose to provide partial credit. If you decide to have students complete the constructed response, use the correct response parameters provided in the Answer Key along with the scoring rubric listed below to assign a score of 0 through 4.

## Score: 4
- The student understands the question/prompt and responds suitably using the appropriate text evidence from the selection or selections.
- The response is an acceptably complete answer to the question/prompt.
- The organization of the response is meaningful.
- The response stays on-topic; ideas are linked to one another with effective transitions.
- The response has correct spelling, grammar, usage, and mechanics, and it is written neatly and legibly.

## Score: 3
- The student understands the question/prompt and responds suitably using the appropriate text evidence from the selection or selections.
- The response is a somewhat complete answer to the question/prompt.
- The organization of the response is somewhat meaningful.
- The response maintains focus; ideas are linked to one another.
- The response has occasional errors in spelling, grammar, usage, and mechanics, and it is, for the most part, written neatly and legibly.

## Score: 2
- The student has partial understanding of the question/prompt and uses some text evidence.
- The response is an incomplete answer to the question/prompt.
- The organization of the response is weak.
- The writing is careless; contains extraneous information and ineffective transitions.
- The response requires effort to read easily.
- The response has noticeable errors in spelling, grammar, usage, and mechanics, and it is written somewhat neatly and legibly.

## Score: 1
- The student has minimal understanding of the question/prompt and uses little to no appropriate text evidence.
- The response is a barely acceptable answer to the question/prompt.
- The response lacks organization.
- The writing is erratic with little focus; ideas are not connected to each other.
- The response is difficult to follow.
- The response has frequent errors in spelling, grammar, usage, and mechanics, and it is written with borderline neatness and legibility.

## Score: 0
- The student fails to compose a response.
- If a response is attempted, it is inaccurate, meaningless, or completely irrelevant.
- The response may be written so poorly that it is neither legible nor understandable.

# Teacher Introduction

# Evaluating Scores

The primary focus of each weekly assessment is to evaluate student progress toward mastery of previously-taught skills and strategies.

The expectation is for students to score 80% or higher on the assessment as a whole. Within this score, the expectation is for students to score 75% or higher on the items assessing Comprehension Skills; score 75% or higher on the items assessing the particular week's Vocabulary Strategy; and "3" or higher on the extended constructed response, if assigned.

For students who do not meet these benchmarks, assign appropriate lessons from the Tier 2 online PDFs. Refer to the weekly "Progress Monitoring" spreads in the Teacher's Editions of *Wonders* for specific lessons.

The Answer Keys in *Weekly Assessments* have been constructed to provide the information you need to aid your understanding of student performance, as well as individualized instructional and intervention needs. Further metadata is available in the online versions of the assessment, including specific test claims and targets.

This column lists the instructional content for the week that is assessed in each item.

| Question | Correct Answer | Content Focus | CCSS | Complexity |
|----------|----------------|---------------|------|------------|

This column lists alignment for each assessment item.

This column lists the Depth of Knowledge associated with each item.

| Question | Correct Answer | Content Focus | CCSS | Complexity |
|----------|----------------|---------------|------|------------|
| 7 | B, E | Main Idea and Key Details | RI.5.2 | DOK 2 |
| 8 | D | Context Clues | L.5.4a | DOK 2 |
| 9A | C | Main Idea and Key Details | RI.5.2 | DOK 2 |
| 9B | B | Main Idea and Key Details/Text Evidence | RI.5.2/RI.5.1 | DOK 2 |

Although all items feature use of text evidence, this is explicitly mentioned in PART B EBSR items.

| | | | |
|---|---|---|---|
| Comprehension 1A, 1B, 4, 5, 6, 7A, 7B, 10 | /12 | | % |
| Vocabulary 2, 3A, 3B, 8, 9 | /8 | | % |
| Total Weekly Assessment Score | /20 | | % |

Scoring rows identify items associated with Reading and Language strands and allow for quick record keeping.

**Read the text "Maddie and the Homeless Pets" before answering Numbers 1 through 5.**

# Maddie and the Homeless Pets

Maddie lives in New Bern, a city near the coast in North Carolina. She likes living in New Bern except when a hurricane moves up the coast. Then she worries about what may happen to her home and family.

One day her school is closed for safety reasons because of an ominous weather forecast that a hurricane is on the way. The torrential rain of a hurricane often causes flooding. Almost ten inches of rain falls on North Carolina. The power is out for hours, but Maddie's family feels lucky. Their home is on high ground and isn't flooded. When the power is restored the next day, Maddie turns on the television for news of the storm. She hears that many dogs and cats got separated from their families and were found wandering around loose after the storm.

The reporter says, "Volunteers and the Humane Society have opened an emergency shelter for lost pets at the county fairgrounds. Anyone who had to leave a home and needs a safe place for a pet can bring it to the shelter to stay for now. The people at the shelter need help from the community and are requesting donations of pet food."

**GO ON →**

Because Maddie really cares about animals, she wants to help. She resolves to find a way. She wonders what she can do to make a difference. She might open a lemonade stand. Then she remembers she did that once. She sold a total of ten glasses of lemonade and made $2.50. It would not be enough to buy much food for the animals.

Next, Maddie thinks about asking her parents for money. Yet, asking them may not be a good idea. She has heard them talking about saving on expenses. Mom lost her job arranging flowers at the floral shop when it went out of business, and Dad's company cut his hours last week. Asking them for money is definitely not a good idea.

Finally, Maddie gets a good idea. Almost everyone likes pets and must feel sorry for the homeless ones. If she can convince her classmates to donate food, she might collect enough. Because she is artistic, Maddie decides to make a poster. At the top, it says, "Help the Pets." She adds a newspaper article about the emergency shelter. Then draws pictures of cats and dogs. She also gives some examples of kinds of pet food the shelter needs. In the garage, Maddie finds a big cardboard box, which she decorates with pictures of animals.

In the morning, Maddie takes her poster and cardboard box to school. She asks her teacher, Ms. Jones, if she can put them in the hall near the door to the room. Ms. Jones says, "This is a great poster and great idea!" She helps Maddie find the best place, so that they will be most visible. She suggests that Maddie make a card to deliver with the food so that all the students who collaborate to help the shelter can sign their names. Finally, Maddie ties three colorful balloons to the box to attract attention to the display.

After the first day, there are only four cans of cat and dog food in the box. On the next day, there are more cans and several bags of food. Maddie already needs to find another box to hold all the contributions.

On Saturday, Maddie's dad drives her to the shelter and helps her carry the boxes inside. The people at the shelter are delighted. Their supplies are unusually low because there are so many homeless pets. They invite Maddie to visit with the pets. She even gets to hold a kitten on her lap for a few minutes.

Driving home, Maddie has a new thought. Maybe she can find a permanent animal shelter that needs donations. It would be fun to have another food drive, especially if everyone pitches in to help.

**GO ON →**

**Now answer Numbers 1 through 5. Base your answers on "Maddie and the Homeless Pets."**

**1**  Read this sentence from the text.

One day her school is closed for safety reasons because of an <u>ominous</u> weather forecast that a hurricane is on the way.

What does <u>ominous</u> mean in the sentence above?

(A)  false

(B)  hopeful

(C)  possible

(D)  threatening

**2**  Read these sentences from the text.

The <u>torrential</u> rain of a hurricane often causes flooding. Almost ten inches of rain falls on North Carolina.

What does <u>torrential</u> mean in the sentence above?

(A)  gentle

(B)  heavy

(C)  unexpected

(D)  welcome

**GO ON →**

**3** This question has two parts. First, answer part A. Then, answer part B.

**Part A:** What is Maddie's first idea about how to help?

(A) Maddie wants to open an emergency shelter for lost pets.

(B) Maddie thinks about opening a lemonade stand.

(C) Maddie asks her parents for money.

(D) Maddie thinks about collecting food from her classmates.

**Part B:** Maddie then thinks that her first idea will not work. Which sentence **best** supports this conclusion?

(A) Her parents are looking to save money.

(B) She needs to convince classmates to give food.

(C) She only made $2.50 selling lemonade.

(D) Her father had his hours cut.

**4** What happens after Maddie decides to convince her classmates to donate pet food? Select **two** options.

(A) Her school is closed.

(B) Her home is flooded.

(C) Many dogs and cats were separated from their families.

(D) She finds a big cardboard box in the garage

(E) Her mom lost her job arranging flowers.

(F) She makes a poster.

**GO ON →**

**5** Look at each sentence below. Complete the graphic organizer with the sentences so that they appear in the sequence in which they occur.

Maddie decorates a cardboard box.

Maddie makes a poster.

Maddie ties a balloon to the box.

Maddie makes a card.

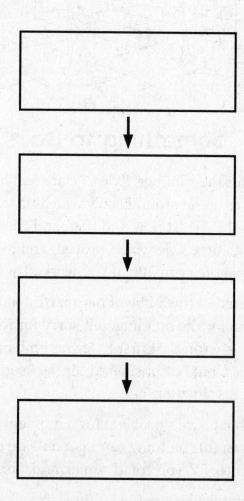

**Read the text "Something to Do" before answering Numbers 6 through 10.**

# Something to Do

Ever since school let out for the summer, Kyle O'Hara had been spending his afternoons being passive as he sat around lazily watching television shows. His dad would tell him to turn off the TV set now and then and tried to convince him to get up and do something. Each time Kyle would protest, and his dad would reply, "I'm not sorry for you; I'd have more sympathy if you worked as hard as I do!"

One afternoon Kyle lingered in the lobby of his apartment building, feeling sad. Mr. Jackson, the custodian for the building, felt sorry for Kyle, and stopped to chat and find out what was wrong. At first Kyle was embarrassed and didn't want to admit how bored he was. But he considered Mr. Jackson a friend after all, and finally he told him about his situation.

The custodian thought about Kyle's problem for a moment. "Well," he began, "several elderly residents in this building can't get outside much anymore. Maybe, instead of watching so much TV, you could run errands for them during the day."

"That's a great idea! It sounds like it could be fun!" exclaimed Kyle. Later that afternoon Kyle posted a flyer on the bulletin board in the lobby announcing his services and told his father about his plan. Several days went by, and he didn't receive a single phone call in response to the flyer. He found this bewildering and wondered what the problem was. In the flyer he had listed really low, reasonable prices for his services. One day Kyle left his apartment in search of Mr. Jackson. The custodian was delivering a package to a resident when he told him he had not received any phone calls.

**GO ON →**

"That's really strange," Mr. Jackson told Kyle. "I know that Mrs. Kim's dog needs exercise, but she can't take her on long walks every day. And Mr. Castelli has an injury, so it is hard for him to get around. He needs someone to pick up his prescriptions at the store. Maybe they just don't have money to spare to pay for someone else to do the jobs."

Kyle could hardly believe his ears. He simply couldn't comprehend that the people living in his building's luxurious apartments were struggling to make ends meet.

Mr. Jackson must have read his mind. He said, "Some of the residents have lived in this building a long time, and it's hard to pay rent that keeps going up when your income stays the same."

Kyle hesitated and then said, "You know, I'm mainly looking for something to keep me busy until school starts. The pay isn't the main consideration for me."

"It is for them, Kyle," Mr. Jackson said.

Kyle understood what he meant. He rode the elevator to the third floor, walked down the hall, and knocked on a door. After a few minutes, Mrs. Kim opened it. But before she could say anything, Kyle asked, "Would you like me to walk your dog for you? There's no charge, and it would be my pleasure."

A little, well-groomed dog peeked at Kyle from around the door and sniffed the air. "Oh, Kyle!" said Mrs. Kim. "That would be so nice. Trixie is a little shy, but she'll take to you quickly. And maybe in the future I can find a way to return the favor."

As Trixie bounded down the street ahead of Kyle, he made sure to keep a tight grip on her leash. When they rounded the corner, they passed Kyle's father, who was coming home from work. Without hesitation, he quickly gave Kyle a broad grin as he walked by.

**GO ON →**

**Now answer Numbers 6 through 10. Base your answers on "Something to Do."**

**6** This question has two parts. First, answer part A. Then, answer part B.

**Part A:** Read this sentence from the text.

Ever since school let out for the summer, Kyle O'Hara had been spending his afternoons being <u>passive</u> as he sat around lazily watching television shows.

What does <u>passive</u> mean in the sentence above?

(A) busy

(B) naughty

(C) inactive

(D) considerate

**Part B:** Which word or phrase from the text **best** supports your answer in part A?

(A) summer

(B) spending

(C) sat around

(D) school let out

**7** Read this sentence from the text.

"I'm not sorry for you; I'd have more <u>sympathy</u> if you worked as hard as I do."

What does <u>sympathy</u> mean in the sentence above?

(A) understanding

(B) anger

(C) happiness

(D) regret

**GO ON →**

**8** What happens before Mr. Jackson tells Kyle that he could run errands for the residents? Select **two** options.

(A) Kyle decides that he is mainly looking for something to do rather than a paid job

(B) Kyle walks Mrs. Kim's dog.

(C) Mr. Jackson stops to talk to Kyle to find out what is wrong.

(D) Mrs. Kim tells Kyle that in the future she may be able to find a way to return the favor.

(E) Kyle passed his father on the street.

(F) Mr. Jackson tells Kyle that some residents can't get out much.

**9** Read this sentence from the text.

He found this <u>bewildering</u> and wondered what the problem was.

What does <u>bewildering</u> mean in the sentence above?

(A) amusing

(B) confusing

(C) embarrassing

(D) exciting

**GO ON →**

**10** Identify what happens **before** Kyle decides that pay is not the main consideration and write it in Column A. Identify what happens **after** he decides that pay is not the main consideration and write it in Column B.

Mr. Jackson tells Kyle that he could run errands for people.

Kyle offers to walk Mrs. Kim's dog for her for no charge.

Kyle learns that some people may not have enough money.

Kyle posted a flyer on the bulletin board in the lobby.

| Column A | Column B |
|----------|----------|
|          |          |
|          |          |
|          |          |

   **Weekly Assessment** · Unit 1, Week 1

Name: _____  Date: _____

**11** In the texts "Maddie and the Homeless Pets" and "Something to Do," how do
the characters achieve their goals? Explain the ways in which Maddie and Kyle
are similar. Use clear text evidence in your response.

_____

_____

_____

_____

_____

_____

_____

_____

_____

_____

_____

_____

_____

# Answer Key

| Question | Correct Answer | Content Focus | CCSS | Complexity |
|---|---|---|---|---|
| 1 | D | Context Clues: Sentence Clues | L.5.4 | DOK 2 |
| 2 | B | Context Clues: Sentence Clues | L.5.4 | DOK 2 |
| 3A | B | Character, Setting, Plot: Sequence | RL.3.3 | DOK 1 |
| 3B | C | Character, Setting, Plot: Sequence/ Text Evidence | RL.3.3/ RL.5.1 | DOK 1 |
| 4 | D,F | Character, Setting, Plot: Sequence | RL.3.3 | DOK 1 |
| 5 | see below | Character, Setting, Plot: Sequence | RL.3.3 | DOK 1 |
| 6A | C | Context Clues: Sentence Clues | L.5.4 | DOK 2 |
| 6B | C | Context Clues: Sentence Clues/ Text Evidence | L.5.4/ RL.5.1 | DOK 2 |
| 7 | A | Context Clues: Sentence Clues | L.5.4 | DOK 2 |
| 8 | C,F | Character, Setting, Plot: Sequence | RL.3.3 | DOK 1 |
| 9 | B | Context Clues: Sentence Clues | L.5.4 | DOK 2 |
| 10 | see below | Character, Setting, Plot: Sequence | RL.3.3 | DOK 1 |
| 11 | see below | Writing About Text | W.5.9a | DOK 4 |

| | | |
|---|---|---|
| **Comprehension** 3A, 3B, 4, 5, 8, 10 | /10 | % |
| **Vocabulary** 1, 2, 6A, 6B, 7, 9 | /10 | % |
| **Total Weekly Assessment Score** | /20 | % |

**5** Students should complete the grahic organizer as follows:
- Maddie makes a poster.
- Maddie decorates a cardboard box.
- Maddie makes a card.
- Maddie ties a balloon to the box.

**10** Students sort the sentences as follows:
- Column A: Mr. Jackson tells Kyle about errands; Kyle learns people might not have money.
- Column B: Kyle offers to walk the dog; Kyle posted a flyer.

**11** To receive full credit for the response, the following information should be included: Maddie and Kyle both figure out ways to help others in need. Maddie delivers food to the shelter to help the pets, and Kyle offers to run errands for no charge to help his neighbors.

**Read the text "On the Trail" before answering Numbers 1 through 5.**

# On the Trail

My name is Luis. Two weeks ago on Saturday, my friend Justin and I were biking along Riverside Trail. The ride along the trail was so peaceful and quiet that Justin and I had barely spoken to one another at all. Then, to my surprise, all at once Justin shouted, "There's something sparkling under those bushes. Let's see what it is!"

We got off our bikes, parked them beside the trail where they would be out of the way, and started searching under the bushes. Justin and I took the opportunity to cool off with a few sips of cold water, when I spotted something bright shining under the foliage and exclaimed, "Oh my gosh! It's a wallet with jewels on it." I went over the the spot, brushed away a few leaves, picked it up, and we saw that the wallet had sparkling imitation jewels.

"We should try to find the owner, so let's see if there is some form of identification inside," I said. "This wallet must be something of great value to someone, and we should try to return it."

After looking inside all the interior pockets of the wallet, we found three photographs, some money, and a library card for Mary Johnson. Justin said, "We can try to find Mary Johnson's phone number on the Internet."

**GO ON →**

We headed for the computer at Justin's house and searched for "Johnson" in a directory for our town. We found eight *Mary Johnsons* and two *M. Johnsons*. There were just too many *Mary* and *M. Johnsons* to complete a successful search. Justin, in a sad and defeated voice asked, "Should we throw in the towel?"

I said, "No, we shouldn't give up; we have only started to look. We could start calling, but what if she lives in another town and only comes here to bike, or what if she has an unlisted number? We should look for other clues first, in order to narrow down the possibilities."

Next, we examined the snapshots that had been carefully preserved inside the wallet. One was very old, and another was of a boy about two years old with "William, 2011" written on the back. The third showed a girl about seven in front of Mount Rushmore, and "Annalee, 2011" was written on the back.

Justin guessed, "William and Annalee might be Mary Johnson's children. On Monday, we could see if she goes to our school. But that's a long time for Mary Johnson to wait for her wallet, so let's look for other clues."

We went through the wallet again and found, tucked in back, an appointment card for an eye examination at a mall in town. The appointment was for two o'clock—that same day! I said, "If we want this plan to succeed, we have to get to the mall before two o'clock, and we have no time to lose."

Justin said, "My mom probably will drive us. I'll ask her."

So that is how we got to the mall at exactly three minutes before two. We hurried into the waiting room at the doctor's office. Almost immediately a worried-looking woman came in. She said, "I have a two o'clock appointment. My name is Mary Johnson."

Justin and I introduced ourselves and showed her the wallet. As soon as Mr. Johnson saw her wallet, the concerned look left her face and her eyes lit up. She smiled at us and said, "What a relief! I have been so upset all day. I have been beside myself!"

Mrs. Johnson thanked us repeatedly. She was elated to have back her money and the photos of her children and great-grandparents.

After we explained where we found the wallet, she said, "I took the children for a bike ride this morning. William was in a cart that I attach to my bike. He must have found the wallet in my bag and tossed it from the cart."

She added, "You two deserve a reward" and handed each of us five dollars. It was worth missing the rest of our Saturday bike ride, and it was fun using clues to solve the problem!

**GO ON →**

**Now answer Numbers 1 through 5. Base your answers on "On the Trail."**

**1** Read this sentence from the text.

Then, to my surprise, <u>all at once</u>, Justin shouted, "There's something sparkling under those bushes."

What does the idiom "all at once" mean?

(A) fearfully

(B) happily

(C) loudly

(D) suddenly

**2** In paragraph 5 of the text, what does the idiom "thrown in the towel" mean?

(A) start calling

(B) ask for help

(C) decide to quit

(D) toss the wallet

**GO ON →**

**3** What reasons does Luis mention for giving up up the plan to call the owner of the wallet? Select **two** choices.

(A) There is not enough time.

(B) There are too many M. or Mary Johnsons

(C) They would rather finish the bike ride.

(D) They decide to keep the wallet.

(E) She may have an unlisted number.

(F) They could not use the Internet.

**4** This question has two parts. First, answer part A. Then, answer part B.

**Part A:** How do Justin and Luis solve the main problem in the text?

(A) They search around in the bushes.

(B) They return the wallet.

(C) They ask Justin's mother for a ride.

(D) They look for "Johnson" in a directory.

**Part B:** Which sentence from the text **best** supports your answer to Part A?

(A) "She smiled at us and said, 'What a relief!'"

(B) "I went over the the spot, brushed away a few leaves, picked it up, and we saw that the wallet had sparkling imitation jewels."

(C) "We should look for other clues first, in order to narrow down the possibilities."

(D) "Justin said, 'My mom probably will drive us.'"

**GO ON →**

**5** Write the letter of the clue from the list below in Column A if it helped solve the problem. If it did not help, write the letter of the clue in Column B.

**A** an appointment card

**B** sparkling imitation jewels

**C** money

**D** a directory

**E** a library card

| Column A | Column B |
|----------|----------|
|          |          |
|          |          |
|          |          |
|          |          |

**GO ON →**

**Read the text "A Saturday Morning Adventure" before answering Numbers 6 through 10.**

# A Saturday Morning Adventure

"These new video games are really cool!" Rasheed exclaims as he sets down his backpack and sits next to Jami in front of the new widescreen monitor that just had been installed in the game room. He and his friend Jami get together to play video games almost every weekend. Without a doubt, their favorites are the ones that take place in outer space. They put on spacesuits and climb into a spaceship; they check the fuel supplies and life-support systems. Then they blast off to begin an unbelievable adventure in which they journey across the galaxy to fight battles against other spaceships and dangerous creatures from outer space. The games are very realistic because the graphics are so amazingly detailed. They are also challenging and require Rasheed and Jami to use their problem-solving skills.

On this particular Saturday, the two kids are playing "Space Attack." In this game, blazing hot meteors zoom from outer space through Earth's atmosphere. Attack ships try to collide with the players' ship to disable it and leave Earth undefended. Players try to avoid the meteors, destroy the attack ships, and defend their home planet from a terrible fate. The game requires quick thinking and lightning-fast reflexes. This is one of Jami and Rasheed's favorite games, as it presents unusual challenges and is never the same game twice. They like joining forces and coming up with new ideas to overcome whatever obstacles arise.

"Look," Jami says. "I just reversed course. Maybe if we go the opposite direction, our spaceship won't get smashed by a meteor or an attack ship. It's good we have our spacesuits on. If our ship gets hit by a meteor, we can just float through space until a robot rescues us. I think we're lucky that this is just a game and not real life."

**GO ON →**

"To continue playing for an additional minute, please pay 100 more tokens at this time," says the robot running the game room. "Otherwise, your game will terminate in 10 seconds."

Rasheed hands the tokens to the robot, which looks almost like a real person. "These new robots can do anything," he says. "They're so much better than the outdated ones of the last century because there have been so many advances in the design of robot technology."

"You can say that again," says Jami. "My grandpa told me stories about the robots that people used when he was young. They couldn't walk as well as they do now. They were jerky, and they talked funny. My grandpa makes me laugh when he imitates them."

Suddenly, Rasheed screams, "Look out! The attack ship just rotated and turned around. Now it's headed right toward us! We'd better do something quick and take evasive actions!"

Realizing that the ball is in her court, Jami calmly pulls up on her joystick. "This is easy," she says, laughing. But her laugh is cut off by the gasp she makes when the joystick fails to respond. "This joystick is broken!" she yells. "The attack ship is gaining on us quickly; we'll never evade it!"

Rasheed rushes over and adjusts the game dials to increase their speed, but the ship still can't move fast enough to avoid the attack. With a sickening thud, the attack ship hits theirs. Jami is thrown forward and then staggers back into her seat. Suddenly, Rasheed is thrust into the air and finds himself dangling from the ceiling. He holds tightly onto his seat belt, and sways slowly back and forth.

Something has gone wrong in the game. But Jami doesn't get bent out of shape. She carefully checks to make sure that her spacesuit hasn't been damaged. Next, she asks Rasheed if he's hurt and tells him to examine his spacesuit. Then, she calmly takes out her tools. She repairs the joystick and adjusts the dials. "All fixed," she announces. She calmly steers the ship into the dock.

When the kids climb out of their spaceship, Rasheed makes a suggestion. "Maybe next week we can go laser-bowling instead of playing video games. After all, variety is the spice of life!"

"No way!" Jami says. "Compared to these new video games, laser-bowling is way too boring!"

**GO ON →**

**Now answer Numbers 6 through 10. Base your answers on "A Saturday Mornig Adventure."**

**6** Read these sentences from the text.

Something has gone wrong in the game. But Jami doesn't get <u>bent out of shape</u>. She carefully checks to make sure that her spacesuit hasn't been damaged.

What does the idiom "bent out of shape" mean?

(A) to start

(B) to laugh

(C) to be upset

(D) to be happy

**GO ON →**

**7** Which statement **best** compares how Jami and Rasheed each react to the problem?

(A) Jami stays calm, and Rasheed panics.

(B) Jami panics, and Rasheed stays calm.

(C) Both children react with excitement; then Jami reacts practically.

(D) Both children react with excitement; then Rasheed reacts practically.

**8** Read these sentences from the text.

"Maybe next week we can go laser-bowling instead of playing video games. After all, variety is the spice of life!"

What does the idiom "variety is the spice of life" mean?

(A) Trying new things in life is difficult

(B) Doing different things makes life interesting.

(C) Only strange people try new things.

(D) You're better off if you always do the same thing.

**GO ON →**

**9** How do Jami and Rasheed attempt to solve their problem? Select **two** choices.

(A) Rasheed hands the tokens to the robot.

(B) Rasheed adjusts the game dials.

(C) Jami tells Rasheed to examine his spacesuit.

(D) Rasheed holds tightly onto his seat belt.

(E) Jami repairs the joystick.

(F) Jami and Rasheed climb out of their spaceship.

**10** Read the sentences and phrases listed below. Select the sentences and phrases that are idioms.

(A) You can say that again.

(B) the ball is in her court

(C) blazing hot meteors

(D) We'd better do something quick.

(E) you game will terminate

(F) Without a doubt.

Name: _____ Date: _____

**Now answer Number 11. Base your answer on "On the Trail" and "A Saturday Morning Adventure."**

**11** How are Luis and Jami similar in the way they solve problems? Provide text evidence in your explanation.

_____

_____

_____

_____

_____

_____

_____

_____

_____

_____

_____

_____

_____

_____

# Answer Key

Name: _____

| Question | Correct Answer | Content Focus | CCSS | Complexity |
|:---:|:---:|:---:|:---:|:---:|
| 1 | D | Idioms | L.5.5b | DOK 2 |
| 2 | C | Idioms | L.5.5b | DOK 2 |
| 3 | B, E | Character, Setting, Plot: Problem and Solution | RL.4.3 | DOK 2 |
| 4A | B | Character, Setting, Plot: Problem and Solution | RL.4.3 | DOK 2 |
| 4B | A | Character, Setting, Plot: Problem and Solution/Text Evidence | RL.4.3/ RL.5.1 | DOK 2 |
| 5 | see below | Character, Setting, Plot: Problem and Solution | RL.4.3 | DOK 2 |
| 6 | C | Idioms | L.5.5b | DOK 2 |
| 7 | C | Character, Setting, Plot: Problem and Solution | RL.4.3 | DOK 2 |
| 8 | B | Idioms | L.5.5b | DOK 2 |
| 9 | B, E | Character, Setting, Plot: Problem and Solution | RL.4.3 | DOK 2 |
| 10 | A, B, F | Idioms | L.5.5b | DOK 2 |
| 11 | see below | Writing About Text | W.5.9a | DOK 4 |

| | | |
|:---|:---:|:---:|
| **Comprehension** 3, 4A, 4B, 5, 7, 9 | /10 | % |
| **Vocabulary** 1, 2, 6, 8, 10 | /10 | % |
| **Total Weekly Assessment Score** | /20 | % |

**5** Students sort the items correctly as follows:
- Column A: A, E
- Column B: B, C, D

**11** To receive full credit for the response, the following information should be included: Both Luis and Jamie remain calm. Luis patiently follows clues in an orderly way to find the owner of a wallet. Jami follows steps in an orderly way to bring the ship safely into dock.

**Read the text "The Burrowing Owl" before answering Numbers 1 through 5.**

# The Burrowing Owl

Have you ever been lucky enough to see an owl in the wild? If it was small and brown with white spots, it could have been a burrowing owl. These owls are found across North America. People often see them at nature preserves or in conservation areas. These wilderness areas are protected natural habitats that are maintained for the benefit of wildlife and the general public, as well. Therefore, these are safe places for the owls to live.

Burrowing owls make an interesting sound. This is a good way to identify them. The sound is similar to someone saying "coo-whooh." It is a quavering, chattering sound that is unlike any other. If a ranger were to conduct a nature walk to show visitors around a nature preserve and teach them about wildlife, he or she might tell them to listen for this sound.

If you were looking for the owl, you would search for a bird with brown feathers that are dappled with white marks. The owl has long legs and bright yellow eyes above curved bills. These sharp beaks vary in color and may be dark yellow or gray. It also has white markings over its eyes. Unlike some other owls, the burrowing owl does not have tufted ears, or ears with upright feathers.

Among the smallest of owls, the burrowing owl is eight to ten inches tall and weighs only about eight ounces. Most owls are night creatures, but burrowing owls are active during the day. People might spot one on the ground or perched in a tree along a nature trail.

**GO ON →**

The burrowing owl got its name because of how it makes its home. This owl does not build a nest in a tree. Instead, it nests in holes and small tunnels under the ground, called burrows, that are no longer used by prairie dogs and ground squirrels. The owl makes the burrows its home after the other animals abandon them. For this reason, burrowing owls are found in grasslands and prairies from southwestern Canada all the way to Mexico. People in the western United States and in Florida often see them. In the western states, the owl moves from place to place, but in Florida the birds do not.

If you are lucky enough to see a burrowing owl, remember to stay away from it. If a human comes near, then the owl may become upset or excited. It will make loud noises and bob its head. The burrowing owl has even been known to dive at people. Some people have heard a frightened owl hissing at them like a snake.

It is important to protect the burrowing owl so that it does not become endangered. In several states, the burrowing owl is listed as a "species of special concern." That does not mean it is endangered yet. If it continues to decrease in numbers though, it will be at risk of becoming extinct in the future. There are fewer burrowing owls today than there were in the past. This is because of a few different reasons. Cities have spread across land once used for farming. As a result, the owls lose their habitats, or natural homes. In areas used for farming, large machines can destroy owl nests in the ground.

People can help save the burrowing owl in a few different ways. They can talk to their family members and friends and tell them not to destroy any burrows they find on their property that the owls may use as their nesting area. People can put up signs to indicate that owls are nesting in the area. They can also encourage others not to use pesticides in gardens to kill insects because burrowing owls eat insects and may be affected by the chemicals. People can spread the word about burrowing owls if they post flyers that inform others about this special bird. We can all do our part to make sure the burrowing owl is here to stay for many years to come.

**GO ON →**

**1** This question has two parts. First, answer part A. Then, answer part B.

**Part A:** In the first paragraph of the text, what reason does the author give to explain why burrowing owls may be living in a nature preserve?

(A) It is a safe place for the owl to live.

(B) Some people are lucky to see the owl.

(C) The owl is found across North America.

(D) The owl is small and brown with white spots.

**Part B:** Which word from the first paragraph **best** supports your answer for Part A?

(A) lucky

(B) nature

(C) habitats

(D) protected

**2** Read this sentence from the text.

It will make loud noises and <u>bob</u> its head.

Which definition of <u>bob</u> fits the sentence above?

(A) to fluff up feathers

(B) to move up and down

(C) to float

(D) to grab at objects with the mouth

**GO ON →**

**3** This question has two parts. First, answer part A. Then, answer part B.

**Part A:** Read this sentence from the text.

If a ranger were to <u>conduct</u> a nature walk to show visitors around a nature preserve and teach them about wildlife, he or she might tell them to listen for this sound.

Which definition fits the homograph <u>conduct</u> in the sentence above?

(A) act a certain way

(B) lead as a guide

(C) transmit energy

(D) direct an orchestra or choir

**Part B:** Which phrase from the sentence **best** supports your answer for Part A?

(A) "show visitors around"

(B) "listen for this sound"

(C) "nature walk"

(D) "nature preserve"

**4** How does the author help the reader understand why burrowing owls are a *species of special concern*? Select **two** options.

(A) by placing signs around their nests

(B) by leading people through nature preserves

(C) by comparing its interesting sound to other owls

(D) by stating that there are fewer burrowing owls today

(E) by explaining that their burrows are important to the environment

(F) by mentioning its loss of habitats

**GO ON →**

**5** Write **all** the items below that may cause the burrowing owl to become endangered in the box.

- large farming machines

- ground squirrels

- pesticides

- rangers

- conservation areas

- expanding cities

**GO ON →**

**Read the text "Wild in the City" before answering Numbers 6 through 10.**

# Wild in the City

As cities grow, people expand into areas where wild animals live. They build their homes, create transportation routes and other structures that are necessary for city life. Well-lit retail locations, restaurants and recreation facilities draw a lot of traffic. When this happens, some animals move away from the lights and noise of city life, but many of them adapt, or change to fit their new situation. For this reason the number of wild animals living in cities is growing.

Wild animals live in parks, on golf courses, and even in backyards. They find food in trash. They drink the water in ponds. They often make homes in hollow logs, trees, or shrubs because they need a safe place to sleep and to raise their young.

## Rats
Throughout history, rats have been city dwellers. Black and brown rats traveled from Asia to Europe. They came to North America on ships. Brown rats live throughout the United States, but most black rats live near the Gulf Coast. They can gnaw through wood and metal. For this reason, they make homes in basements and sewers. They are not picky about food and will eat both plants and animals. Rats live in big groups. Sometimes they band together to attack their prey.

## Birds
Many birds live in cities too. One is the nighthawk. These birds nest on flat roofs. They eat insects and dive to catch them. Another is the pigeon. Many pigeons were brought to America as pets. Others were used to carry messages. Later they were freed, and the numbers grew rapidly. In cities, they pick through trash for food. They nest on windowsills, the ledges of tall buildings, or under eaves. They are often seen in large flocks in the heart of a big city like Chicago or New York.

**GO ON →**

**Weekly Assessment · Unit 1, Week 3**

### Coyotes

Once coyotes lived in grasslands, mountains, and open prairies. As cities grew and took over open land, coyotes learned to live near people. Since they are intelligent, they adapted well to city life. In some cities, the numbers of coyotes are growing at an alarming rate because they are good at finding food in trash. Like rats, they will eat almost anything. People should be alert when coyotes are reported in a neighborhood since they have attacked small animals. Coyotes may attack a human to protect their pups. People can hear them whine at night. They also growl and bark when threatened.

### Bears

Surprisingly, black bears now wander in built-up neighborhoods. It is not unusual to see video or read a story in the news about one of these wild animals making an unexpected appearance in a residential area. In an area of New Jersey only forty miles from New York City, they are seen regularly. Like other city animals that adapt well, black bears eat almost anything. They are found in the United States, Canada, and Mexico. While many people fear them because of their large size, they usually do not attack unless threatened. In most areas, the number of bears is either growing or remaining steady. However, the status of the Louisiana black bear and the Florida black bear is "threatened species."

### Cougars

At one time, cougars lived across North America. Also called *mountain lion*, *puma*, and *panther*, the cougar is a large cat. They are active mostly at night when they stalk their prey. Cities spread into the foothills of mountains in the West. As a result, cougars adapted and now live in neighborhoods near wooded areas and canyons. Many live in Colorado and California. Their numbers are growing rapidly in the western states.

Although people enjoy watching wildlife, they often feel threatened by it. In order to protect themselves, people should be careful not to leave out food. They should put garbage in a covered can. They should also keep dogs and cats indoors most of the time.

**GO ON →**

**Now answer Numbers 6 through 10. Base your answers on "Wild in the City."**

**6** Which statements **best** explain why the number of wild animals living in North American cities is growing? Select **all** that apply.

(A) Cities expand into areas where wild animals live.

(B) Many cities provide protected habitats for wild animals.

(C) Wild animals move away from the light and noise of city life.

(D) Many wild animals adapt to their situation.

(E) They can find food and water in or near cities.

(F) Wild animals need cities to raise their young.

**7** Read this sentence from the text.

In cities, they <u>pick</u> through trash for food.

Which definition fits <u>pick</u> in the sentence above?

(A) to follow after

(B) to break up into small pieces

(C) to proceed carefully

(D) to choose and pull from

**GO ON →**

**8** This question has two parts. First, answer part A. Then, answer part B.

**Part A:** Read this sentence from the text.

Since they are intelligent, they adapted <u>well</u> to city life.

Which definition fits <u>well</u> in the sentence above?

(A) in a safe way

(B) in a familiar way

(C) to a high degree

(D) an underground source of water

**Part B:** Which sentence from the text **best** supports your answer to part A?

(A) "Once coyotes lived in grasslands, mountains, and open prairies."

(B) "In some cities, the numbers of coyotes are growing at an alarming rate."

(C) "Like rats, they will eat almost anything."

(D) "Coyotes may attack a human to protect their pups."

**GO ON →**

Name: _____ Date: _____

**9** Which word from the text that means a short, sharp sound is a homograph for the word defined below?

the tough, outer covering of a tree

(A) bark

(B) gnaw

(C) growl

(D) whine

**10** Draw a line form the animal to the characteristic that has enabled it to live in cities.

rats                    make their home in basements and sewers

birds                   live in neighborhoods near wooded areas
                        and canyons

coyotes                 nest on buildings

cougars                 good at finding food in trash

STOP

Name: _____ Date: _____

**Now answer Number 11. Base your answer on "The Burrowing Owl" and "Wild in the City."**

**11** How do the ways that people use land affect the wildlife in "The Burrowing Owl" and "Wild in the City"? Use text evidence in your response.

_____

_____

_____

_____

_____

_____

_____

_____

_____

_____

_____

_____

_____

_____

_____

# Answer Key

Name: _____

| Question | Correct Answer | Content Focus | CCSS | Complexity |
|----------|----------------|---------------|------|------------|
| 1A | A | Text Structure: Cause and Effect | RI.5.3 | DOK 2 |
| 1B | D | Text Structure: Cause and Effect/ Text Evidence | RI.5.3/ RI.5.1 | DOK 2 |
| 2 | B | Homographs | L.5.5c | DOK 1 |
| 3A | B | Homographs | L.5.5c | DOK 1 |
| 3B | A | Homographs/Text Evidence | L.5.5c/ RI.5.1 | DOK 1 |
| 4 | D, F | Text Structure: Cause and Effect | RI.5.3 | DOK 2 |
| 5 | see below | Text Structure: Cause and Effect | RI.5.3 | DOK 2 |
| 6 | A, D, E | Text Structure: Cause and Effect | RI.5.3 | DOK 2 |
| 7 | D | Homographs | L.5.5c | DOK 1 |
| 8A | C | Homographs | L.5.5c | DOK 1 |
| 8B | B | Homographs/Text Evidence | L.5.5c/ RI.5.1 | DOK 1 |
| 9 | A | Homographs | L.5.5c | DOK 1 |
| 10 | see below | Text Structure: Cause and Effect | RI.5.3 | DOK 2 |
| 11 | see below | Writing About Text | W.5.9b | DOK 4 |

| | | | |
|---|---|---|---|
| **Comprehension** 1A, 1B, 4–6, 10 | | /10 | % |
| **Vocabulary** 2, 3A, 3B, 7, 8A, 8B, 9 | | /10 | % |
| **Total Weekly Assessment Score** | | /20 | % |

**5**
- large farming machines
- pesticides
- expanding cities

**10** Students match the items correctly as follows:
- rats: basements and sewers
- birds: nest on buildings
- coyotes: good at finding food
- cougars: live in neighborhoods

**11** In "the Burrowing Owl, "burrowing owls lost their habitats and their numbers decreased because people developed land. Birds, coyotes, black bears, and cougars in "Wild in the City" adapted when they lost their habitats, and the effect is that now people and wild animals live in cities across America.

**Read the text "Bicycles, Then and Now" before answering Numbers 1 through 5.**

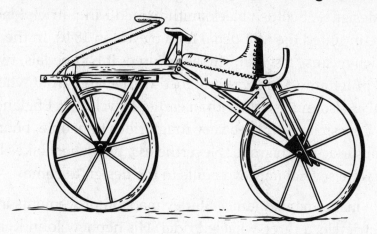

# Bicycles, Then and Now

Sometimes, today's modern products have a very remarkable resemblance to things that were invented a long time ago. Today's balance bikes for children look remarkably like an early model by Baron Karl von Drais Sauerbrun. Bicycles began with this German inventor. A biography of him reveals that he was born in 1785, worked for his uncle, was given the title of professor of mechanics, and even worked on an early version of the typewriter. The bicycle-like contraption he made in 1817 had two wheels and was made of wood. It had a seat but no pedals. To move, the rider had to use his legs to push the machine forward. It weighed about 50 pounds! It must have been like riding a very heavy scooter.

Drais exhibited his running machine in 1818 and was given a patent for it the same year. In Germany, it was called the *Draisine*. In France, it became the *Draisienne*, and in England, it was called a hobby horse. For a number of reasons, this early bicycle was popular only a short time. Riders' boots wore out too quickly. It was hard to steer. There were very few evenly paved streets, and many roads were often rutted, sunken and full of holes at this time in history. Therefore, it was even more difficult to balance on these new inventions. Riders who decided to use sidewalks instead were crashing into pedestrians and causing injuries.

**GO ON →**

The history of bicycles shows the chronological order of events as inventors kept improving the design. A Scottish blacksmith named Kirkpatrick Macmillan is believed to have invented the foot pedal for a bicycle in 1840. In the 1860s, the velocipede, which means "fast feet," first appeared. It had pedals, two wooden wheels, and an iron frame. One was designed with a large front wheel and a small back wheel. It was also much lighter than earlier bicycles. In England, it given the nickname "the Boneshaker." It gave very rough rides to people, bouncing and rattling over the surface of the road. Nevertheless, two-wheel bikes became popular. There were several improvements to the design to come.

A British bicycle maker named James Starley made improvements in both the bicycle and the tricycle, a three-wheeled rider. His nephew John Kemp Starley worked for him, and the younger man, who had extraordinary mechanical skills, built the Rover in 1885. It is often described as the first modern bicycle. It had two 26-inch wheels, ball bearings and rubber tires for a smooth and more stable ride. It had a chain drive, as well. The chain drive had been used before on other machines, but not on bicycles. The chain that transfers power from one part of the machine to another. On bicycles, it distributes power between the two wheels.

In the United States, an amazing number of bicycles were produced in the late 1800s. This spectacular growth led to more inventions. During the 1900s, the wooden wheels were replaced with air-filled rubber wheels, which made for a much more comfortable ride. Other improvements followed, including the invention of two-speed and three-speed bicycles, which improved efficiency.

The market for bicycles decreased because cars and motorcycles became a faster and more convenient way to get around. As a result, in the 1920s through the 1950s, children became the primary target market for bicycle manufacturers, and many bicycles were designed to appeal to a America's youth. In the 1960s and 1970s, adults grew more interested in fitness and preserving the environment. Then the industry began growing again. Some bikes were made especially for racing, and others for rough, mountainous land.

Balance bikes are a recent bicycle development These are amazingly similar to Baron Karl von Draise Sauerbrun's *Draisine*. Sometimes balance bikes are called push bikes or run bikes. Like the old-fashioned *Draisine*, they have no pedals. Children start by walking the bike and pushing it along, then they can glide along. After the young children gain confidence, they can move on to bikes with pedals.

**GO ON →**

**Base your answers on "Bicycles, Then and Now."**

**1** Read this sentence from the text.

A <u>biography</u> of him reveals that he was born in 1785, worked for his uncle, was given the title of professor of mechanics, and even worked on an early version of the typewriter.

The word <u>biography</u> comes from two Greek roots, *bio* and *graph*. *Bio* means "life." The root *graph* can mean "write." What does <u>biography</u> mean?

(A) spending a lifetime reading

(B) a story told with illustrations and photographs

(C) a written story about a person's life

(D) something written in two sections

**2** This question has two parts. First, answer part A. Then, answer part B.

**Part A:** How does the author help the reader understand that the design of bicycles improved through the years?

(A) by comparing different bicycles

(B) by telling the sequence of improvements

(C) by contrasting the Draisine and balance bikes

(D) by explaining what caused people to start using cars

**Part B:** Which sentence from the text **best** supports your answer in Part A?

(A) "It must have been like riding a very heavy scooter."

(B) "For a number of reasons, this early bicycle was popular only a short time."

(C) "Riders who decided to use sidewalks instead were crashing into pedestrians and causing injuries."

(D) "The history of bicycles shows the chronological order of events as inventors kept improving the design."

**GO ON →**

**3** This question has two parts. First, answer part A. Then, answer part B.

**Part A:** The root of chronological is *chron*, meaning "time." What does chronological mean?

Ⓐ importance

Ⓑ interest

Ⓒ when things happen

Ⓓ why things happen

**Part B:** Which phrase from the text **best** supports your answer to Part A?

Ⓐ "order of events"

Ⓑ "much lighter"

Ⓒ "became popular"

Ⓓ "improving the design"

**4** What **two** events led to the increase in the bicycle's popularity in the 1960s and 1970s ?

Ⓐ Rubber wheels replaced wooden ones.

Ⓑ Bicyles were built with chain drives.

Ⓒ People became interested in fitness.

Ⓓ Cars became a convenient way to get around.

Ⓔ There was concern for the environment.

Ⓕ Balance bikes were made for children.

**GO ON →**

**5** Write the text into the graphic organizer so that events appear in the sequence in which they occur.

The chain drive was added to the bicycle.

Children became the primary market for bicycles.

Kirkpatrick Macmillan invented the pedal for the bike.

Air-filled rubber tires replaced wooden wheels.

Drais received a patent for his running machine.

Cars became a convenient way to get around.

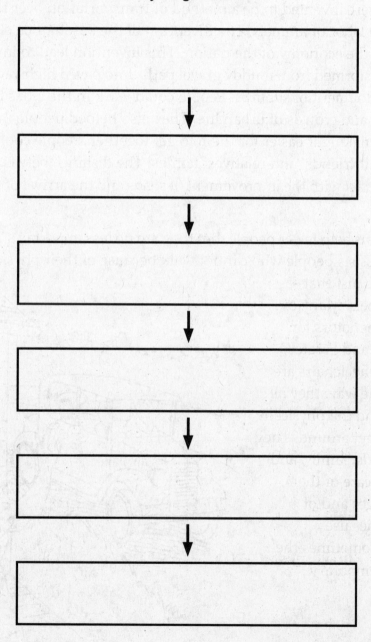

**GO ON →**

Read the text "Living Better, Thanks to Inventions!" before answering Numbers 6 through 10.

# Living Better, Thanks to Inventions!

Inventions improve people's lives in many ways. People use inventions every day but they never pause to consider who made them or how they were made. Life would be quite different without the many inventions we have come to rely on.

## Automobiles

Automobiles were invented to be a method of transportation over land that did not require the labor of animals. The invention of the automobile changed the landscape and the economy of the nation. This invention lead to improved roads. They were transformed from muddy gravel paths into paved highways. Automobiles led to the development of suburbs. People could work in the cities but live away from the noise and crowds of urban life. They also helped people interact with each other by making it easier for them to get together. People could drive to their jobs and to their friends' and relatives' homes. The distance between places seemed to contract with the improvement of roads and the arrival of the automobile.

## Wheelchairs

Other inventions help fewer people, but they are no less important. The wheelchair, for example, assists people who cannot walk because of their physical condition.

A wheelchair is just that—a chair with wheels. Many of them also have motors for independence and greater mobility. All wheelchairs are the same in one way: they all help injured and the physically challenged to get around. They also help friends, family, and others to take care of them. People of all ages and of different abilities use wheelchairs. Sometimes the need is only temporary.

**GO ON →**

## Telephones

The next time someone gets in touch with you with a message through your telephone, express your thanks to Alexander Graham Bell. He was the man who invented this device. Bell first tested his machine on March 10, 1876. It quickly became popular. His invention opened up a whole new way of communicating. It allowed people to communicate over distances almost instantaneously. Before telephones, most people communicated by writing and by sending letters through the mail. If you can consider such a thing, contemplate what life would be like without telephones.

## Computers

Today, computers perform many of the tasks that only telephones could once do. Much of the work of transmitting phone calls, and thousands of other tasks, is done by computers. Computers are everywhere in the United States, and the country could not function without them. We depend upon them to perform many necessary tasks. If computers suddenly shut down, businesses, digital banking and shopping, and travel by airplane and car would halt. Most people would be without energy and communication. Lights would go out, and things could get out of control.

## Photography

An invention that has changed our way of seeing ourselves and the world around us is photography. Early photographs captured images of people and events in history. In traditional photography, the light leaves an impression on surfaces coated with chemicals. People used to paint and draw pictures to record people and events in history. Photographs allow us to observe what was there, rather than an artist's interpretation in pencil, paint, or ink. Today we take digital photographs to record the events of our daily lives as well as the extraordinary events that we witness.

## Taking It Forward

Many inventions have been combined in order to make life easier. Cell phones have built-in cameras so people can take photographs on the go. Using a computer and the Internet, people can share those photographs with friends and family right away. People can use their computers to have video telephone calls. They can talk with friends, family, and coworkers around the world as if they were sitting across the table from them. Without the invention of the photograph, telephone, or computer, these tasks would not be possible.

Because these inventions are so familiar to us and we use them every day, they may seem simple. Actually, they are not simple at all, but they have simplified and improved our lives.

**GO ON →**

Name: _____ Date: _____

**Base your answers on "Living Better, Thanks to Inventions!."**

**6** The origin of the word automobile comes from the Greek roots *auto* meaning "self" and *mobile* meaning "capable of moving." What does this suggests about the automobile?

- Ⓐ It can only be used by one driver in a family.
- Ⓑ It is available to any independent person.
- Ⓒ It is large enough to move smoothly on bad roads.
- Ⓓ It can move without being pulled by an animal.

**7** The word photography comes from Greek roots meaning "light" and "draw, write." What is the meaning of photography?

- Ⓐ making a picture using light
- Ⓑ making a picture using paints
- Ⓒ making a picture using a laser
- Ⓓ making a picture using a pencil

**GO ON →**

**8** Read this sentence from the text.

If you can imagine such a thing, contemplate what life would be like without <u>telephones</u>.

<u>Telephone</u> comes from the Greek *tele* meaning "far off" and *phon* meaning "sound." What is the meaning of <u>telephone</u>?

**(A)** a device for sounds that are close by

**(B)** a device that helps sound travel a long way

**(C)** a device for very loud sounds

**(D)** a device that helps sound travel quietly

**9** This question has two parts. First, answer part A. Then, answer part B.

**Part A:** Why does the author write about the telephone before the computer?

**(A)** to show that communication was impossible before the invention of the telephone

**(B)** to argue that Alexander Graham Bell would have invented the computer

**(C)** to point out that computers were invented after the telephone

**(D)** to prove that the telephone was a more important invention

**Part B:** Which sentence **best** supports your answer to Part A?

**(A)** "Today, computers perform many of the tasks that only telephones could once do."

**(B)** "Most people would be without energy and communication."

**(C)** "People can use their computers to have video telephone calls."

**(D)** "Many inventions have been combined in order to make life easier."

**GO ON →**

Name: _____ Date: _____

**10** The inventions in this text came before changes to how people lived. Draw a line between the invention and the change that followed.

automobiles                          independence for those who
                                     could not walk

wheelchairs                          digital banking

telephones                           instantaneous communication

computers                            record images of world events

photography                          development of the suburbs

**Now answer Number 11. Base your answer on "Bicycles, Then and Now" and "Living Better, Thanks to Inventions."**

**11** Use text evidence from "Bicycles, Then and Now" and "Living Better, Thanks to Inventions!" to show how the sequence in each text helps to explain the authors' ideas.

_____

_____

_____

_____

_____

_____

_____

_____

_____

_____

_____

_____

_____

_____

_____

_____

# Answer Key

Name: _____

| Question | Correct Answer | Content Focus | CCSS | Complexity |
|:---:|:---:|:---:|:---:|:---:|
| 1 | C | Greek Roots | L.5.4b | DOK 1 |
| 2A | B | Text Structure: Sequence | RI.5.5 | DOK 2 |
| 2B | D | Text Structure: Sequence/Text Evidence | RI.5.5/ RI.5.1 | DOK 2 |
| 3A | C | Greek Roots | L.5.4b | DOK 1 |
| 3B | A | Greek Roots/Text Evidence | L.5.4b/ RI.5.1 | DOK 1 |
| 4 | C, E | Text Structure: Sequence | RI.5.5 | DOK 2 |
| 5 | see below | Text Structure: Sequence | RI.5.5 | DOK 2 |
| 6 | D | Greek Roots | L.5.4b | DOK 1 |
| 7 | A | Greek Roots | L.5.4b | DOK 1 |
| 8 | B | Greek Roots | L.5.4b | DOK 1 |
| 9A | C | Text Structure: Sequence | RI.5.5 | DOK 2 |
| 9B | A | Text Structure: Sequence/Text Evidence | RI.5.5/ RI.5.1 | DOK 2 |
| 10 | see below | Text Structure: Sequence | RI.5.5 | DOK 2 |
| 11 | see below | Writing About Text | W.5.9b | DOK 4 |

| | | |
|:---|:---:|:---:|
| **Comprehension** 2A, 2B, 4, 5, 9A, 9B, 10 | /10 | % |
| **Vocabulary** 1, 3A, 3B, 6, 7, 8 | /10 | % |
| **Total Weekly Assessment Score** | /20 | % |

**5** Correct sequence, first to last:
Drais received a patent for his running machine. Kirkpatrick Macmillan invented the foot pedal for the bike. The chain drive was added to the bicycle. Air-filled rubber tires replaced wooden wheels. Cars became a convenient way to get around. Children became the primary market for bicycles.

**10** Students match the items correctly as follows:
- automobiles: development of suburbs
- wheelchairs: independence for those who could not walk
- telephones: instantaneous communication
- computers: digital banking
- photography: record images of world events

**11** In "Bicycles, Then and Now," the author tells about the history of bicycles in chronological order. This helps the reader understand how bicycles slowly changed over a period of time. In "Living Better, Thanks to Inventions!" the author presents earlier invetions first and more modern inventions later to show how inventions progressed over time and were eventually combined to create our newest inventions today.

**Read the text "Smart Cars for Clean Air" before answering Numbers 1 through 5.**

# Smart Cars for Clean Air

Cars take us to school, work, and anywhere else we want to go. We rely on cars to get us to a wide variety of places...and fast! There is no doubt that the automobile has made our lives easier in a number of ways. But there is also no doubt that cars are slowly killing our planet. It is clearly time to rethink how we use cars in our daily lives.

While cars have given us the convenience of easy travel, the pollution they cause is a serious consequence. The Environmental Protection Agency, or EPA, says that gas-powered vehicles such as cars, trucks, and bulldozers are the main cause of air pollution in large cities in the United States. In fact, they cause air pollution throughout the entire world. Environmentalists have talked about the dangerous effects of air pollution for decades. One way to stop this pollution is to buy hybrids. These are cars that run on both gasoline and electricity.

Vehicles are responsible for air pollution because they run on a fossil fuel. When this fuel is burned in the process of running a car, pollutants are released into the air. As long ago as the 1900s, some experts said that burning gasoline in automobiles could damage the environment. Studies show that we are now paying the price with our quality of air today. Those experts were right!

**GO ON →**

Hybrid vehicles currently coexist with gas-powered cars. Hybrids could significantly reduce the pollution we release into the air. It is true that these cars still use gasoline. But they certainly use a lot less of it. Hybrid cars utilize a combination of gasoline and electricity. One specific type of hybrid is a particularly good choice. This is because this type relies mostly on electric power. An electric motor turns the car's wheels, and gasoline is used to generate the electricity. The car is recharged by plugging it into an electrical outlet.

If everyone were required to drive a hybrid car, the amount of pollution from the use of gas would be hugely reduced. The government could make it a precondition that all new car owners buy hybrids. Drivers would not be allowed to buy cars that only run on gasoline. We would also be conserving our fossil fuels for other machines.

Hybrid cars have other advantages, too. Since they use gasoline, they can be refueled at any gas station so that the driver is not left stranded if there is nowhere to charge the battery. They are a great choice because they do not require a huge lifestyle change for drivers. They are very similar to the gas-powered cars that we are so familiar with. They just have one major difference: they greatly improve the environment in which we live.

Hybrid cars are the best choice to reduce air pollution around the world. Transcontinental car manufacturers should be required to stop selling the gas-guzzling cars of yesterday. Instead, they should sell hybrids at reasonable prices so that all people will be able to buy them. The future of our planet is at stake!

**GO ON →**

**Now answer Numbers 1 through 5. Base your answers on "Smart Cars for Clean Air."**

**1** This question has two parts. First answer part A. Then answer part B.

**Part A:** What reason from the text best supports the author's point of view that cars make life better for people?

(A) Hybrid cars can run on gasoline.

(B) Burning gasoline damages the environment.

(C) Hybrid cars do not require a lifestyle change.

(D) We rely on cars to take us to a number of places.

**Part B:** What sentence from the text **best** supports your answer to Part A?

(A) "Cars take us to school, work, and anywhere else we want to go."

(B) "Hybrid cars are the best choice to reduce air pollution around the world."

(C) "While cars have given us the convenience of easy travel, the pollution they cause is a serious consequence."

(D) "But there is also no doubt that cars are slowly killing our planet."

**2** Read this sentence from the text.

Hybrid vehicles currently coexist with gas-powered cars.

What does coexist mean in the sentence above?

(A) exit

(B) pollute

(C) run both on gas and electricity

(D) are used together

**GO ON →**

**3** Which statements support the author's point of view on transportation? Select **two** options.

(A) It is not necessary to change driving habits.

(B) Cars are a convenient way to travel.

(C) People rarely use their cars

(D) Cars are more important than the prblems of pollution.

(E) Hybrid cars would reduce pollution.

(F) Gasoline is used to generate electricity.

**4** Read these sentences from the text.

The government could make it a <u>precondition</u> that all new car owners buy hybrids. Drivers would not be allowed to buy cars that only run on gasoline.

Based on this sentence, you can tell the prefix *pre-* in precondition means

(A) after.

(B) against.

(C) before.

(D) wihout.

**GO ON →**

Name: _____ Date: _____

**5** Choose the sentences that are true for both gas-powered and hybrid vehicles.

(A) They are a convenient way to travel.

(B) They are responsible for air pollution because they run only on gasoline.

(C) They are recharged by plugging it into an electrical outlet.

(D) They can be refuled at any gas station.

(E) They are sold at reasonable prices.

(F) They could significantly reduce air pollution.

**GO ON →**

**Read the text "Fewer Cars for Clean Air" before answering Numbers 6 through 10.**

# Fewer Cars for Clean Air

Cars are a major part of most of our lives. People count on their cars to do the things they need to do every day. But there is a downside to having so many cars on the road. As gasoline is burned, it releases pollution and harmful gases into the air. These get trapped in our atmosphere and increase the temperature of Earth. As the temperature goes up, ice melts and ocean levels rise. This can create international problems for people who live on coastlines. Rising temperatures affect people, animals, and plants around the world.

The intake of polluted air can be harmful to people. If people were to burn less gasoline, there would be fewer carbon emissions from our cars. This in turn would create less air pollution. Public transportation is the solution to our air pollution problem. People need to stop using their cars and find other ways to get places.

Public transportation is the use of buses, trains, subways, ferries, and other vehicles meant to carry a group of passengers. The benefit of public transportation is that only one vehicle releases air pollutants. Consider if 50 people rode a bus instead of driving their cars. That would eliminate a lot of gasoline and emissions!

**GO ON →**

Public transportation has other benefits, too. If this mode of travel were put into effect everywhere in the United States, it could greatly improve traffic problems on the streets. It would also save people money that they would be spending at the gas pump. Having fewer cars on the road also reduces the use of fossil fuels that are slowly being used up. These fossil fuels are not renewable resources. We cannot create more fuel once it is all gone.

Some people have supported the use of electric or hybrid cars as an alternative to gas-powered cars, but I disagree. These vehicles still involve the use of gas in some cases. They are also expensive and are still being perfected. Public transportation has already been proven to work and to improve the quality of our environment.

Public transportation may require a slight change in lifestyle. But do not misjudge the amount of help it can do. Isn't it worth it to ride a train or bus when you are helping to keep the air you breathe as clean as possible? We owe it to the planet to try to protect and respect it. After all, Earth is the only home we have. Let's do our part to improve the world in which we live.

**GO ON →**

**Now answer Numbers 6 through 10. Base your answers on "Fewer Cars for Clean Air."**

**6** Which of the following sentences from the text supports the author's point of view? Select **three** options.

(A) "But there is a downside to having so many cars on the road."

(B) "People need to stop using their cars and find other ways to get places."

(C) "Public transportation is the use of buses, trains, subways ferries, and other vehicles meant to carry a group of passengers."

(D) "These fossil fules are not renewable resources."

(E) "Public transportation has already been proven to work and to improve the quality of our environment."

**7** Read this sentence from the text.

This can create dangerous <u>international</u> problems for people who live on coastlines.

*Inter* means "between." What are <u>international</u> problems?

(A) problems in one town

(B) problems in one city

(C) problems in at least two countries

(D) problems in a large country

**GO ON →**

**8** This question has two parts. First, answer part A. Then, answer part B.

**Part A:** According to the text, what is one effect of using public transportation?

(A) People would be happier.

(B) Public transportation can be cheaper.

(C) Public transportation is easier.

(D) People would get to their destinations faster.

**Part B:** Which sentence supports your answer to part A?

(A) "People count on their cars to do the things they need to do every day."

(B) "It would also save people money that they would be spending at the gas pump."

(C) "Public transportation may require a slight change of lifestyle."

(D) "Let's do our part to improve the world in which we live."

**GO ON →**

**9** Read these sentences from the text.

Public transportation may require a slight change in lifestyle. But do not misjudge the amount of help it can do. Isn't it worth it to ride a train or bus when you are helping to keep the air you breathe as clean as possible?

The prefix *mis-* in misjudge is a negative prefix. What dose it mean to misjudge?

(A) to think carefully about something

(B) to think correctly about something

(C) to think wrongly about something

(D) to think quickly about something

**10** Why does the author believe that hybrid cars are poor solutions? Select **two** options that **best** support the author's point of view.

(A) "Public transportation has other benfits, too."

(B) "Having fewer cars on the road also reduces the use of fossil fuels that are slowly being used up."

(C) "They are also expensive and are still being perfected."

(D) "As gasoline is burned, it releases dangerous pollution and harmful gases into the air."

(E) "These vehicles still involve the use of gas in some cases."

(F) "That would eliminate a lot of gasoline and emissions."

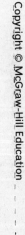

**Now answer Number 11. Base your answer on "Smart Cars for Clean Air" and "Fewer Cars for Clean Air."**

**11** Compare and contrast the points of view of the authors of "Smart Cars for Clean Air" and "Fewer Cars for Clean Air." Use text evidence from both texts to explain how the viewpoints are similar and different.

_____

_____

_____

_____

_____

_____

_____

_____

_____

_____

_____

_____

_____

_____

_____

| Question | Correct Answer | Content Focus | CCSS | Complexity |
|---|---|---|---|---|
| 1A | D | Author's Point of View | RI.6.6 | DOK 3 |
| 1B | A | Author's Point of View/ Text Evidence | RI.6.6/ RI.5.1 | DOK 3 |
| 2 | D | Greek and Latin Prefixes | L.5.4b | DOK 1 |
| 3 | B, E | Author's Point of View | RI.6.6 | DOK 3 |
| 4 | C | Greek and Latin Prefixes | L.5.4b | DOK 1 |
| 5 | A, D | Author's Point of View | RI.6.6 | DOK 3 |
| 6 | B, D, E | Author's Point of View | RI.6.6 | DOK 3 |
| 7 | C | Greek and Latin Prefixes | L.5.4b | DOK 1 |
| 8A | B | Author's Point of View | RI.6.6 | DOK 3 |
| 8B | B | Author's Point of View/ Text Evidence | RI.6.6/ RI.5.1 | DOK 3 |
| 9 | C | Greek and Latin Prefixes | L.5.4b | DOK 1 |
| 10 | C, E | Author's Point of View | RI.6.6 | DOK 3 |
| 11 | see below | Writing About Text | W.5.9b | DOK 3 |

| | | |
|---|---|---|
| **Comprehension** 1A, 1B, 3, 5, 6, 8A, 8B, 10 | /12 | % |
| **Vocabulary** 2, 4, 7, 9 | /8 | % |
| **Total Weekly Assessment Score** | /20 | % |

11 To receive full credit for the response, the following information should be included: Both authors believe that air pollution is a major problem that is due primarily to the use of gas-powered cars. Both authors believe that these cars should be replaced, but they disagree on how to reduce air pollution. The author of "Smart Cars for Clean Air" thanks that hybrids are the best way to cut back on polluting the air. The author of "Fewer Cars for Clean Air" thinks that cars should be replaced with public transportation to reduce emissions and the pollution that enters the air.

**Read the article "Compromise" before answering Numbers 1 through 5.**

# Compromise

In the year 1850, disagreement between the North and the South about slavery was growing. An earlier settlement called the Missouri Compromise had helped to solve the problem for some thirty years. As in any compromise, neither side was completely satisfied, but each got part of what it wanted. Then in 1849, California asked to join the Union as a free state. There were 15 slave states and 15 free states. Adding another free state would upset the balance.

Henry Clay was known as the "Great Compromiser." He worked to keep the states united. In 1849, Clay was elected to the U.S. Senate from Kentucky. As a senator, he wanted to find a way to solve the controversy (serious arguments) between the North and South. A number of issues needed to be resolved.

- The first was statehood for California. Congress was not likely to approve admission for another free state.

- The United States had been at war with Mexico, and as a result, the federal government got new territory. Should the territory allow slavery or not?

- Texas claimed that its territory extended to Santa Fe. The government disagreed; that is, it disputed Texas's right to expand into what is now New Mexico.

- Slaves were traded in Washington, D.C. Many believed that was wrong in the capital of the nation.

Clay presented his ideas in the Senate, hoping to keep the country united. Not everyone agreed with Clay's ideas, and a debate lasted for months.

Clay asked that California become a state, but Congress could not decide whether it would be free or slave. Clay proposed that the people living in a territory set up on land gained in the war with Mexico could decide the question of slavery for themselves. Also, the borders of Texas would not include any part of New Mexico. In return, Texas would be paid for the land in dispute. Slavery in the District of Columbia could not be ended without the people's consent. However, slaves could no longer be traded in the nation's capital. Laws would provide for the return of runaway slaves. Finally, Congress would have no power over the trading of slaves between slave states.

Months of debate in the Senate followed Clay's proposals. John C. Calhoun, Senator from South Carolina, was leader of the opposition. He wrote a response but was too ill to deliver it, so another senator read it for him. Clay's legislation was voted down, but then Daniel Webster, a senator from Massachusetts, and Stephen A. Douglas, a senator from Illinois, helped win approval for a compromise. Douglas later became famous for his debates with Abraham Lincoln.

The Compromise of 1850 included five acts of Congress. The laws covered the main issues that had come up because of California's request to become a free state. They were based on Clay's resolutions. California could join the Union as a free state. The settlers in the territories of New Mexico and Utah would be able to vote on whether they would allow slavery or not. Texas received ten million dollars. In return, Texas had to give up claims to disputed territories. The Fugitive Slave Law went into effect. Runaway slaves were to be returned if they were caught, but the slave trade ended in the District of Columbia.

The Compromise of 1850 solved the problem for a time, but conflicts soon grew again. A major point of contention, that is, a point that caused a great deal of argument, was the Fugitive Slave Act. Northerners believed it was too unfair to slaves. Many still helped slaves escape to Canada through the Underground Railroad. Because of the Fugitive Slave Law, another compromise was not possible. Eventually the Civil War broke out in 1861, and North and South fought in battle after battle until the war ended in 1865.

**GO ON →**

**Now answer Numbers 1 through 5. Base your answers on "Compromise."**

**1** This question has two parts. First, answer part A. Then, answer part B.

**Part A:** Why does the author examine the issue of slavery at the beginning of the article?

- (A) to discuss the rise of California as a major state
- (B) to show the conflict between states and territories
- (C) to discuss the effects of a labor shortage on farming
- (D) to show the growing division between the North and the South

**Part B:** Which sentence from the article **best** supports your answer in part A?

- (A) "An earlier settlement called the Missouri Compromise had helped to solve the problem for some thirty years."
- (B) "Then in 1849, California asked to join the Union as a free state."
- (C) "As a senator, he wanted to find a way to solve the controversy (serious arguments) between the North and South."
- (D) "The United States had been at war with Mexico, and as a result, the federal government got new territory."

**2** Read the sentence from the article.

As in any compromise, neither side was completely satisfied, but each got part of what it wanted.

What does compromise mean in the sentence above?

- (A) a promise to stand behind your word
- (B) both sides refuse to reach an agreement
- (C) something that gives hope of success in the future
- (D) both sides agree to give up something to solve a conflict

**GO ON →**

**3** How does the author help the reader understand Clay's difficulty in reaching a lasting compromise? Select **two** options.

Ⓐ by describing the election of Clay to the U.S. Senate

Ⓑ by explaining the actions of the Underground Railroad

Ⓒ by describing the argument about the Fugitive Slave Law

Ⓓ by explaining the dispute over the Missouri Compromise

Ⓔ by discussing the admission of New Mexico to the Union

Ⓕ by discussing the angry debate about California's borders

**4** Put the events in history in the correct sequence. Write each event in the correct section of the chart.

| | |
|---|---|
| **First** | |
| **Second** | |
| **Third** | |
| **Fourth** | |

**Events:**

Clay was elected to the Senate.

The Civil War broke out.

California became a state in the Union.

War broke out between the U.S. and Mexico.

**GO ON →**

**5** This question has two parts. First, answer part A. Then, answer part B.

**Part A:** Read the sentence from the article.

A major point of <u>contention</u>, that is, a point that caused a great deal of argument, was the Fugitive Slave Act.

What does <u>contention</u> mean in the sentence above?

(A) approval

(B) disagreement

(C) mistake

(D) unhappiness

**Part B:** Which word from the sentence restates what <u>contention</u> means?

(A) major

(B) deal

(C) argument

(D) fugitive

**GO ON →**

**Read the article "Democracy in the United States" before answering Numbers 6 through 10.**

# Democracy in the United States

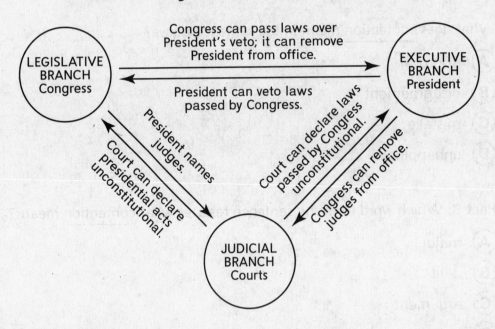

Before the United States became its own country, it was made up of 13 British colonies that were ruled by the king of England. Many colonists demanded a say in making the laws they had to follow. They didn't like the fact that a king had so much control over their lives. So the colonists decided to break away from England and form a new nation called the United States of America.

The United States is a democracy, which is a form of government. It is a government for the people. In a democracy, the people choose their leaders by voting. The leaders then share the responsibility of running the country. This prevents one person or group of people from having all of the power. Not all countries are democracies. In some, a king or queen has the lion's share of the power. Because others have little power, he or she can do almost anything. The people who wrote the Constitution of the United States set up a democracy because they wanted their government to be different. The Constitution is a written statement of the rules that the U.S. government must follow. Those who created it wanted every voter to have an equal voice in the decisions made by the government because it takes many people working together to make a government work well.

**GO ON →**

The U.S. government has three parts, or "branches." One is the executive branch, which includes the president and the cabinet. The president's cabinet is made up of people who advise the president. They help the president deal with problems in the country and in the world. The president and the cabinet members work together as a team to make important decisions and carry out the laws.

The legislative branch of government creates the laws. The main part of this branch is the Congress, which is made up of two groups of people that form the Senate and the House of Representatives. These people represent, or act for, the people in the states that elected them. Members of each group create ideas for laws. When an idea is written down to be presented, it is called a bill. The bill is discussed and may be changed in several or many ways. Finally, it is voted on. If it passes in one group, then it goes to the other and must also pass there. If it passes in the House of Representatives and the Senate, it goes to the president to be signed and become a law. Not all bills become laws.

The third branch of government is the judicial branch. It includes the Supreme Court, which has nine justices. These judges explain the laws if there are disagreements about them. They also may agree to hear arguments about a case decided in a lower court. To do their jobs, the judges must understand the Constitution. They decide how the laws of the Constitution apply to certain situations.

Though each branch of the government has its own leaders, these branches must work together to make a democracy work. Each branch of government must check the actions of the other two branches to prevent one branch from having too much power.

The U.S. government has survived for more than 200 years, but it takes more than good leaders for a democracy to last. Citizens must get involved in the government, too. In the United States, citizens may vote when they reach 18 years of age. Then they can help elect the country's leaders. They can vote for the president of the United States. They can also vote for leaders who represent them in Congress. People who take part affect the whole country. They have an impact on what happens in the United States.

**GO ON →**

**Now answer Numbers 6 through 10. Base your answers on "Democracy in the United States."**

**6** Read the sentences from the article.

In a <u>democracy</u>, the people choose their leaders by voting. The leaders then share the responsibility of running the country.

What does <u>democracy</u> mean in the sentences above?

(A) a government that makes laws

(B) a government that is permanent

(C) a government with a single leader

(D) a government created by the people

**7** Complete the sentence about the beginning of the article. Write the number of the correct phrase in each part of the sentence.

The author begins this article by referring to _____ in order to explain

_____.

> **Phrases:**
>
> 1 – the history of democracy in the Western world
>
> 2 – democracy's deep roots in American history
>
> 3 – the American colonists' break with England
>
> 4 – America's many different governments

**GO ON →**

**8** This question has two parts. First, answer part A. Then, answer part B.

**Part A:** Read the sentences from the article.

One is the executive branch, which includes the president and the <u>cabinet</u>. The president's cabinet is made up of people who advise the president.

What does <u>cabinet</u> mean in the sentences above?

Ⓐ a group of advisors

Ⓑ a group of citizens

Ⓒ a storage case

Ⓓ Congress

**Part B:** Which phrase from the sentence provides a definition of <u>cabinet</u>?

Ⓐ "the executive branch"

Ⓑ "includes the president"

Ⓒ "the president's cabinet is made up of"

Ⓓ "people who advise the president"

**GO ON →**

**9** This question has two parts. First, answer part A. Then, answer part B.

**Part A:** Why does each branch of government check the other branches?

(A) so that no single branch has too much power

(B) so that American citizens have a say in government

(C) so that the president cannot take control of the government

(D) so that powers are divided between the federal government and the states

**Part B:** Which sentence from the article supports your answer in part A?

(A) "Though each branch of the government has its own leaders, these branches must work together to make a democracy work."

(B) "Each branch of government must check the actions of the other two branches to prevent one branch from having too much power."

(C) "The U.S. government has survived for more than 200 years, but it takes more than good leaders for a democracy to last."

(D) "They can also vote for leaders who represent them in Congress."

**10** Why does the author end the article by discussing voting? Select **two** choices.

(A) to explain how government has changed through the years

(B) to show that people can have a voice in government

(C) to stress the importance of citizens' involvement

(D) to compare voting today with voting in the past

(E) to analyze how people voted in recent elections

(F) to list voting qualifications

**Now answer Number 11. Base your answer on "Compromise" and
"Democracy in the United States."**

**11** How do the authors of "Compromise" and "Democracy in the United States"
use the ideas of democracy to help readers understand how they can help solve
national problems? Support your answer with details from both texts.

_____

_____

_____

_____

_____

_____

_____

_____

_____

_____

_____

_____

| Question | Correct Answer | Content Focus | CCSS | Complexity |
|---|---|---|---|---|
| 1A | D | Text Structure: Problem and Solution | RI.5.3 | DOK 3 |
| 1B | C | Text Structure: Problem and Solution/ Text Evidence | RI.5.3/ RI.5.1 | DOK 3 |
| 2 | D | Context Clues: Definitions and Restatements | L.5.4a | DOK 2 |
| 3 | B, C | Text Structure: Problem and Solution | RI.5.3 | DOK 3 |
| 4 | see below | Sequence | RI.5.3 | DOK 2 |
| 5A | B | Context Clues: Definitions and Restatements | L.5.4a | DOK 2 |
| 5B | C | Context Clues: Definitions and Restatements/Text Evidence | L.5.4a/ RI.5.1 | DOK 2 |
| 6 | D | Context Clues: Definitions and Restatements | L.5.4a | DOK 2 |
| 7 | see below | Text Structure: Problem and Solution | RI.5.3 | DOK 3 |
| 8A | A | Context Clues: Definitions and Restatements | L.5.4a | DOK 2 |
| 8B | D | Context Clues: Definitions and Restatements/Text Evidence | L.5.4a/ RI.5.1 | DOK 2 |
| 9A | A | Text Structure: Problem and Solution | RI.5.3 | DOK 3 |
| 9B | B | Text Structure: Problem and Solution/ Text Evidence | RI.5.3/ RI.5.1 | DOK 3 |
| 10 | B, C | Text Structure: Problem and Solution | RI.5.3 | DOK 2 |
| 11 | see below | Writing About Text | W.5.9b | DOK 4 |

| | | | |
|---|---|---|---|
| **Comprehension** 1A, 1B, 3, 4, 7, 9A, 9B, 10 | | /12 | % |
| **Vocabulary** 2, 5A, 5B, 6, 8A, 8B | | /8 | % |
| **Total Weekly Assessment Score** | | /20 | % |

4 Students should complete the chart as follows:
- First: War broke out between the U.S. and Mexico.
- Second: Clay was elected to the Senate.
- Third: California became a state in the Union.
- Fourth: The Civil War broke out.

7 Students should write the numbers 3 and 2 to complete the sentence as follows:
- The author begins this article by referring to *the American colonists' break with England* in order to explain *democracy's deep roots in American history*.

11 To receive full credit for the response, the following information should be included: In "Compromise," conflict between states was temporarily solved in the Compromise of 1850 when each side gave up things to keep one nation. In "Democracy in the United States," the problem of creating a new nation was solved when a government of three power-sharing branches was formed.

**Read the passage "Yellowstone Adventure" before answering Numbers 1 through 5.**

# Yellowstone Adventure

"Hey, Olivia," says Jayden, "I overheard Mom and Dad planning a trip to Boise to see our grandparents."

"We have never been to Boise. Do you know where it is?" asks Olivia.

"It is in Idaho," says Jayden, "and I do not want to go because all my friends will be here this summer."

"It could be fun," Olivia disagrees.

That night, Mom talks about the car trip and asks Jayden and Olivia to do some research to learn about a national park they can visit along the way.

"Great!" Olivia says. She looks at maps, but Jayden is too busy. Olivia discovers they will go through South Dakota and Wyoming to get to Boise. Next, she looks up national parks on the Internet and finds four good possibilities. Two are in South Dakota: Wind Cave National Park and Badlands National Park. Grand Teton National Park is in Wyoming, and Yellowstone National Park is in Wyoming, with parts in Montana and Idaho.

Olivia does some more research and learns that if they want to see an unusual cave, they should stop at Wind Cave. For cliffs and wildflowers, Badlands National Park is the best choice, but to see forests and mountains with high peaks, they should stop at Grand Teton. Yellowstone has animals and waterfalls, and it is enormous.

She tells Jayden what she has found, and he says, "You are a walking encyclopedia! You choose because I really do not want to go anyway." Olivia chooses Yellowstone, and her parents agree.

Nothing much happens the first day on the road. Jayden says to Olivia, "Just as I predicted, this is going to be one boring trip."

On the second day of driving, Dad says, "We will make a stop at Wind Cave National Park since it is on the way."

**GO ON →**

They find a camping area for the night, and the next day take a tour of the cave. Olivia is fascinated by the formations of crystals on the walls and ceiling. The patterns are like the honeycombs where bees store honey. Mom says, "Outside, the wind is roaring like a lion, but inside here, it sounds like a purring kitten."

After two more days of driving, they get to Yellowstone. It is a huge park, with parts in three states. Dad suggests that Jayden and Olivia try the Junior Ranger Program, where they hike a trail and find a waterfall as loud as thunder. Jayden and Olivia test their skills in the Yellowstone Wildlife Olympics by moving like different animals that live in the park. Afterwards, they meet with a ranger who gives them badges. They are having a good time, but Jayden is not yet convinced about this trip.

The following day, the family is off to see Old Faithful. It is a geyser, a spout of hot spring water heated to boiling under the ground and forced into the air. It usually erupts about once every hour and a quarter. When he sees it, Jayden shouts, "Cool!"

They are exhausted from the hiking, and after a picnic dinner, they only want to sleep. First, however, they hang their leftover food in a bag high up in a tree. That's what the ranger has told them to do. During the night, Olivia awakens to a terrible, crashing sound. Suddenly, everyone is awake and frightened that a bear may cause them harm. Dad whispers, "We have to frighten that animal away, so let's sing as loud as we can." As they sing, Dad peeks out of the tent and says, "There are two raccoons running away."

Jayden stops singing and starts to guffaw. In between his howls of laughter, he says, "Our singing must have hurt their ears!" In the morning, they see that their empty cooler has been overturned. Jayden starts laughing again. "We could make a CD of ourselves singing," he says. "We could sell it to scare away animals. I can't wait to tell my friends. This is the greatest vacation ever!"

**GO ON →**

**Now answer Numbers 1 through 5. Base your answers on "Yellowstone Adventure."**

**1** Read the sentence from the passage.

She tells Jayden what she has found, and he says, "You are <u>a walking encyclopedia</u>!"

What does Jayden mean when he calls Olivia "a walking encyclopedia"?

(A) Olivia likes to read books.

(B) Olivia is not very interesting.

(C) Olivia spends a lot of time at the library.

(D) Olivia knows a lot of facts and information.

**2** How are Badlands National Park and Wind Cave different?

(A) Badlands has more cliffs and wildflowers.

(B) Wind Cave does not allow camping.

(C) Only Badlands is a national park.

(D) They are in different states.

**GO ON →**

**3** Read the sentence from the passage.

Mom says, "Outside, the wind is roaring like a lion, but inside here, it sounds like a purring kitten."

What does Mom want to show by using the comparison in the sentence above? Select **two** choices.

(A) The family is in danger.

(B) Wind can be very tricky.

(C) It is a bad storm outside.

(D) It is soft and fuzzy inside.

(E) They are safe from the storm inside.

(F) Lions roar whenever there are storms.

**4** This question has two parts. First, answer part A. Then, answer part B.

**Part A:** Why does the family think the crashing sound is a problem?

(A) They are afraid they are in danger from the bear.

(B) They did not want to be awakened from sleep.

(C) They do not want to lose their food supplies.

(D) They are worried about a thunderstorm.

**Part B:** Which sentence from the passage supports your answer in part A?

(A) "They are exhausted from the hiking, and after a picnic dinner, they only want to sleep."

(B) "First, however, they hang their leftover food in a bag high up in a tree."

(C) "During the night, Olivia awakens to a terrible, crashing sound."

(D) "Suddenly, everyone is awake and frightened that a bear may cause them harm."

**GO ON →**

**5** How is Jayden's attitude toward the trip different at the beginning and end of the passage? Write the details and text evidence from the box into the correct locations on the chart to compare and contrast his attitude. Not all details and text evidence will be used.

|  | **Jayden's Attitude** | **Text Evidence** |
|---|---|---|
| *Beginning* |  |  |
| *End* |  |  |

**Jayden's Attitude:**

excited

surprised

uninterested

**Text Evidence:**

"'It is in Idaho . . .'"

"'. . . all my friends will be here this summer.'"

"'This is the greatest vacation ever!'"

**GO ON →**

**Read the passage "A Good Defense" before answering Numbers 6 through 10.**

# A Good Defense

One cool Saturday morning, Will slipped into his favorite jacket with worn, frayed edges and hiked to one of the deep arroyos around Albuquerque. Will had lived in New Mexico his whole life, yet he never got tired of the beauty of the arroyo, a gully carved from the ground by flowing water. In the summer, the season of sudden storms, the arroyos were full. But now, in early November, the arroyo was as dry as a bone.

Outdoors provided a soothing place to reflect, but Will's thoughts were not calm or happy. He was thinking about the bully who had chased him from the schoolyard on Friday afternoon, and worse, he was thinking about how he had fled from the older boy. His face was on fire at the memory. Why had he run away? Sure, Sam was obviously much stronger than Will, but Will should have stayed and defended himself. He did not want to be a coward.

Will had told his grandfather about what happened. "Every moment in life presents a choice," his grandfather said. "Every choice creates a new moment."

Will considered that. "But I chose to run away," he replied. "How do I know if that was the right choice to make?"

"Think about the moments that came as a result of your choice," said his grandfather. "If you had made the choice to stay and fight, would those moments have been better or worse?"

Will had thought about it, but he was not sure. All he knew for certain was that he felt bad about what had happened.

**GO ON →**

Will sat down at the edge of the arroyo, where weeds and flowers grew freely. The breeze blew softly, and the air was clean and cool. The banks of the arroyo offered a protected home for the small animals that hid from larger animals. Snakes, ground squirrels, and rabbits lived in the soft soil bed of the arroyo. Will sat silently while the life of the arroyo went on around him. He gazed at a jackrabbit nibbling the tall grasses and smiled at the creature's long ears, twitching nervously as it listened for enemies. A jackrabbit was prey for a lot of different animals. Then Will fought down a sinking feeling: he was just like a jackrabbit himself. It was an upsetting thought.

Suddenly, a shadow crossed over him, and Will glanced up to see a large hawk wheeling overhead. It hung in the sky for an instant like a threatening cloud. Will realized the bird had gotten a glimpse of the jackrabbit, which froze like a statue to avoid arousing the hawk's attention. Some animals defended themselves this way, while others turned to fight.

The hawk hovered lower in the sky. Will knew that if that rabbit did not want to be the hawk's meal, it had better move fast, but the little brown fellow seemed stunned by the nearness of the hawk and remained motionless. So the two creatures had recognized one another: hunter and hunted.

As the bird swooped lower, Will could hesitate no longer. As quick as a flash, he grabbed a small stone and flung it right at the jackrabbit. Stunned into movement, the desperate rabbit leaped away for denser cover in the underbrush.

"Good for you," Will thought. "You're not a coward; you just needed to escape." Sometimes, he realized, it was the wiser choice to run from trouble.

**GO ON →**

**Now answer Numbers 6 through 10. Base your answers on "A Good Defense."**

**6** This question has two parts. First, answer part A. Then, answer part B.

**Part A:** How is the arroyo in summer different from the arroyo in fall?

(A) In summer, it is full of water. In fall, it is dry.

(B) In summer, snakes live there. In fall, snakes hibernate.

(C) In summer, flowers grow freely. In fall, the flowers dry up.

(D) In summer, a big river flows through it. In fall, the river is a small stream.

**Part B:** Which **two** sentences from the passage support your answer in part A?

(A) "One cool Saturday morning, Will slipped into his favorite jacket with worn, frayed edges and hiked to one of the deep arroyos around Albuquerque."

(B) "Will had lived in New Mexico his whole life, yet he never got tired of the beauty of the arroyo, a gully carved from the ground by flowing water."

(C) "In the summer, the season of sudden storms, the arroyos were full."

(D) "But now, in early November, the arroyo was as dry as a bone."

(E) "Outdoors provided a soothing place to reflect, but Will's thoughts were not calm or happy."

(F) "He was thinking about the bully who had chased him from the schoolyard on Friday afternoon, and worse, he was thinking about how he had fled from the older boy."

**GO ON →**

**7** Read the sentence from the passage.

His face was on fire at the memory.

What does this sentence mean?

(A) Will was very hot.

(B) Will was blushing.

(C) Will was sunburned.

(D) Will was too close to a fire.

**8** This question has two parts. First, answer part A. Then, answer part B.

**Part A:** How are Will and the jackrabbit alike?

(A) Both are very fast runners.

(B) Both are afraid of their enemies.

(C) Both believe that the hawk is a bully.

(D) Both feel badly about what they have done.

**Part B:** Which detail from the passage shows that Will and the jackrabbit are alike?

(A) Will realizes that the jackrabbit is prey for others.

(B) Will tries to scare the jackrabbit away to save its life.

(C) Will watches the jackrabbit as it nibbles grass nearby.

(D) Will sees that the hawk has caught sight of the jackrabbit.

**GO ON →**

**9**  How are the hawk and Sam the bully alike?

Ⓐ  Both can fly.

Ⓑ  Both are hungry.

Ⓒ  Both threaten weaker creatures.

Ⓓ  Both are taller than other creatures.

**10**  Determine the meaning of each underlined simile. Draw a line from the sentence with the simile on the left to the simile's correct meaning on the right.

| It hung in the sky for an instant "like a threatening cloud." | | very fast |
|---|---|---|

| Will realized the bird had gotten a glimpse of the jackrabbit, which froze "like a statue" to avoid arousing the hawk's attention. | | dangerous |
|---|---|---|

| "As quick as a flash," he grabbed a small stone and flung it right at the jackrabbit. | | very still |
|---|---|---|

**STOP**

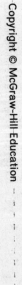

**Now answer Number 11. Base your answer on "Yellowstone Adventure" and "A Good Defense."**

**11** Compare how Jayden in "Yellowstone Adventure" and Will in "A Good Defense" change from the beginning to the end of the passages. Support your answer with details from both texts.

_____

_____

_____

_____

_____

_____

_____

_____

_____

_____

_____

_____

_____

# Answer Key

Name: _____

| Question | Correct Answer | Content Focus | CCSS | Complexity |
|:---:|:---:|:---:|:---:|:---:|
| 1 | D | Metaphor | L.5.5a | DOK 2 |
| 2 | A | Character, Setting, Plot: Compare and Contrast | RL.5.3 | DOK 2 |
| 3 | C, E | Simile | L.5.5a | DOK 2 |
| 4A | A | Character, Setting, Plot: Problem and Solution | RL.4.3 | DOK 2 |
| 4B | D | Character, Setting, Plot: Problem and Solution/Text Evidence | RL.4.3/RL.5.1 | DOK 2 |
| 5 | see below | Character, Setting, Plot: Compare and Contrast | RL.5.3 | DOK 3 |
| 6A | A | Character, Setting, Plot: Compare and Contrast | RL.5.3 | DOK 2 |
| 6B | C, D | Character, Setting, Plot: Compare and Contrast/Text Evidence | RL.5.3/RL.5.1 | DOK 2 |
| 7 | B | Metaphor | L.5.5a | DOK 2 |
| 8A | B | Character, Setting, Plot: Compare and Contrast | RL.5.3 | DOK 2 |
| 8B | A | Character, Setting, Plot: Compare and Contrast/Text Evidence | RL.5.3/RL.5.1 | DOK 2 |
| 9 | C | Character, Setting, Plot: Compare and Contrast | RL.5.3 | DOK 2 |
| 10 | see below | Simile | L.5.5a | DOK 2 |
| 11 | see below | Writing About Text | W.5.9a | DOK 4 |

| | | |
|:---|:---:|:---:|
| **Comprehension** 2, 4A, 4B, 5, 6A, 6B, 8A, 8B, 9 | /12 | % |
| **Vocabulary** 1, 3, 7, 10 | /8 | % |
| **Total Weekly Assessment Score** | /20 | % |

**5** Students should complete the chart as follows:
- Beginning—Jayden's Attitude: uninterested; Text Evidence: "'. . . all my friends will be here this summer.'"
- End—Jayden's Attitude: excited; Text Evidence: "'This is the greatest vacation ever!'"

**10** Students should make the following matches:
- "It hung in the sky for an instant *like a threatening cloud*."—dangerous
- "Will realized the bird had gotten a glimpse of the jackrabbit, which froze *like a statue* to avoid arousing the hawk's attention."—very still
- "*As quick as a flash*, he grabbed a small stone and flung it right at the jackrabbit."—very fast

**11** To receive full credit for the response, the following information should be included: The reader can infer that both boys feel different about their situations in the end. Jayden is no longer sorry he had to go on the trip, and Will feels better about his decision to run from Sam when he sees how the jackrabbit avoids danger.

**Read the article "Watching Earth from Space" before answering Numbers 1 through 5.**

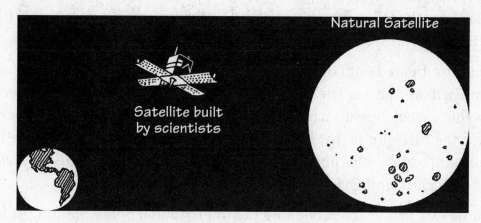

# Watching Earth from Space

We are learning about life on Earth from a large satellite in space. Scientists built the satellite and used a rocket to launch it into space in 1998. It is the International Space Station, or ISS. Fifteen countries cooperated to build and operate it. The space station is about 250 miles above Earth and orbits, or circles, Earth sixteen times a day. It is a little longer than a United States football field and weighs almost one million pounds.

Since 2000, people have lived and been active on the space station. One purpose of the ISS is to learn about living in space. Another is to conduct experiments. The findings should make life better for people on Earth. Crews live on the ISS to gather information about space and Earth. A part that is like a big sunroom was attached to the space station in 2010. From here, astronauts can view Earth from space. They can observe lights of cities on Earth. They can watch other astronauts walking in space and study objects like asteroids in space. It is like having an eye on the universe.

In 2011, a new camera was placed on the space station that records happenings on Earth. The camera gives scientists a better tool to research natural events on Earth, such as lightning. It also gives information about the effects of human activities on our planet.

Space exploration began more than fifty years ago when Russia sent the first human-made satellite into orbit. In 1962, John Glenn, an American, orbited Earth. Then in 1969, people around the world watched Neil Armstrong's walk on the surface of the moon.

**GO ON →**

The Skylab space station was launched in 1973. It had no human passengers. Later, a crew went to live on Skylab for a month. Three crews of astronauts lived on Skylab over the following nine months. Skylab proved it was possible for people to survive in space, but more importantly, they could work in orbit.

Scientists also figured out how to make a vehicle that could go back and forth between Earth and space. The next step was building such a space shuttle. Having such a vehicle would greatly simplify space exploration. *Columbia*, launched in 1981, was the first shuttle that carried astronauts. The space shuttles were larger than the earlier spaceships and they carried both pilots and scientists. *Challenger*, *Discovery*, *Atlantis*, and *Endeavour* later joined the fleet of shuttles.

The shuttle was important in building the International Space Station. At first, shuttle flights brought construction parts into space. Later, flights brought crews to live on the space station. Shuttles continue to serve as transportation for crews and supplies.

For more than ten years, the ISS's space laboratory has given new information that will improve our future on Earth. Studies about infectious diseases have opened new ways to prevent those diseases. The benefits of ultrasound have increased due to its use on the space station. Ultrasound has deepened understanding about gravity's effects on the human body. It also has helped to discover the health problems of people living on the space station.

We have learned new ways to treat heart disease, cancer, and bone disease as a result of research on the ISS. Experiments with plants have shown they can grow and be used as food on space expeditions. Moreover, they are a way to make air and water clean. We have already seen many good things come from experiments on the ISS. Scientists believe we will continue to benefit from work done in space.

**GO ON →**

**Now answer Numbers 1 through 5. Base your answers on "Watching Earth from Space."**

**1** Read the sentence from the article.

Since 2000, people have lived and been active on the space station.

The suffix *-ive*, as in *active*, means "tending to or being likely to." What would someone who is <u>communicative</u> probably enjoy?

(A) eating

(B) playing

(C) reading

(D) talking

**2** This question has two parts. First, answer part A. Then, answer part B.

**Part A:** How does the author organize "Watching Earth from Space"?

(A) by showing causes and effects in space

(B) by comparing and contrasting Earth and space

(C) by explaining sequence of events in exploring space

(D) by discussing problems and solutions in using a camera in space

**Part B:** Which sentence from the article **best** shows how the text is organized?

(A) "The space station is about 250 miles above Earth and orbits, or circles, Earth sixteen times a day."

(B) "The camera gives scientists a better tool to research natural events on Earth, such as lightning."

(C) "*Columbia*, launched in 1981, was the first shuttle that carried astronauts."

(D) "Shuttles continue to serve as transportation for crews and supplies."

**GO ON →**

**3** Read the sentence from the article.

Having such a vehicle would greatly <u>simplify</u> space exploration.

What does the word <u>simplify</u> mean?

(A) to make something simpler

(B) to make something not simple

(C) to make something less simple

(D) to make something simple again

**4** Put the events from the article in the correct sequence by numbering them from 1 to 4. Write the correct number in front of each event.

_____ | A camera was placed on the ISS.

_____ | People started living on the space station.

_____ | The ISS was launched into space.

_____ | A part was added to the space station.

**GO ON →**

**5** What are some effects of experiments done on the International Space Station? Select **two** choices.

(A) We have learned how to keep a satellite in orbit.

(B) We have learned new ways to treat some diseases.

(C) Scientists figured out how to make a space vehicle.

(D) Astronauts have been able to walk on Earth's moon.

(E) We have discovered how to grow and use plants in space.

(F) People from many countries have learned how to cooperate.

**GO ON →**

**Read the article "The Life of a Hurricane" before answering Numbers 6 through 10.**

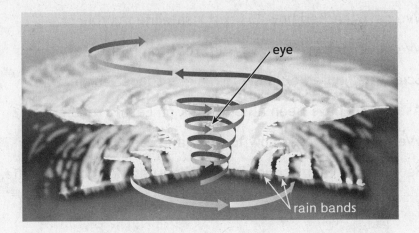

# The Life of a Hurricane

What do hurricanes, cyclones, and typhoons have in common? They are all different names for the same severe tropical storm that is known as a tropical cyclone. In this article, the word *hurricane* will be used to discuss this type of storm.

What creates the possibility for a hurricane to develop over ocean water? At least three elements must be present. First, the water must be warm enough to give off heat and moisture into the atmosphere. Second, water already in the air must mix with the heat and moisture from the ocean. Finally, easterly winds must be blowing. Conditions are usually best for hurricanes in the late summer or early fall.

The warm, wet air rises because warm air is lighter than cold air. The wind moves the heat and water high into the atmosphere. Then, Earth's turning begins to work against the easterly winds, twisting the growing storm into a tube shape. The center of this tube is called the eye. The heat and moisture from the ocean's surface come into contact with the cooler air higher up, creating thunderstorms. Then, the cooler air travels back toward the ocean's surface and pulls more moisture from the ocean. Once that moisture rises into the thunderclouds, it is released as heavy rain. This type of rain usually accompanies hurricanes.

The winds increase in speed and begin to move the enormous storm across the ocean. As long as hurricanes remain over water, they have the ability to keep increasing in size and strength.

**GO ON →**

Usually the weather is calm in the eye of the hurricane. The eye may range from 2 miles to 200 miles across, and the hurricane itself might be as big as 400 to 500 miles across. Rain bands spin toward the center of the hurricane. They often bring high winds and heavy rainfall. Calmer weather is found between the rain bands.

A tropical storm qualifies as a hurricane when its winds reach 74 miles an hour. Scientists have measured winds in hurricanes that move at more than twice that speed. Hurricanes have been given names since 1950. The names of the worst storms are retired—that is, they are not used again.

Hurricanes are given a number from 1 to 5. Hurricanes with the number 1 are the least dangerous. Those given a 5 are the most dangerous. The strongest hurricane ever to hit the United States struck Florida in 1935. The second strongest was Hurricane Katrina, which struck Louisiana in 2005.

What causes the storm to end? Sometimes the power of a hurricane diminishes, or fades, when it travels into the path of strong westerly winds. This disturbs its course, and can cause the storm to move over cooler northern waters. The storm no longer gets power from the warm ocean water, and it finally dies out.

At other times, a hurricane travels until it hits land. Once it is over land, it causes almost unbelievable damage. Tornadoes may form in the rain bands. High winds knock over structures. The ocean can flood towns. These floods are responsible for a great deal of damage. Cars, houses, and businesses are often destroyed. But a hurricane over land doesn't have the warm ocean water to help it grow. It will quickly lose power. At last, it ends up as nothing more than rain showers.

Scientists study hurricanes to understand them and predict them better. They use weather satellites to find out more about the storms. Sometimes, they fly planes right into the eye of the hurricane to get information! What they learn will help people when these terrible storms threaten.

**GO ON →**

**Now answer Numbers 6 through 10. Base your answers on "The Life of a Hurricane."**

**6** Read the sentence from the passage.

What creates the possibility for a hurricane to develop over ocean water?

The suffix -ity, as in possibility, means "state or quality of." What are you told to do if you are told to show civility?

(A) be brave

(B) be polite

(C) be funny

(D) be careful

**7** This question has two parts. First, answer part A. Then, answer part B.

**Part A:** Why does the author of "The Life of a Hurricane" consider the blowing of easterly winds to be an important occurrence?

(A) It contributes to flooding.

(B) It causes hurricanes to end.

(C) It creates the eye of the hurricane.

(D) It contributes to hurricane formation.

**Part B:** Which sentence from the article **best** supports your answer in part A?

(A) "At least three elements must be present."

(B) "The center of this tube is called the eye."

(C) "This type of rain usually accompanies hurricanes."

(D) "Calmer weather is found between the rain bands."

**GO ON →**

**8** What happens before a growing storm twists into a tube shape? Select **two** options.

(A) Warm air rises.

(B) Heavy rain falls.

(C) The storm is named.

(D) The storm gets a number.

(E) Wind moves the heat and water up.

(F) Cooler air travels back to the ocean surface.

**9** What happens after the warm air and moisture meet cooler air? Underline the sentence that states what happens next.

The warm, wet air rises because warm air is lighter than cold air. The wind moves the heat and water high into the atmosphere. Then, Earth's turning begins to work against the easterly winds, twisting the growing storm into a tube shape. The center of this tube is called the eye. The heat and moisture from the ocean's surface come into contact with the cooler air higher up, creating thunderstorms. Then, the cooler air travels back toward the ocean's surface and pulls more moisture from the ocean. Once that moisture rises into the thunderclouds, it is released as heavy rain. This type of rain usually accompanies hurricanes.

**GO ON →**

Name: _____ Date: _____

**10** Read the sentence from the passage.

Hurricanes with the number 1 are the least <u>dangerous</u>.

Based on the suffix *-ous*, what does the word <u>dangerous</u> mean?

Ⓐ after danger

Ⓑ before danger

Ⓒ marked by danger

Ⓓ without any danger

**Now answer Number 11. Base your answer on "Watching Earth from Space" and "The Life of a Hurricane."**

**11** Compare and contrast how the authors use sequence in the articles. Support your answer with details from both texts.

_____

_____

_____

_____

_____

_____

_____

_____

_____

_____

_____

_____

_____

_____

# Answer Key

Name: _____

| Question | Correct Answer | Content Focus | CCSS | Complexity |
|---|---|---|---|---|
| 1 | D | Greek and Latin Suffixes | L.5.4b | DOK 1 |
| 2A | C | Text Structure: Sequence | RI.5.5 | DOK 3 |
| 2B | C | Text Structure: Sequence/ Text Evidence | RI.5.5/ RI.5.1 | DOK 3 |
| 3 | A | Greek and Latin Suffixes | L.5.4b | DOK 1 |
| 4 | see below | Text Structure: Sequence | RI.5.5 | DOK 2 |
| 5 | B, E | Cause and Effect | RI.5.3 | DOK 2 |
| 6 | B | Greek and Latin Suffixes | L.5.4b | DOK 1 |
| 7A | D | Text Structure: Sequence | RI.5.5 | DOK 3 |
| 7B | A | Text Structure: Sequence/ Text Evidence | RI.5.5/ RI.5.1 | DOK 3 |
| 8 | A, E | Sequence | RI.5.3 | DOK 2 |
| 9 | see below | Sequence | RI.5.3 | DOK 2 |
| 10 | C | Greek and Latin Suffixes | L.5.4b | DOK 1 |
| 11 | see below | Writing About Text | W.5.9b | DOK 4 |

| | | |
|---|---|---|
| **Comprehension** 2A, 2B, 4, 5, 7A, 7B, 8, 9 | /12 | % |
| **Vocabulary** 1, 3, 6, 10 | /8 | % |
| **Total Weekly Assessment Score** | /20 | % |

**4** Students should order the events as follows:
- 1: The ISS was launched into space.
- 2: People started living on the space station.
- 3: A part was added to the space station.
- 4: A camera was placed on the ISS

**9** Students should underline the following sentence:
- The heat and moisture from the ocean's surface come into contact with the cooler air higher up, creating thunderstorms.

**11** To receive full credit for the response, the following information should be included: Both authors organize the texts by showing the sequence in which things happen. In "Watching Earth from Space," the author shows developments from early space flights to recent experiments on the ISS. In "The Life of a Hurricane," the author shows the stages in the development of a hurricane.

**Read the passage "The Spider Monkey and the Marmoset" before answering Numbers 1 through 5.**

# The Spider Monkey and the Marmoset

*Based on Aesop's Fable "The Ant and the Grasshopper"*

In the rainforests of Brazil lived two friends, Spider Monkey and Marmoset. Spider Monkey loved to spend his days swinging through the trees, eating as much fruit as his belly could hold. The generous trees provided Spider Monkey with lots of delicious fruit.

Marmoset loved to eat fruit, but knew he had to plan for the future. The elder marmosets spoke of times when finding fruit was difficult. Sometimes, the fruit would get a terrible disease, or cruel, vicious winds would whip through the branches and knock the fruit to the ground. So, Marmoset saved two bites of fruit for every bite he ate.

Spider Monkey laughed at Marmoset as he saw him carrying fruit, shrieking, "Silly Marmoset! We will never be out of fruit, for it leaps off the tree, glad to be your snack."

Marmoset ignored Spider Monkey and still collected fruit. "Someday," Marmoset would say, "Spider Monkey will regret making fun of me." Soon, Marmoset's storage place was full and Marmoset smiled with contentment.

**GO ON →**

Not long after this, Marmoset and Spider Monkey noticed the fruit drooping on the branches. One day, great numbers of fruit plummeted to the ground. That is, it fell off the branches fast and hard. Soon after this, it began to become difficult to find fruit to eat.

At first, Spider Monkey was amused, chortling, "It makes for a great game! The fruit is playing hide and seek with me." But in a short time, Spider Monkey realized that it would not be easy to find enough fruit to fill his belly.

Then he remembered the storage place of his friend, Marmoset. "I know!" Spider Monkey said excitedly. "I'll just ask Marmoset to share with me. He is such a great friend that I know he will be generous."

Spider Monkey swung through the trees to find Marmoset, who was resting near his storage place. When Spider Monkey approached, Marmoset opened one eye and looked at him warily, asking, "How can I help you, Spider Monkey?"

"I have come to share your fruit," Spider Monkey announced triumphantly. "You were so smart to plan ahead, and I am forever grateful for your planning."

Marmoset slowly shook his head before responding. "Spider Monkey," he began, "this fruit is for my family. We don't know how long it will be difficult to find fruit, so I can't share what I've gathered. I'm sorry, but you will have to find food elsewhere. You should have been planning for a day like this yourself." Marmoset turned from Spider Monkey and took his place in front of the entrance to the storage place. He set up his position as guard in front of the food.

Spider Monkey's mouth hung open, for he was not expecting this from his friend. Slowly, he turned to walk away from Marmoset. As he swung through the trees, in search of food, he thought of Marmoset's words. "Maybe," he thought, "I should plan ahead."

**GO ON →**

Name: _____ Date: _____

**1** Read the sentence from the passage.

The generous trees provided Spider Monkey with lots of delicious fruits.

Why does the author make the tree seem human?

(A) to show that the tree grew different types of fruits

(B) to show that the tree handed fruit to Spider Monkey

(C) to show that Spider Monkey made the tree give him fruit

(D) to show that Spider Monkey took a lot of fruit from the tree

**2** Read the sentence from the passage.

"We will never be out of fruit, for it leaps off the tree, glad to be your snack."

Which **two** words from the sentence describe the fruit with human qualities? Write the words in the chart below.

| Words that Describe the Fruit with Human Qualities |
| --- |
| |
| |

**GO ON →**

**3** This question has two parts. First, answer part A. Then, answer part B.

**Part A:** When does Spider Monkey realize that he has behaved foolishly?

(A) when Marmoset refuses to share his family's food with him

(B) when he remembers Marmoset's storage place

(C) when he sees Marmoset storing up fruit

(D) when the fruit becomes hard to find

**Part B:** Which sentence from the story shows that Spider Monkey realizes his mistake?

(A) "Marmoset slowly shook his head before responding."

(B) "'I'm sorry, but you will have to find food elsewhere.'"

(C) "He set up his position as guard in front of the food."

(D) "'Maybe,' he thought, 'I should plan ahead.'"

**4** How is Spider Monkey different from Marmoset? Select **two** options.

(A) Marmoset is selfish; Spider Monkey shares.

(B) Marmoset is practical; Spider Monkey is not.

(C) Spider Monkey doesn't need much to eat; Marmoset does.

(D) Spider Monkey likes to eat fruit; Marmoset does not like fruit.

(E) Marmoset thinks of the future; Spider Monkey thinks of the present.

(F) Spider Monkey knows how to have fun; Marmoset only knows how to work.

**GO ON →**

**5** This question has two parts. First, answer part A. Then, answer part B.

**Part A:** What is the theme of "The Spider Monkey and the Marmoset"?

(A) Friends don't always share.

(B) Needs can be hard to fulfill.

(C) Always eat one bite, save two.

(D) One must prepare for the future.

**Part B:** Which sentence from the passage **best** supports the theme?

(A) "'I'll just ask Marmoset to share with me.'"

(B) "Spider Monkey swung through the trees to find Marmoset, who was resting near his storage place."

(C) "'You should have been planning for a day like this yourself.'"

(D) "Spider Monkey's mouth hung open, for he was not expecting this from his friend."

**GO ON →**

**Read the passage "Raven the Trickster and Fish Hawk" before answering Numbers 6 through 10.**

# Raven the Trickster and Fish Hawk

*A Retelling of a Native American Tale*

Tricksters have ways of getting what they want. However, trouble is a close companion of tricksters. One day, a bird named Fish Hawk was unfortunate enough to meet Raven on the riverbank. Raven acted very kindly toward Fish Hawk, hoping the bird would do him a favor.

"Ah, my dearest friend," Raven greeted Fish Hawk. "The wind is howling along the shore of the river, and the weather has turned cold and bitter. The warmth of your house is calling to me. Let us go there."

Fish Hawk was too polite to refuse, but it was without enthusiasm that he led Raven to his home. Once inside, Raven glanced about slyly and noticed that the hawk had laid in a large supply of food. Fish Hawk also had a very inviting home. He had made his home quite comfortable with soft blankets of leaves and grasses.

"What a lot of things you have here," sneaky Raven said. "You could open your own store and sell what you have!"

When Fish Hawk said nothing in response, Raven continued. "All the birds that have wasted the summer singing and flitting about, instead of storing food for the winter, would be eager to buy some of this. You will need a treasurer to help you with sales and to help you collect profits on these goods. That requires a lot of time and effort! Why don't I visit with you during the winter months? We can share some of the burdens of keeping shop and housekeeping."

**GO ON →**

Fish Hawk doubted the wisdom of this plan, but he let Raven stay with him. It soon became clear that Raven would not lift a feather to help his kind host. In time, Fish Hawk grew tired of his lazy guest, but Raven talked to him sweetly, saying, "Don't worry, dear friend. This beach will wear a thick cloak of fish, and you will not have to catch them. I'll get our dinner for us while you rest." However, he never did, and Fish Hawk's life just got harder and harder.

Weeks passed by and Raven did nothing to help. He made his host gather food for both of them while he slept and ate up the meals. Thanking Fish Hawk many times after each large dinner, he would say, "What a rich, wise friend you are! I have so much appreciation for your kindness. Words can hardly express my feelings." Raven's flattery was ceaseless. He would always end his speeches by again assuring Fish Hawk that he would catch fish, but, of course, nothing came of this empty promise.

Fish Hawk finally grew disgusted by Raven's laziness and greed. He flew away from his own house, towards a sun that was peeking around clouds. "That will teach you, Raven!" he called out. "Now you will have to fend for yourself!" He hoped to educate Raven by teaching him a lesson, yet deep in his heart, he knew that the old trickster would never change.

Fish Hawk soon built himself a cozy new home, and Raven had to find his own dinner from then on.

**GO ON →**

**Now answer Numbers 6 through 10. Base your answers on "Raven the Trickster and Fish Hawk."**

**6** Read the sentence from the passage.

"The warmth of your house is calling to me."

What does Raven mean when he says this to Fish Hawk?

(A) He wants to go to Fish Hawk's house where it is warm.

(B) He has heard that Fish Hawk's house is very warm.

(C) Fish Hawk's house is making some kind of noise.

(D) Fish Hawk's house is very close to where he is.

**7** Select **two** ways that Raven is a problem for Fish Hawk.

(A) He will not leave Fish Hawk's home.

(B) He does not flatter Fish Hawk enough.

(C) He uses all of Fish Hawk's soft blankets.

(D) He eats all of Fish Hawk's food supplies.

(E) He brings friends over to Fish Hawk's home.

(F) He takes up too much room in Fish Hawk's home.

**GO ON →**

**8** Read the sentence from the passage.

"This beach will <u>wear a thick cloak of fish</u>, and you will not have to catch them."

What does "wear a thick cloak of fish" mean?

(A) Fish will be hard to find.

(B) Fish will cover the beach.

(C) There will be a cloak made of fish.

(D) There will be a few fish on the beach.

**9** Raven causes a lot of trouble for Fish Hawk in the passage. Underline two sentences in the paragraph below that support this idea.

Weeks passed by and Raven did nothing to help. He made his host gather food for both of them while he slept and ate up the meals. Thanking Fish Hawk many times after each large dinner, he would say, "What a rich, wise friend you are! I have so much appreciation for your kindness. Words can hardly express my feelings." . . .

**GO ON →**

**10** This question has two parts. First, answer part A. Then, answer part B.

**Part A:** What is the theme of "Raven the Trickster and Fish Hawk"?

(A) Tricksters often change their ways.

(B) Visitors always help with the chores.

(C) Tricksters always keep their promises.

(D) Tricksters often cause problems for others.

**Part B:** Which sentence from the passage **best** supports the theme?

(A) "Fish Hawk was too polite to refuse, but it was without enthusiasm that he led Raven to his home."

(B) "Fish Hawk doubted the wisdom of this plan, but he let Raven stay with him."

(C) "Fish Hawk finally grew disgusted by Raven's laziness and greed."

(D) "Fish Hawk soon built himself a cozy new home, and Raven had to find his own dinner from then on."

**STOP**

Name: _____ Date: _____

**Now answer Number 11. Base your answer on "The Spider Monkey and the Marmoset" and "Raven the Trickster and Fish Hawk."**

**11** Using details from both texts, compare the themes of "The Spider Monkey and the Marmoset" and "Raven the Trickster and Fish Hawk." How do Marmoset and Fish Hawk respond when their plans are challenged by Spider Monkey and Raven?

_____

_____

_____

_____

_____

_____

_____

_____

_____

_____

_____

_____

# Answer Key

| Question | Correct Answer | Content Focus | CCSS | Complexity |
|---|---|---|---|---|
| 1 | D | Personification | L.5.5a | DOK 2 |
| 2 | see below | Personification | L.5.5a | DOK 2 |
| 3A | A | Theme | RL.5.2 | DOK 3 |
| 3B | D | Theme/Text Evidence | RL.5.2/ RL.5.1 | DOK 3 |
| 4 | B, E | Character, Setting, Plot: Compare and Contrast | RL.5.3 | DOK 3 |
| 5A | D | Theme | RL.5.2 | DOK 3 |
| 5B | C | Theme/Text Evidence | RL.5.2/ RL.5.1 | DOK 3 |
| 6 | A | Personification | L.5.5a | DOK 2 |
| 7 | A, D | Theme | RL.5.2 | DOK 3 |
| 8 | B | Personification | L.5.5a | DOK 2 |
| 9 | see below | Theme | RL.5.2 | DOK 3 |
| 10A | D | Theme | RL.5.2 | DOK 3 |
| 10B | C | Theme/Text Evidence | RL.5.2/ RL.5.1 | DOK 3 |
| 11 | see below | Writing About Text | W.5.9a | DOK 4 |

| | | |
|---|---|---|
| **Comprehension** 3A, 3B, 4, 5A, 5B, 7, 9, 10A, 10B | /12 | % |
| **Vocabulary** 1, 2, 6, 8 | /8 | % |
| **Total Weekly Assessment Score** | /20 | % |

**2** Students should complete the chart with the following words:

- leaps
- glad

**9** Students should underline the following sentences:

- Weeks passed by and Raven did nothing to help.
- He made his host gather food for both of them while he slept and ate up the meals.

**11** To receive full credit for the response, the following information should be included: Marmoset planned ahead. He did not share with Spider Monkey because Spider Monkey did not plan. Fish Hawk prepared for winter and as a result, Raven tricked Fish Hawk into letting him stay with him. Fish Hawk realized he was being tricked and so he left his own home and made Raven fend for himself.

**Read the passage "Four Short Weeks" before answering Numbers 1 through 5.**

# Four Short Weeks

Audra scanned the directions for her social studies assignment as her teacher read. They were supposed to research and report on one of the fifty states. The project was due in one month and included a five-page report, a poster, and an oral report. Audra feared she would never complete this in four short weeks.

"Mrs. Peterson, do you have advice for starting this project?" Audra asked. She tried to console herself a little, though she couldn't soothe herself much.

Mrs. Peterson smiled as she explained, "Plan how you will complete each part of the project, and write your plan down. Break the assignment into smaller pieces, and do not wait until the last minute to start!"

Later that afternoon, Audra walked through her front door and almost ran into her older brother, Gus.

"Sorry," Audra muttered as she dug the directions for the project out of her backpack and put them on the dining room table. Then she plopped on a chair and began to contract, or become smaller, into a little ball. She wished she had someone to commiserate with about the project so that they could each express sorrow for the other.

"Is something wrong?" Gus asked, sitting down beside her.

"Why do teachers subject us to difficult assignments?" Audra wailed. "This assignment is due in a month, and I will never finish it on time!"

Gus smiled and said, "Let me see if I can help you." Audra slid the directions towards him and Gus skimmed the top sheet.

**GO ON →**

"Audra, this is not so bad," Gus began. When Audra started to protest, he put up his hand to stop her. "I am not trying to bluff you, because it is a big project and you will have to work hard, but you can break the project down into little ones with shorter due dates."

Gus pulled a blue notebook from a desk drawer. He said, "Today is October 1 and the entire project is due on October 30. If you spend one week on each of the four parts, you will finish the project on time."

Audra watched as Gus opened the notebook and drew a two-column chart. In the left column, he wrote a requirement for the project. In the right column, he wrote a date that was a few weeks before the final due date for the project.

| Requirement | Due Date for Each Part |
|---|---|
| Five page research report, typed | October 15 |
| Oral Presentation, 2–3 minutes in length | October 29 |

As Audra looked at Gus's schedule, she began to feel as though this project might be possible after all.

For the next four weeks, Audra followed Gus's schedule. Whenever she started to feel overwhelmed, she looked at her schedule and relaxed. It would all get done, she told herself, and she was right!

The night before the project's due date, Audra thanked her brother with the following poem:

> Racing thoughts, beating heart
> What do do, how to start?
> Wringing hands, the hour's late,
> Four short weeks to my due date.

> Gus arrives to save the day.
> "Make a date each week away."
> "Plan to do one thing a week."
> Suddenly it's not so bleak.

> Thanks to Gus there's time to spare.
> I even wrote a rhyme to share.
> If you plan you'll get things done.
> And even have some time for fun!

**GO ON →**

**Now answer Numbers 1 through 5. Base your answers on "Four Short Weeks."**

**1** Read the sentence from the passage.

She tried to <u>console</u> herself a little, though she couldn't soothe herself much.

Which definition fits the word <u>console</u> as it is used in the sentence above?

(A) cabinet

(B) case

(C) comfort

(D) help

**2** What is responsible for changing Audra's attitude from hopeless to cautiously hopeful? Select **two** choices.

(A) her own past experiences

(B) her brother's past experiences

(C) her conversation with her brother

(D) the chart her brother makes for her

(E) her conversation with Mrs. Peterson

(F) the directions on her class assignment

**GO ON →**

**3** This question has two parts. First, answer part A. Then, answer part B.

**Part A:** Read the sentence from the passage.

"Why do teachers <u>subject</u> us to difficult assignments?" Audra wailed.

Which definition fits <u>subject</u> as it is used in the sentence above?

(A) topic

(B) one who is ruled over

(C) force to suffer through

(D) something that is studied

**Part B:** Which sentence uses the word <u>subject</u> in the same way it is used in part A?

(A) What is your favorite subject in school?

(B) Please do not subject me to this boring movie.

(C) The cows in the field are interesting subjects to paint.

(D) This ruler is much kinder to his subjects than the last one was.

**4** Put the events from the passage in the correct sequence by numbering them from 1 to 4. Write the correct number in front of each event.

_____   | Audra finishes her report. |

_____   | Audra reads her poem. |

_____   | Audra makes a plan. |

_____   | Audra gets her assignment. |

**GO ON →**

**5** This question has two parts. First, answer part A. Then, answer part B.

**Part A:** What is the theme of "Four Short Weeks"?

(A) When feeling overwhelmed, it is good if others feel the same way.

(B) When completing a large project, it is good to have a plan.

(C) Nothing is done well if left to the last minute.

(D) Older brothers have all the answers.

**Part B:** Which sentence from the passage **best** supports the theme?

(A) "'Break the assignment into smaller pieces, and do not wait until the last minute to start!'"

(B) "'This assignment is due in a month, and I will never finish it on time!'"

(C) "Audra slid the directions towards him and Gus skimmed the top sheet."

(D) "When Audra started to protest, he put up his hand to stop her."

**GO ON →**

**Read the passage "The Big Contest" before answering Numbers 6 through 10.**

# The Big Contest

"We will win this contest," José bragged to Aisha at recess.

"I don't want to have a dispute with you because a quarrel won't get us anywhere, but I disagree," Aisha said. "How can we win? We're not experts. Why did the fifth grade pick us to represent everyone in the Big Bake-Off?"

"You should give us more credit," José said. "We are capable kids who can follow directions, so we should be able to use a recipe. The contest has many different categories, and I have a plan."

Aisha remembered the last time she listened to José's big plan. They had gotten into trouble because José made his own rules, and they were thrown out of the contest altogether.

"Aisha, are you listening to me?" asked José.

Aisha shook herself back into the present and asked, "What is your plan?"

"We will bake a gigantic cake that will be larger than all the other cakes! It will be so huge that we will get the prize for the biggest cake," he said. "It won't matter what it tastes like!"

Aisha said, "That is an excellent plan, José, and I think you are on to something!"

**GO ON →**

The next day, Aisha and José went to the grocery store and bought the ingredients for their gigantic cake. At Aisha's house, they set everything on the counter and started working.

"We will bake a few square cakes at a time and then we will put them together and spruce them up with a lot of frosting," Aisha said.

Aisha measured flour, sugar, baking soda, and other ingredients while José cracked eggs into a bowl. They mixed the batter, poured it into pans, and placed two pans in the oven. While those cakes were in the oven, they started on the next batch, and worked until two rows of cakes stood on the table and a huge bowl of frosting was made. The kids slumped against the counter, for they were very tired.

"My back hurts," moaned José as he put all the cakes on a large board. "I'll never be able to stand up straight again." Aisha brushed a strand of hair from her eyes before spreading the frosting on the cake.

The next day, with the help of Aisha's father and José's mother, the two kids took the huge cake to the school. They left it on one of the special tables set up in the cafeteria for the contest, surrounded by many smaller cakes.

That day felt like the longest school day ever. Finally, it was the last period of the day and time for the contest to begin! All the students at the school went to the cafeteria, where they watched as the judges tasted each of the cakes. José and Aisha saw the judges, but they couldn't tell what the judges were thinking. Both kids waited with their hearts pounding.

"Well, now, the judging is over, and I am really nervous," Aisha said. "Maybe putting regular cakes together won't count as one cake," she fretted. José didn't reply because he was worried, too. One of the judges cleared his throat and announced, "The prize for the biggest cake goes to . . . Aisha Thomas and José Mora, representing the fifth grade!"

"I told you we were bound to win!" José said to Aisha with a smile. "I never doubted it for a minute!"

**GO ON →**

**Now answer Numbers 6 through 10. Base your answers on "The Big Contest."**

**6** Circle the paragraph that shows how José plans to win the contest.

Aisha remembered the last time she listened to José's big plan. They had gotten into trouble because José made his own rules, and they were thrown out of the contest altogether.

"Aisha, are you listening to me?" asked José.

Aisha shook herself back into the present and asked, "What is your plan?"

"We will bake a gigantic cake that will be larger than all the other cakes! It will be so huge that we will get the prize for the biggest cake," he said. "It won't matter what it tastes like!"

Aisha said, "That is an excellent plan, José, and I think you are on to something!"

**7** Read the sentence from the passage.

While those cakes were in the oven, they started on the next batch, and worked until two rows of cakes stood on the table and a huge bowl of frosting was made.

Which definition fits the word rows as it is used in the sentence above?

(A) streets or ways

(B) moves with oars

(C) noisy quarrels or disturbances

(D) objects arranged in straight lines

**GO ON →**

**8** Select **two** reasons why Aisha **most likely** trusts José and his plan.

(A) José is her friend.

(B) José can bake well.

(C) José always has good ideas.

(D) José's plan makes sense to her.

(E) She knows what the judges want.

(F) She has made many cakes before.

**9** Read the definition.

to leap or jump

Which word from the passage means "sure" and is also a homograph for the word defined above?

(A) bound

(B) contest

(C) count

(D) trouble

**GO ON →**

**10** This question has two parts. First, answer part A. Then, answer part B.

**Part A:** What is the theme of "The Big Contest"?

(A) Big things are always better than small things.

(B) You will always win if you follow directions.

(C) Having a plan helps to achieve goals.

(D) Always listen to your friends.

**Part B:** Which sentence from the passage **best** supports the theme?

(A) "'We are capable kids who can follow directions, so we should be able to use a recipe.'"

(B) "Aisha said, 'That is an excellent plan, José, and I think you are on to something!'"

(C) "The kids slumped against the counter, for they were very tired."

(D) "Aisha brushed a strand of hair from her eyes before spreading the frosting on the cake."

**STOP**

Name: _____ Date: _____

**Now answer Number 11. Base your answer on "Four Short Weeks" and "The Big Contest."**

**11** Using details from both texts, compare the themes of "Four Short Weeks" and "The Big Contest." How does having a plan help Audra with her project and Aisha and José win a prize in the contest?

_____

_____

_____

_____

_____

_____

_____

_____

_____

_____

_____

_____

_____

# Answer Key

| Question | Correct Answer | Content Focus | CCSS | Complexity |
|----------|---------------|---------------|------|------------|
| 1 | C | Homographs | L.5.5c | DOK 1 |
| 2 | C, D | Theme | RL.5.2 | DOK 3 |
| 3A | C | Homographs | L.5.5c | DOK 1 |
| 3B | B | Homographs | L.5.5c | DOK 1 |
| 4 | see below | Character, Setting, Plot: Sequence | RL.3.3 | DOK 2 |
| 5A | B | Theme | RL.5.2 | DOK 3 |
| 5B | A | Theme/Text Evidence | RL.5.2/RL.5.1 | DOK 3 |
| 6 | see below | Theme | RL.5.2 | DOK 3 |
| 7 | D | Homographs | L.5.5c | DOK 1 |
| 8 | A, D | Theme | RL.5.2 | DOK 3 |
| 9 | A | Homographs | L.5.5c | DOK 1 |
| 10A | C | Theme | RL.5.2 | DOK 3 |
| 10B | B | Theme/Text Evidence | RL.5.2/RL.5.1 | DOK 3 |
| 11 | see below | Writing About Text | W.5.9a | DOK 4 |

| | | |
|---|---|---|
| **Comprehension** 2, 4, 5A, 5B, 6, 8, 10A, 10B | /12 | % |
| **Vocabulary** 1, 3A, 3B, 7, 9 | /8 | % |
| **Total Weekly Assessment Score** | /20 | % |

**4** Students should order the events as follows:
- 1: Audra gets her assignment.
- 2: Audra makes a plan.
- 3: Audra finishes her report.
- 4: Audra reads her poem.

**6** Students should circle the following paragraph:
- "We will bake a gigantic cake that will be larger than all the other cakes! It will be so huge that we will get the prize for the biggest cake," he said. "It won't matter what it tastes like!"

**11** To receive full credit for the response, the following information should be included: Audra is able to finish her project because she breaks the large project into four smaller projects. Aisha and José are able to win the contest because they have a plan in mind to bake the biggest cake rather than the best-tasting one.

**Read the passage "The Bake Sale" before answering Numbers 1 through 5.**

# The Bake Sale

Ms. Cross's fifth-grade class was planning a bake sale to make money for new equipment for the school grounds. Maia said, "Let's all bring some cookies to sell."

Jared put up his hand, "What if we sold bread? It is something almost everyone likes and we could make a variety of kinds."

Josie added, "Why don't we bring different breads that our families enjoy?"

Ms. Cross said, "What a great idea! You could each choose bread you would like to make. Some of you may want to work in pairs or teams along with an adult to help with the baking. Wash all the equipment you use so it will be sanitary."

Sophia said, "This is an important project, and our project has a better chance to succeed if we choose a good location."

Juan suggested setting up a table in front of the big grocery store near the school. The class started making plans. Because there would be customers, everyone could work a one-hour shift as a salesperson.

Ms. Cross reminded students that they would have to set a price for their breads and mark the prices on them, so Maddie suggested that a committee go to grocery stores to take notes about the cost of bread. Another committee could find a long table, and other students were needed to get cards and markers to use for labeling.

Jake said, "Are we sure we want all this work?"

Tim said, "Of course we do! We need new soccer balls and other things too, and this is the only way we'll get them. The exertion will make us tired, but it will be worth it."

So they all agreed to help. Everyone got busy checking recipes for what they needed for ingredients. Since they would need advice on some things, they had to enlist parents to help them.

**GO ON →**

Liane loved the *mantou*, or steamed buns, that her grandmother learned to make in China before coming to America. Her grandmother offered to help her make a batch early Saturday morning so they would be fresh. When Liane got to her grandmother's house, the dough of water, a little sugar, yeast, and flour was mixed and rising. The yeast in the dough would make it rise. Grandmother told her to punch the dough down. Then they covered it and let it rise again. After about 20 minutes, Grandmother showed Liane how to knead the dough and shape it into rolls. They boiled water and placed the rolls in the steamer. In 10 minutes, the first batch of buns was cooked. They looked perfect, and Liane was proud of them.

When Liane got to the bake sale, several classmates were already there. Mauricio showed her the Cuban bread his grandfather had helped him make. He had started it with yeast, warm water, and flour like the steamed buns. The dough had to rest in the refrigerator for 24 hours. On Saturday morning, they added other ingredients to the "starter." They kneaded it, let it rise, and formed the dough into loaves. The loaves were baked, not steamed.

Carissa showed the Italian focaccia bread she made with her grandmother's help. It had similar ingredients to the other breads but more spices, including garlic and basil and some cheese. Erik brought crusty rye sourdough bread. His mother helped him make it the way her mother from Germany had taught her. Wendy made scones with her mother, whose family came from England in the seventeenth century. Scones are rich biscuits made without yeast.

Jay brought some chapati, a flatbread he learned about in India last summer. Patrick brought his mother's Irish soda bread with caraway seeds. David and Sarah brought challah, a bread traditionally served on Jewish holidays. With help from Sarah's mom, David and Sarah rolled the dough into "snakes" and braided them. Jake participated by bringing a loaf of whole wheat bread his father had helped him make and several dozen homemade rolls.

The bake sale was a huge success! The breads sold quickly, and the class made $370 for new equipment. Ms. Cross observed that bread is an important part of cultures around the world.

**GO ON →**

**Now answer Numbers 1 through 5. Base your answers on "The Bake Sale."**

**1** Which sentences **best** explain how the characters in the passage are alike? Select **two** options.

(A) They all ask Ms. Cross to help them bake their bread.

(B) They all worry about the amount of work involved.

(C) They all recently came from different countries.

(D) They all want to have a successful bake sale.

(E) They all become experts in making bread.

(F) They all participate in the project.

**2** This question has two parts. First, answer part A. Then, answer part B.

**Part A:** Read the sentence from the text.

"Wash all the equipment you use so it will be sanitary."

What does sanitary mean in the sentence?

(A) clean

(B) fresh

(C) tasty

(D) useful

**Part B:** Which word in the sentence explains why the equipment is sanitary?

(A) wash

(B) all

(C) you

(D) use

**GO ON →**

**3** This question has two parts. First, answer part A. Then, answer part B.

**Part A:** Which statement **best** summarizes the theme of the text?

(A) Most bread contains flour and water.

(B) A successful project needs help from parents.

(C) A bake sale featuring bread will always be a success.

(D) People from different countries have things in common.

**Part B:** Which sentence from the text **best** supports your answer in part A?

(A) "Ms. Cross's fifth-grade class was planning a bake sale to make money for new equipment for the school grounds."

(B) "Another committee could find a long table, and other students were needed to get cards and markers to use for labeling."

(C) "With help from Sarah's mom, David and Sarah rolled the dough into "snakes" and braided them."

(D) "Ms. Cross observed that bread is an important part of cultures around the world."

**4** Read the sentence from the text.

"The exertion will make us tired, but it will be worth it."

What does exertion mean in the sentence?

(A) bread

(B) effort

(C) game

(D) viewpoint

**GO ON →**

**5** Circle **two** paragraphs that **best** support the major theme in the passage.

Ms. Cross's fifth-grade class was planning a bake sale to make money for new equipment for the school grounds. Maia said, "Let's all bring some cookies to sell."

Jared put up his hand, "What if we sold bread? It is something almost everyone likes and we could make a variety of kinds."

Josie added, "Why don't we bring different breads that our families enjoy?"

Ms. Cross said, "What a great idea! You could each choose bread you would like to make. Some of you may want to work in pairs or teams along with an adult to help with the baking. Wash all the equipment you use so it will be sanitary."

Sophia said, "This is an important project, and our project has a better chance to succeed if we choose a good location."

**GO ON →**

**Read the passage "Fourteen Days in Tokyo" before answering Numbers 6 through 10.**

# Fourteen Days in Tokyo

It was July, and Todd wanted to hang out with his friends. Yet, on Friday, Todd and his family were flying to Tokyo, Japan. They would visit his grandmother, Obaasan. She liked being called by the Japanese word for *grandmother*. Obaasan promised to show them around Tokyo, but Todd really did not want to leave San Francisco.

First of all, they arrived early and had to sit in the airport for two hours before the flight. Finally they took off and were airborne, but it was still another eleven hours before they would land in Tokyo. Todd's mother was petite, so she didn't suffer from the small amount of space each passenger had, but his father was soon complaining about leg cramps. This trip was even worse than Todd had expected.

After a taxi ride, they were at Obaasan's apartment in a modern building. She met them with a big hug. Inside her apartment, there were no doors, but rather screens that separated the rooms. Instead of carpets, straw mats were on the floors. The furnishings with cushions for seating and a low dining table were different from the kind of furniture in Todd's home. Obaasan also had flowers in every room.

Obaasan had prepared a special meal for them. Todd liked the rice and grilled tuna, but he didn't care for the cake of soybeans called tofu. He had never eaten pickled vegetables, but the taste was not bad.

**GO ON →**

Due to being awake during the protracted flight, Todd was exhausted and slept well. Obaasan served them breakfast and then took them to the Tokyo Metropolitan Government Building, the tallest building in the city. The observatory decks at the top are the best place to view all of Tokyo. It was a clear morning, so they could see Mount Fuji, the tallest mountain in Japan and a kind of volcano. Todd had never seen such a view! Maybe this trip would not be boring after all.

Afterwards, they ate at a restaurant in the building. Everyone ordered sushi, a small, tasty food and a delicacy. Some pieces were rice rolled with fish and others were rice rolled with vegetables. The sushi in San Francisco was not nearly as good.

The next day, Obaasan took everyone to Sunshine City, a city within the city with shops, restaurants, and an indoor theme park with games and rides. It had a number of food theme areas like Ice Cream City where shops sell ice cream. While Obaasan and Mom went shopping, Dad and Todd visited the theme park where Todd played video games. Then they went to the aquarium to see sea animals. The stingrays were Todd's favorite.

Everything was turning out to be more interesting than Todd expected, but his best time was at a *bunraku*, or puppet theater. The puppets were as big as people and seemed to be alive. The people who worked the puppets were right on stage in front of the audience. Because the puppets were so large, everything they said and did seemed exaggerated. Todd loved the colorful costumes and sets.

When it was time to return to America, Todd did not want to leave. It had been the best two weeks of his life! He asked Obaasan if he could come back next summer, and she said, "I would love that."

**GO ON →**

**Now answer Numbers 6 through 10. Base your answers on "Fourteen Days in Tokyo."**

**6** This question has two parts. First, answer part A. Then, answer part B.

**Part A:** Which statement **best** summarizes the theme of the text?

(A) Tokyo is the best city in the world.

(B) It is a long way from San Francisco to Tokyo.

(C) Sometimes we have to try something new to enjoy it.

(D) Many things in Japan are different from what an American is used to.

**Part B:** Which sentence from the text **best** supports your answer in part A?

(A) "It was July, and Todd wanted to hang out with his friends."

(B) "He had never eaten pickled vegetables, but the taste was not bad."

(C) "Maybe this trip would not be boring after all."

(D) "The sushi in San Francisco was not nearly as good."

**7** Read the sentence from the text.

Todd's mother was petite, so she didn't suffer from the small amount of space each passenger had, but his father was soon complaining about leg cramps.

What does the word petite mean?

(A) cheerful

(B) eager

(C) patient

(D) small

**GO ON →**

**8** Complete the sentence about the message of the passage. Write the number of the correct phrase in each part of the sentence.

At first, Todd _____, but by the end of the passage he _____.

> **Phrases:**
> 1 – is excited about visiting Obaasan
> 2 – can't wait to go back to Tokyo
> 3 – looks forward to returning home
> 4 – does not want to travel to Japan

**9** This question has two parts. First, answer part A. Then, answer part B.

**Part A:** Read the sentence from the text.

Because the puppets were so large, everything they said and did seemed exaggerated.

What does exaggerated mean?

(A) magnified

(B) played down

(C) spoken loudly

(D) decreased in size

**Part B:** Which word in the sentence explains why the puppets are exaggerated?

(A) because

(B) large

(C) everything

(D) seemed

**GO ON →**

**10** Which details **best** support the theme of the passage? Select **two** choices.

(A) the length of the trip to Japan

(B) Todd's new experiences in Tokyo

(C) the description of Obaasan's home

(D) Obaasan's efforts to show her affection

(E) the way Todd feels about his trip to Tokyo

(F) the differences between Japanese and American food

**STOP**

Name: _____ Date: _____

**Now answer Number 11. Base your answer on "The Bake Sale" and "Fourteen Days in Tokyo."**

**11** Compare and contrast the themes of "The Bake Sale" and "Fourteen Days in Tokyo." Support your answer with details from both texts.

_____

_____

_____

_____

_____

_____

_____

_____

_____

_____

_____

_____

_____

_____

_____

_____

# Answer Key

Name: _____

| Question | Correct Answer | Content Focus | CCSS | Complexity |
|---|---|---|---|---|
| 1 | D, F | Character, Setting, Plot: Compare and Contrast | RL.5.3 | DOK 3 |
| 2A | A | Context Clues: Cause and Effect | L.5.4a | DOK 2 |
| 2B | A | Context Clues: Cause and Effect/ Text Evidence | L.5.4a/ RL.5.1 | DOK 2 |
| 3A | D | Theme | RL.5.2 | DOK 3 |
| 3B | D | Theme/Text Evidence | RL.5.2/ RL.5.1 | DOK 3 |
| 4 | B | Context Clues: Cause and Effect | L.5.4a | DOK 2 |
| 5 | see below | Theme | RL.5.2 | DOK 3 |
| 6A | C | Theme | RL.5.2 | DOK 3 |
| 6B | B | Theme/Text Evidence | RL.5.2/ RL.5.1 | DOK 3 |
| 7 | D | Context Clues: Cause and Effect | L.5.4a | DOK 2 |
| 8 | see below | Theme | RL.5.2 | DOK 3 |
| 9A | A | Context Clues: Cause and Effect | L.5.4a | DOK 2 |
| 9B | B | Context Clues: Cause and Effect/ Text Evidence | L.5.4a/ RL.5.1 | DOK 2 |
| 10 | B, E | Theme | RL.5.2 | DOK 3 |
| 11 | see below | Writing About Text | W.5.9a | DOK 4 |

| | | | |
|---|---|---|---|
| **Comprehension** 1, 3A, 3B, 5, 6A, 6B, 8, 10 | | /12 | % |
| **Vocabulary** 2A, 2B, 4, 7, 9A, 9B | | /8 | % |
| **Total Weekly Assessment Score** | | /20 | % |

**5** Students should circle the following two paragraphs:
- Jared put up his hand, "What if we sold bread? It is something almost everyone likes and we could make a variety of kinds."
- Josie added, "Why don't we bring different breads that our families enjoy?"

**8** Students should write the numbers 4 and 2 to complete the sentence as follows:
- At first, Todd does not want to travel to Japan, but by the end of the passage he can't wait to go back to Tokyo.

**11** To receive full credit for the response, the following information should be included: The themes of "The Bake Sale" and "Fourteen Days in Tokyo" are similar in that characters in each story learn about other cultures and discover that people from different places have things in common. In "The Bake Sale," the students discover that people from many countries make and enjoy bread. In "Fourteen Days in Tokyo," Todd has a good time visiting new places and trying new foods in Japan.

**Read the passage "The Stag at the Pool" before answering Numbers 1 through 5.**

# The Stag at the Pool

There was once a Stag who was tremendously proud of his beautiful horns. They were large and well-formed, with many points. He rubbed them often on the bark of trees, keeping them glossy and razor-sharp. The other animals of the forest bowed to him, and they often spoke of his antlers with admiration. "How beautiful your horns are!" the Fox and the Rabbit would say. "They are as glossy as satin or sunlight reflecting off water!" The Stag would bow his head, making sure his antlers caught the light of the sun so they would flash and glow. He knew the other animals were right, and he felt that their high regard was well deserved. No other Stag, and certainly none of the other animals, had such stunning horns.

Whenever the Stag passed a pool of water, he would stop to look in and admire his magnificent horns. One day, while passing through a meadow, he came to a clear pond and bent to the water. There was his reflection, as glorious as ever. "No one in the world has such astonishing antlers as mine!" he said, preening as he turned this way and that.

For the first time, though, he noticed his legs reflected in the water. He frowned, and his reflection frowned back. "How lean my legs are!" he said. "I wish they were thicker and stronger. My wonderful antlers look ridiculous atop a body with such weak-looking legs!" For the first time he felt jealous of the Fox, with its short, thick limbs. He even envied the Rabbit, who could leap high into the air on its funny legs.

The Stag was so engrossed that he did not notice that a Lion had crept up alongside him. Suddenly, he saw the Lion reflected in the pond, and for a moment the two animals stared at each other in the water. The Lion displayed his teeth, flaunting them as if he were bragging. The Stag leaped away, terrified, and the Lion immediately gave chase.

**GO ON →**

Through the meadow the Stag raced, gasping in fear. The ground was flat and even, and the Stag moved with the velocity of an arrow shot from a bow. His legs kept him far ahead of the Lion, whose legs were much shorter and thicker than his own. From a distance, the other animals watched the chase.

"The Stag will surely outrun the Lion!" the Fox cried.

The Rabbit said, "Oh, he must, he must!" But then the Stag entered the forest, dense with trees.

Weaving among the trees, the Stag kept ahead of the Lion at first. He was not fatigued at all, for his long legs could carry him far and fast without tiring, but the branches of some of the trees hung low, and vines curled around them. The vines clutched at the Stag's antlers as he dodged among the trees. Before he knew it, the Stag had caught his antlers in the branches and vines. He struggled mightily, but the tangled vines held him tight. Closer and closer the Lion came, smiling with its sharp teeth showing. The Stag, knowing his end was near, closed his eyes and sighed deeply.

"Oh," he said, "how I have fooled myself! The long legs that I hated would have saved me, but the antlers that I loved have led to my destruction!"

**GO ON →**

**Now answer Numbers 1 through 5. Base your answers on "The Stag at the Pool."**

**1** Read the sentence from the text.

"They are as <u>glossy</u> as satin or sunlight reflecting off water!"

What does the word <u>glossy</u> mean in the sentence?

(A) pointed

(B) shiny

(C) small

(D) strong

**2** This question has two parts. First, answer part A. Then, answer part B.

**Part A:** Which statement **best** summarizes the theme of the text?

(A) You do not always recognize what is most valuable.

(B) Keep your friends close, but your enemies closer.

(C) Fine possessions do not make a fine person.

(D) The best things come in small packages.

**Part B:** Which evidence from the text **best** supports your answer in part A?

(A) "The other animals of the forest bowed to him, and they often spoke of his antlers with admiration."

(B) "The Stag was so engrossed that he did not notice that a Lion had crept up alongside him."

(C) ". . . but the branches of some of the trees hung low, and vines curled around them."

(D) "The long legs that I hated would have saved me, but the antlers that I loved have led to my destruction!"

**GO ON →**

**3** This question has two parts. First, answer part A. Then, answer part B.

**Part A:** Read the sentence from the text.

The ground was flat and even, and the Stag moved with the velocity of an arrow shot from a bow.

What does the word velocity mean?

(A) curve

(B) direction

(C) sharpness

(D) speed

**Part B:** Which phrase in the sentence **best** explains the meaning of velocity?

(A) "flat and even"

(B) "the Stag moved"

(C) "an arrow shot"

(D) "a bow"

**4** Read the sentence from the text. Then, answer the question.

Before he knew it, the Stag had caught his antlers in the branches and vines.

How does the sentence support the theme of the passage? Select **two** choices.

(A) It describes how dangerous nature can be.

(B) It tells how the Stag's legs could not help him.

(C) It reveals that the Stag values the wrong things.

(D) It shows that the Stag's antlers lead to his downfall.

(E) It suggests that the Lion will take the Stag's antlers.

(F) It explains how the Stag was not as fast as he thought.

**GO ON →**

**5** Both the Stag and the Lion contribute to the theme of the passage. Write the details and text evidence from the box into the correct locations on the chart to show how they contribute. Not all details and text evidence will be used.

|  | **The Stag** | **The Lion** |
|---|---|---|
| *How Contributes to Theme* |  |  |
| *Text Evidence* |  |  |

**How Contributes to Theme:**

Learns lesson

Teaches lesson

Offers compliments

Offers encouragement

**Text Evidence:**

"Through the meadow the Stag raced, gasping in fear."

"'The Stag will surely outrun the Lion!'"

"Closer and closer the Lion came, smiling with its sharp teeth showing."

"'Oh,' he said, 'how I have fooled myself!'"

**GO ON →**

**Read the passage "Hans in Luck" before answering Numbers 6 through 10.**

# Hans in Luck

Long ago, young men worked to learn a trade. When they were done, they were paid by their master and then went off to find work or open their own shops. After seven years of hard work, a young man named Hans asked for his wages. The master gave him a big piece of gold, which Hans thought must surely be the most valuable thing in the world. The young man left immediately to return to his village to see his mother, for he yearned to see her like a homesick child.

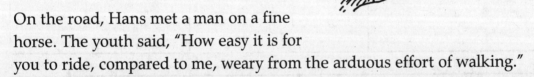

On the road, Hans met a man on a fine horse. The youth said, "How easy it is for you to ride, compared to me, weary from the arduous effort of walking."

The rider got down from the animal and proposed a trade, saying, "I'll exchange my steed for that piece of gold in your hand."

When Hans agreed, the rider thrust the horse's bridle into the young man's hands. "Just utter 'C'ck! C'ck!' and the horse will gallop like lightning," the rider instructed and walked away.

Hans rode only for the briefest moment before the steed instantly threw him off, and he landed in a ditch beside the road.

Soon a woman happened to pass by, leading a cow. She was startled to see a young man in the ditch. Hans rubbed a sore arm and leg and said, "You have a nice, quiet cow that no doubt gives refreshing milk. I'd rather have your cow than this brute of a horse."

**GO ON →**

The peasant woman liked this idea and agreed to trade her cow for the horse. So Hans continued along the route to his village, driving the cow along and whistling merrily.

Hans grew thirsty and tried to milk the cow, but he went about it in a crude way, and the animal gave him a swift kick.

Sweating, thirsty, and bruised, Hans was in great despair by this point. Then along came a butcher driving a horse-drawn cart, and in the cart was a pig. It was gargantuan, seeming to be the size of a house. Hans told the butcher, "How I wish I had a pig. I'd have it butchered to make sausages and other delicacies."

"I'd be happy to trade you this prime pig for that worthless looking cow," offered the butcher. Of course, the cow was exactly what he wanted. The deal was quickly completed.

Before twilight fell, Hans met a man carrying a goose. "What an ancient pig!" the man exclaimed. "It would make a fine pet for my children." He smiled to himself as he offered his goose to Hans in exchange for the pig.

"My mother can use the goose's soft feathers to stuff a pillow," Hans told himself.

Finally he entered his village and the first person he saw was a scissors-grinder at his trade. "Where did you get that goose?" the man asked Hans.

"I exchanged it for my pig," Hans replied. Then he worked backward to relate all his adventures to the scissors-grinder. The man recommended that Hans trade the goose for his grinding stone. Then Hans would have a way to make money, sharpening scissors and knife blades. Hans agreed to the trade.

But with each step Hans took, the stone seemed to grow heavier. Soon he laid it by a stream that ran through the village, and when he stooped to drink, the weighty stone tumbled into the water.

Free of any tiresome burdens now, Hans exclaimed, "I'm the luckiest man alive!" Then with the fleetness of a racer, he headed home to see his mother.

**GO ON →**

Name: _____ Date: _____

**Now answer Numbers 6 through 10. Base your answers on "Hans in Luck."**

**6** Put the events in the story in the correct sequence. Write each event in the correct section of the chart.

| | |
|---|---|
| **First** | |
| **Second** | |
| **Third** | |
| **Fourth** | |
| **Fifth** | |

**Events:**
Hans loses the heavy stone.
Hans makes a trade for a pig.
Hans falls from a horse.
Hans arrives at his village.
Hans meets a peasant woman.

**GO ON →**

**7** Read the sentence from the text.

The youth said, "How easy it is for you to ride, compared to me, weary from the <u>arduous</u> effort of walking."

What does the word <u>arduous</u> mean?

Ⓐ basic

Ⓑ difficult

Ⓒ proper

Ⓓ unlucky

**8** This question has two parts. First, answer part A. Then, answer part B.

**Part A:** Which statement **best** summarizes the theme?

Ⓐ Fine possessions do not make a fine person.

Ⓑ You do not need possessions to be happy.

Ⓒ The best things come in small packages.

Ⓓ Beware of people who offer you gifts.

**Part B:** Which evidence from the text **best** supports your answer in part A?

Ⓐ "Before twilight fell, Hans met a man carrying a goose."

Ⓑ "Finally he entered his village and the first person he saw was a scissors-grinder at his trade."

Ⓒ "Then he worked backward to relate all his adventures to the scissors-grinder."

Ⓓ "Free of any tiresome burdens now, Hans exclaimed, 'I'm the luckiest man alive!'"

**GO ON →**

**9** This question has two parts. First, answer part A. Then, answer part B.

**Part A:** Read the sentence from the text.

It was gargantuan, seeming to be the size of a house.

What does <u>gargantuan</u> mean?

(A) expensive

(B) huge

(C) lively

(D) ugly

**Part B:** Which word in the sentence gives the **best** clue to the meaning of <u>gargantuan</u>?

(A) it

(B) seeming

(C) size

(D) house

**10** Read the sentence from the text. Then, answer the question.

But with each step Hans took, the stone seemed to grow heavier.

Which statements **best** explain how the sentence supports the theme? Select **two** choices.

(A) It hints that Hans will never be a good scissors-grinder.

(B) It suggests that Hans does not know what he wants in life.

(C) It explains that, no matter what he does, Hans is always miserable.

(D) It describes how owning the sharpening stone makes Hans unhappy.

(E) It points out that Hans can never be happy until he has reached home.

(F) It shows that Hans does not gain any satisfaction from making a trade.

**Now answer Number 11. Base your answer on "The Stag at the Pool" and "Hans in Luck."**

**11** What lessons do the Stag and Hans learn in "The Stag at the Pool" and "Hans in Luck"? Support your answer with details from both texts.

_____

_____

_____

_____

_____

_____

_____

_____

_____

_____

_____

_____

_____

_____

_____

_____

# Answer Key

Name: _____

| Question | Correct Answer | Content Focus | CCSS | Complexity |
|:---:|:---:|:---:|:---:|:---:|
| 1 | B | Context Clues: Comparison | L.5.4a | DOK 2 |
| 2A | A | Theme | RL.5.2 | DOK 3 |
| 2B | D | Theme/Text Evidence | RL.5.2/ RL.5.1 | DOK 3 |
| 3A | D | Context Clues: Comparison | L.5.4a | DOK 2 |
| 3B | C | Context Clues: Comparison/ Text Evidence | L.5.4a/ RL.5.1 | DOK 2 |
| 4 | C, D | Theme | RL.5.2 | DOK 3 |
| 5 | see below | Theme | RL.5.2 | DOK 3 |
| 6 | see below | Character, Setting, Plot: Sequence | RL.5.3 | DOK 1 |
| 7 | B | Context Clues: Comparison | L.5.4a | DOK 2 |
| 8A | B | Theme | RL.5.2 | DOK 3 |
| 8B | D | Theme/Text Evidence | RL.5.2/ RL.5.1 | DOK 3 |
| 9A | B | Context Clues: Comparison | L.5.4a | DOK 2 |
| 9B | D | Context Clues: Comparison/ Text Evidence | L.5.4a/ RL.5.1 | DOK 2 |
| 10 | D, E | Theme | RL.5.2 | DOK 3 |
| 11 | see below | Writing About Text | W.5.9a | DOK 4 |

| | | | |
|:---|:---:|:---:|
| **Comprehension** 2A, 2B, 4, 5, 6, 8A, 8B, 10 | /12 | % |
| **Vocabulary** 1, 3A, 3B, 7, 9A, 9B | /8 | % |
| **Total Weekly Assessment Score** | /20 | % |

**5** Students should complete the chart as follows:
- The Stag—How Contributes to Theme: Learns lesson; Text Evidence: "'Oh,' he said, 'how I have fooled myself!'"
- The Lion— How Contributes to Theme: Teaches lesson; Text Evidence: "Closer and closer the Lion came, smiling with its sharp teeth showing."

**6** Students should write the events in the following order:
- First—Hans falls from a horse.
- Second—Hans meets a peasant woman.
- Third—Hans makes a trade for a pig.
- Fourth—Hans arrives at his village.
- Fifth—Hans loses the heavy stone.

**11** To receive full credit for the response, the following information should be included: The Stag and Hans both learn that the things they thought were of great value turned out to be not as valuable to them as they had believed.

**Read the article "The Fall of the Giants" before answering Numbers 1 through 5.**

# The Fall of the Giants

The Sequoia National Forest in California's Sierra Nevada Mountains is home to the most massive trees in the world. At its entrance is the Trail of 100 Giants, a short, easy, paved trail that people can walk. It gives visitors great views of more than a hundred sequoias. These trees grow only in the special geology of the slopes of the Sierra Nevadas. The largest of the trees is 20 feet around and 220 feet tall. You almost need a telescope to see the top of it!

The sequoia trees that line the Trail of 100 Giants have stood for generations. Many of these botanical wonders started growing in the Middle Ages. The trees watched the first Europeans settle in California and they grew while America fought its revolution and its civil war. They grew through the Gold Rush in the mid-1800s and two world wars. The trees were declared a national monument in 2000.

Then, in October 2011, two of the giants fell. There were only a few tourists nearby. One photographer from Germany used a video camera to record the trees crashing to the ground. Luckily, nobody was hurt, but watchers were astonished that these enormous trees could topple like babies trying to take their first steps. One explanation was that the summer had been very wet, and the ground was quite hydrated. The earth may have been too soggy to hold the shallow roots of the trees.

Some officials fear that the foot traffic from tourists might have weakened the trees. Even pollution from cars visiting the park could have damaged them. Three to four million people a year visit Yosemite National Park, where the Trail of 100 Giants is located. It might be, though, that the trees were simply old and it was the time in their life cycle to die.

**GO ON →**

The trees may have been as much as 1,500 years old. They were more than 200 feet tall. The two that fell were connected at their base, and most park scientists believe that when the first one fell, it brought the second one down with it.

The question now is, what should be done with the fallen trees? They fell across a popular path, crushing a bridge and blocking the walkway. The trunks are too big for most walkers to climb over, though some have tried. The path they block is designed for people in wheelchairs, and there is no other path that these people can use. The Park Service asked the public what they thought.

People's ideas have been varied. Many biologists think the trees should be left just as they are, letting nature take its course. Some people feel that the Forest Service should drill a tunnel through the trunk so people can simply walk through. Some want to build a bridge over the trees, but the bridge would have to be one that wheelchairs could use. Some think the path should go around the trees. And some believe the trees should be cut up for firewood.

Park officials have decided to take their time deciding what to do. In the past, they have had to cut down dead trees to be sure that visitors to the park would be safe. Since the trees are national monuments now, though, any decision must be carefully considered. The sequoias are a rare treasure, and even in death, they should be treated with respect.

**GO ON →**

**Now answer Numbers 1 through 5. Base your answers on "The Fall of the Giants."**

**1** Read the sentence from the text.

These trees grow only in the special <u>geology</u> of the slopes of the Sierra Nevadas.

The root of <u>geology</u> is *geo,* which means "earth." What is studied in <u>geology</u>?

(A) animals

(B) land

(C) people

(D) trees

**2** Read the paragraph.

The sequoia trees that line the Trail of 100 Giants have stood for generations. Many of these botanical wonders started growing in the Middle Ages. The trees watched the first Europeans settle in California and they grew while America fought its revolution and its civil war. They grew through the Gold Rush in the mid-1800s and two world wars. The trees were declared a national monument in 2000.

Which detail would **best** support the main idea of the paragraph?

(A) The trees grow taller and taller every day.

(B) Sequoias have seen much of our country's history.

(C) The Gold Rush was responsible in part for the migration west.

(D) The Sierra Nevada Mountains are in the western part of the U.S.

**GO ON →**

Name: _____ Date: _____

**3** This question has two parts. First, answer part A. Then, answer part B.

Read the paragraph. Then, answer the questions.

Then, in October 2011, two of the giants fell. There were only a few tourists nearby. One photographer from Germany used a video camera to record the trees crashing to the ground. Luckily, nobody was hurt, but watchers were astonished that these enormous trees could topple like babies trying to take their first steps. One explanation was that the summer had been very wet, and the ground was quite hydrated. The earth may have been too soggy to hold the shallow roots of the trees.

**Part A:** What is the main idea of the paragraph?

(A) A German photographer took a video of a sequoia falling.

(B) Walking through the sequoias can be dangerous.

(C) Two sequoias fell down recently in the park.

(D) Sequoias fall down easily when they get old.

**Part B:** Which sentence from the paragraph **best** states the main idea?

(A) "Then, in October 2011, two of the giants fell."

(B) "There were only a few tourists nearby."

(C) "One photographer from Germany used a video camera to record the trees crashing to the ground."

(D) "Luckily, nobody was hurt, but watchers were astonished that these enormous trees could topple like babies trying to take their first steps."

**GO ON →**

**4** Determine the meaning of the Greek root in each underlined word. Draw a line from the sentence with the word on the left to the meaning of the Greek root on the right.

| Many of these <u>botanical</u> wonders started growing in the Middle Ages. | | water |
|---|---|---|

| One explanation was that the summer had been very wet, and the ground was quite <u>hydrated</u>. | | circle |
|---|---|---|

| It might be, though, that the trees were simply old and it was the time in their life <u>cycle</u> to die. | | plant |
|---|---|---|

**5** This question has two parts. First, answer part A. Then, answer part B.

**Part A:** What is the central idea of the article?

(A) People should do more to help save the sequoias.

(B) It is lucky nobody was hurt when the sequoias fell.

(C) The death of a sequoia is an important natural event.

(D) Not many people have the chance to see a sequoia fall.

**Part B:** Read the sentence.

The earth may have been too soggy to hold the shallow roots of the trees.

How does the sentence support the central idea of the article?

(A) It provides details about what happened after the sequoias fell.

(B) It shows how giant sequoias are able to grow as large as they do.

(C) It gives information about what the Sequoia National Forest looks like.

(D) It suggests a reason why two giant sequoias fell in the Sequoia National Forest.

**GO ON →**

**Read the article "Super Snakes" before answering Numbers 6 through 10.**

# Super Snakes

Many people have a snake phobia because they know only the common myths about these reptiles. Few snakes are deadly, but poisonous species have certainly given snakes a bad reputation! Here are some facts about snakes that will help you better understand these members of the animal kingdom living in our biosphere.

Snakes can survive in many geographic areas. They are not found in the polar regions of the world, though, because snakes are cold-blooded. Their body thermostat changes their body temperature to match how hot or cold the air is. A snake would freeze and die in the Arctic or Antarctic.

Nature has given this creature many gifts, one of which is the way its skin looks. Its patterns and coloring help the reptile hide from animals that will attack and eat it. Many snake species have skin the dull color of the ground. The kinds that slither up trees may be bright green, like leaves.

Snakes can go for weeks or even months between meals, and some snakes eat only once or twice a year. Because of this, they do not need to hunt constantly for food.

The snake's flickering tongue may look frightening as it vibrates, but it is part of an important sense organ for the snake. This special organ is located on the roof of its mouth. The snake uses it to smell prey and to find a mate. Some snakes, like the python, have special cells on top of their heads. These microscopic cells help them locate warm-blooded animals.

**GO ON →**

Snakes use the muscles along the sides of their bodies to slither from place to place. They have four different ways to move. Some snakes bunch themselves up and then thrust themselves forward. Some push off and move in a wave-like motion. Some move the middle of their bodies up and down. This pushes their heads forward. And some grip the ground with their scales, using the scales and their muscles to push themselves forward.

Most snakes feed on small mammals. Big snakes, like pythons, will attack much larger prey. Constrictor snakes wrap themselves around large prey and compress it like a belt that is much too tight. Snakes will often win what look like impossible battles. Because they can move so rapidly and quietly, snakes are very effective hunters. The same muscles that move the snake along help to move the snake's meal through its system.

Snakes have many enemies themselves. Raccoons, birds, foxes, coyotes, and even other snakes eat snakes, and humans can be their enemies, too. Many humans are afraid of snakes and will hunt them to get rid of them. Humans also build communities in snake territory. With each generation, snakes have less and less room to live.

It is true that some snakes are poisonous. They use their poison to stun their prey before eating it. It is always best to be careful around snakes. Only an expert can tell which snakes are harmless and which are dangerous. However, a person can be careful around snakes without having a fear of them. The best advice is to find out if any poisonous snakes live in your area. In addition, if you are going camping or hiking, check to find out if the area has poisonous snakes.

If any poisonous snakes are found where you live or where you will be visiting, use photographs to learn to identify them. Also learn what steps to take when you come across a poisonous snake. With knowledge like this, you can replace your fear with caution.

**GO ON →**

**Now answer Numbers 6 through 10. Base your answers on "Super Snakes."**

**6** Read the sentence from the passage.

Many people have a snake <u>phobia</u> because they know only the common myths about these reptiles.

The root of <u>phobia</u> is *phob,* meaning "fear." What is someone with a <u>phobia</u> **most likely** to do?

(A) laugh

(B) scream

(C) sigh

(D) yawn

**7** Which details belong in a summary of the article? Write **three** details from the box into the chart. Not all of the details will be used.

| Summary of "Super Snakes" |
|---|
|  |
|  |
|  |

**Details:**

Snakes can push off from the ground to move.

Snakes have amazing ways to survive.

Find out what to do if you see a snake.

Few snakes are dangerous.

Many people fear snakes.

Some birds eat snakes.

**GO ON →**

**8** This question has two parts. First, answer part A. Then, answer part B.

Part A: Which sentence **best** summarizes the main idea of the article?

(A) If you are careless, you can be hurt or killed by a snake.

(B) Snakes have many gifts from nature, such as their skin.

(C) Snakes can be both dangerous and very interesting.

(D) Many people are very afraid of snakes.

Part B: Which sentence from the text **best** supports your answer in part A?

(A) "Here are some facts about snakes that will help you better understand these members of the animal kingdom living in our biosphere."

(B) "Snakes can go for weeks or even months between meals, and some snakes eat only once or twice a year."

(C) "Raccoons, birds, foxes, coyotes, and even other snakes eat snakes, and humans can be their enemies, too."

(D) "In addition, if you are going camping or hiking, check to find out if the area has poisonous snakes."

**GO ON →**

**9** Read the sentence from the text.

These <u>microscopic</u> cells help them locate warm-blooded animals.

The word microscopic comes from the Greek roots *micro*, meaning "small," and *scop*, meaning "see." What does this suggest about <u>microscopic</u> cells?

(A) They are hard to see.

(B) They are easily found.

(C) They are created by scientists.

(D) They are always changing in size.

**10** Which statements **best** explain what results from learning more about snakes? Select **two** choices.

(A) The reader fears snakes less.

(B) The reader begins to fear snakes.

(C) The reader begins to love snakes.

(D) The reader understands snakes better.

(E) The reader can find snakes more easily.

(F) The reader no longer avoids snakes in the wild.

STOP

Name: _____ Date: _____

**Now answer Number 11. Base your answer on "The Fall of the Giants" and "Super Snakes."**

**11** Describe one interesting fact or detail in "The Fall of the Giants" and "Super Snakes." Support your answer with details from both texts.

_____

_____

_____

_____

_____

_____

_____

_____

_____

_____

_____

_____

_____

_____

# Answer Key

Name: _____

| Question | Correct Answer | Content Focus | CCSS | Complexity |
|:---:|:---:|:---:|:---:|:---:|
| 1 | B | Greek Roots | L.5.4b | DOK 1 |
| 2 | B | Main Idea and Key Details | RI.5.2 | DOK 2 |
| 3A | C | Main Idea and Key Details | RI.5.2 | DOK 2 |
| 3B | A | Main Idea and Key Details/ Text Evidence | RI.5.2/ RI.5.1 | DOK 2 |
| 4 | see below | Greek Roots | L.5.4b | DOK 1 |
| 5A | C | Main Idea and Key Details | RI.5.2 | DOK 2 |
| 5B | D | Main Idea and Key Details/ Text Evidence | RI.5.2/ RI.5.1 | DOK 2 |
| 6 | B | Greek Roots | L.5.4b | DOK 1 |
| 7 | see below | Main Idea and Key Details | RI.5.2 | DOK 2 |
| 8A | C | Main Idea and Key Details | RI.5.2 | DOK 2 |
| 8B | B | Main Idea and Key Details/ Text Evidence | RI.5.2/ RI.5.1 | DOK 2 |
| 9 | A | Greek Roots | L.5.4b | DOK 1 |
| 10 | A, D | Text Structure: Cause and Effect | RI.5.3 | DOK 2 |
| 11 | see below | Writing About Text | W.5.9b | DOK 4 |

| | | | |
|---|---|:---:|:---:|
| **Comprehension** 2, 3A, 3B, 5A, 5B, 7, 8A, 8B, 10 | | /12 | % |
| **Vocabulary** 1, 4, 6, 9 | | /8 | % |
| **Total Weekly Assessment Score** | | /20 | % |

**4** Students should draw lines to make the following matches:
- botanical—plant
- hydrated—water
- cycle—circle

**7** Students should write the following sentences to include in a summary:
- Snakes have amazing ways to survive.
- Few snakes are dangerous.
- Many people fear snakes.

**11** To receive full credit for the response, the following information should be included: (Answers may vary but text evidence must be included from each article as well as an explanation of why the student finds it interesting. Examples follow.) Sequoias can be so big that tunnels can be made in fallen trees through which people can walk. Some snakes eat only once or twice a year.

Copyright © McGraw-Hill Education

**Read the article "Make a Model of the Water Cycle" before answering Numbers 1 through 5.**

# Make a Model of the Water Cycle

You can volunteer with three or four friends to do a team experiment. It will show you how heat evaporates water, changes it into droplets, and then turns it back to water. First, you need to know a little about the water cycle. Water moves from the oceans into the air. From the air, it falls as rain or snow back into the ocean or onto land. If it falls on land, it eventually works its way back into the ocean as an overflow of water called runoff. (See the diagram below.)

The water cycle starts when the sun heats ocean water. The sun converts the water into small, invisible particles of moisture called water vapor. The sun and wind cause the water vapor to rise into the air, where it cools off in the atmosphere, or the air that surrounds Earth. Then it changes to drops of water that cluster, or hold together, forming a cloud.

The water in the cloud falls as rain or snow. It may fall back into the ocean, or it may fall on land and eventually work its way back to the ocean as a water overflow called runoff. One way water does this is by falling into tributaries, which are rivers and streams that flow into larger bodies of water. The water may also collect in an underground layer of earth or rock. The rock must be porous enough to let the water flow through it. This water is called groundwater, and it, too, eventually finds its way to the ocean. Then the water cycle starts over again.

## THE WATER CYCLE

**GO ON →**

As you begin your experiment, remember this amazing fact. The amount of water on Earth now is the same as it was in the past and will be in the future. This means that the water you drank yesterday may once have been the water in the Delaware River when General Washington's troops crossed it during the Revolutionary War. About 71% of Earth's surface is water. This includes not only the water in oceans, rivers, and lakes. It also includes the water in clouds, rain, snow, and groundwater and in the icy regions at the North and South Poles.

Make a model of the water cycle with a partner or small group. Use the instructions below.

## Water Cycle Baggie

**Materials:**

A plastic bag that seals

A small, clear plastic cup

Water

Red food color

A permanent marker

**Steps:**

1. Fill cup about halfway with water. Add red food color to the water. Stir. Use the marker to show water level.

2. Place the cup in the baggie. Seal the bag.

3. Place the baggie in a sunny window.

Observe what happens to the water in the cup. Check the mark showing the water level. You should see that the water level becomes gradually lower. You should also begin to see droplets of water on the sides and bottom of the bag. The water is evaporating from the heat and then changing from the gas created by evaporation to water drops on the sides of the bag. The drops run down the sides and will begin to collect at the bottom. This is what happens when the sun heats the ocean. Particles of moisture rise and form clouds. The drops running down the sides of the bag are like rain falling on Earth.

**GO ON →**

**Now answer Numbers 1 through 5. Base your answers on "Make a Model of the Water Cycle."**

**1** This question has two parts. First, answer part A. Then, answer part B.

**Part A:** Read the sentence from the text.

The sun <u>converts</u> the water into small, invisible particles of moisture called water vapor.

The Latin root of <u>converts</u> is *vert*, meaning "to turn." What does <u>converts</u> mean?

(A) allows

(B) changes

(C) helps

(D) repeats

**Part B:** Which other word includes the same root as <u>converts</u>?

(A) convict

(B) overtime

(C) revert

(D) very

**GO ON →**

**2** This question has two parts. First, answer part A. Then, answer part B.

**Part A:** Which sentence **best** summarizes the main idea of the article?

(A) You can do an experiment with a baggie, cup, water, food color, and a marker.

(B) When the water in a cloud falls as precipitation, it may fall on land or water.

(C) In the water cycle, water evaporates, condenses, and falls as precipitation.

(D) Water is about 71% of Earth's surface and needed by plants and animals.

**Part B:** Which evidence from the text **best** supports the main idea?

(A) "You can volunteer with three or four friends to do a team experiment."

(B) "The amount of water on Earth now is the same as it was in the past and will be in the future."

(C) "This includes not only the water in oceans, rivers, and lakes."

(D) "The drops running down the sides of the bag are like rain falling on Earth."

**3** Read the sentence from the article.

One way water does this is by falling into tributaries, which are rivers and streams that flow into larger bodies of water.

The Latin root of tributaries is *trib*, meaning "pay." Which word is **most likely** to come from the same root as tributaries?

(A) allowance

(B) contribute

(C) salary

(D) tribe

**GO ON →**

Copyright © McGraw-Hill Education

**Weekly Assessment** · Unit 3, Week 4

**4** Choose **one** sentence that states the main idea of the section titled "Water Cycle Baggie." Then choose **two** sentences that support the main idea and write them in the chart. Write the number of each sentence in the chart.

| Main Idea of "Water Cycle Baggie" | Supporting Details |
|---|---|
| | |
| | |

**Sentences:**

1 – An important part of the experiment is adding the food color before putting the sealed plastic bag in a warm place.

2 – You need a plastic bag, clear cup, water, red food color, and a marker before setting up the experiment.

3 – An experiment with a plastic bag, cup, and water can show how water evaporates and then turns back to water.

**5** How did the author organize the steps to make the water cycle model? Select **two** choices.

(A) by including numbered directions

(B) by asking and answering questions

(C) by showing the cause of evaporation

(D) by listing the steps in the order they should be done

(E) by solving the problem of what causes condensation

(F) by comparing and contrasting water and water vapor

**GO ON →**

**Read the article "Be Prepared!" before answering Numbers 6 through 10.**

# Be Prepared!

Disasters happen all over the world. They include floods, tornadoes, hurricanes, earthquakes, landslides, and wildfires. Every family needs a plan in case an unexpected disaster strikes their home or community. Disaster plans will vary, and each family should consider the type of emergency most likely to occur.

Flooding is a common emergency. Some floods, called flash floods, develop quickly following heavy rainfall, and they usually affect only a limited area. Other floods develop slowly and affect large areas. Although some floods occur in places never affected before, many places flood consistently. If you live in such an area, your family should be prepared at all times. Have an emergency kit, food and water, and a plan for evacuation, or leaving the affected area.

Hurricanes usually occur in coastal states. They are predicted several days to as much as a week ahead of time. When a hurricane strikes, high winds can cause serious destruction, and flooding is possible. Flooding results from a surge of water from the ocean or gulf. Authorities may mandate that you go to a different location, so it is good to have an evacuation route planned. You may want to arrange to stay with friends or relatives. Many communities open centers that are safer than homes in a hurricane. If your center does not accept pets, you will need an alternate plan for the pet. Ahead of time, make sure your pet has had immunizations. An ID tag will help if you and your pet get separated, and a carrier or cage will protect your pet.

**GO ON →**

Tornadoes are violent storms, and they can do serious damage. They may develop with little advance warning. Just before one touches down, you may notice one or more of the following:

- dark sky
- large-size hail
- air that is ominously still
- a low cloud that may be rotating, or turning in a circle
- a loud roar

If you are in a building during either a hurricane or tornado, go to a basement or to an inside room. Experts say that you should stay away from windows and outside walls. If you are outside, lie flat in the lowest place. Cover your head with your hands.

There are steps everyone should take no matter what the risks are in your particular area. First, hold a family meeting to make a plan. All family members need to know where the emergency supplies are kept. Decide on a place for everyone to meet following a disaster. In an emergency, like a fire, plan to meet at a location right outside. Remember that family members may be in school and at work when a disaster strikes, so plan to go to a place where you can meet if you cannot return home. It is good to have a charged cell phone handy.

Below is a checklist you can use to be prepared for an emergency.

### Gather Emergency Supplies

- For each person, 1 gallon of water a day for 3–7 days
- Packaged and canned meats and fish, fruits, and vegetables
- Manual can opener
- Special foods for family members, such as baby food
- Pet food if you have a pet
- First aid kit with bandages, gauze pads, antiseptic, and scissors
- Portable radio
- Flashlight/batteries

### Other Items

- Paper cups, plates, and plastic utensils
- Paper towels and other paper products
- Trash bags
- Sturdy shoes and warm clothing
- Blankets/sleeping bags

Knowing what to expect and being prepared for the worst will help you and your family survive.

**GO ON →**

**Now answer Numbers 6 through 10. Base your answers on "Be Prepared!"**

**6** This question has two parts. First, answer part A. Then, answer part B.

**Part A:** Read the sentence from the article.

Authorities may <u>mandate</u> that you go to a different location.

The Latin root of <u>mandate</u> is *mand*, which means "to order." What is a <u>mandate</u>?

Ⓐ a suggestion

Ⓑ a requirement

Ⓒ something unclear

Ⓓ something unexpected

**Part B:** Which other word includes the same root as <u>mandate</u>?

Ⓐ demand

Ⓑ human

Ⓒ manual

Ⓓ mend

**GO ON →**

**7** This question has two parts. First, answer part A. Then, answer part B.

**Part A:** What is the main idea of the article?

(A) Emergency supplies include canned food and water.

(B) It is important for your family to have a plan in case of a disaster.

(C) Flooding, tornadoes, and hurricanes can do serious damage to homes.

(D) Be sure to have sturdy shoes, warm clothing, and blankets with your supplies.

**Part B:** Which evidence from the text **best** supports the main idea?

(A) "Disasters happen all over the world."

(B) "Other floods develop slowly and affect large areas."

(C) "Many communities open centers that are safer than homes in a hurricane."

(D) "All family members need to know where the emergency supplies are kept."

**8** Read the phrase from the article.

<u>Manual</u> can opener

The word <u>manual</u> comes from the Latin root *man*, meaning "hand." What does this tell you about a <u>manual</u> can opener?

(A) It cannot be bought.

(B) It must be plugged in.

(C) It cannot open small cans.

(D) It operates by turning a lever.

**GO ON →**

Name: _____ Date: _____

**9** Which **two** sentences **best** describe how to find a family member after a disaster?

Ⓐ Listen to the radio for news.

Ⓑ Find a working flashlight and water.

Ⓒ Pack emergency supplies beforehand.

Ⓓ Decide beforehand on a place to meet.

Ⓔ Wear sturdy shoes and warm clothing.

Ⓕ Have everyone meet at a decided place.

**10** Sort the items from the list into the chart. Write each item in the correct part of the chart based on information in the article.

| Emergency Supplies | Other Items |
|---|---|
|  |  |

**Items:**

First aid kit

Paper cups

Blanket

Pet food

Canned food

Trash bags

Weekly Assessment • Unit 3, Week 4

Name: _____ Date: _____

**Now answer Number 11. Base your answer on "Make a Model of the Water Cycle" and "Be Prepared!"**

**11** Identify the main ideas of "Make a Model of the Water Cycle" and "Be Prepared!" Then explain how both are related to weather. Support your answer with details from both texts.

_____

_____

_____

_____

_____

_____

_____

_____

_____

_____

_____

_____

_____

_____

_____

_____

# Answer Key

Name: _____

| Question | Correct Answer | Content Focus | CCSS | Complexity |
|---|---|---|---|---|
| 1A | B | Latin Roots | L.5.4b | DOK 1 |
| 1B | C | Latin Roots | L.5.4b | DOK 1 |
| 2A | C | Main Idea and Key Details | RI.5.2 | DOK 2 |
| 2B | B | Main Idea and Key Details/ Text Evidence | RI.5.2/ RI.5.1 | DOK 2 |
| 3 | B | Latin Roots | L.5.4b | DOK 1 |
| 4 | see below | Main Idea and Key Details | RI.5.2 | DOK 2 |
| 5 | A, D | Text Structure: Sequence | RI.5.5 | DOK 2 |
| 6A | B | Latin Roots | L.5.4b | DOK 1 |
| 6B | A | Latin Roots | L.5.4b | DOK 1 |
| 7A | B | Main Idea and Key Details | RI.5.2 | DOK 2 |
| 7B | D | Main Idea and Key Details/ Text Evidence | RI.5.2/ RI.5.1 | DOK 2 |
| 8 | D | Latin Roots | L.5.4b | DOK 1 |
| 9 | D, F | Main Idea and Key Details | RI.5.1 | DOK 1 |
| 10 | see below | Main Idea and Key Details | RI.5.1 | DOK 1 |
| 11 | see below | Writing About Text | W.5.9b | DOK 4 |

| | | |
|---|---|---|
| **Comprehension** 2A, 2B, 4, 5, 7A, 7B, 9, 10 | /12 | % |
| **Vocabulary** 1A, 1B, 3, 6A, 6B, 8 | /8 | % |
| **Total Weekly Assessment Score** | /20 | % |

**4** Students should complete the chart with the following sentences:
- Main Idea of "Water Cycle Baggie"—3 – An experiment with a plastic bag, cup, and water can show how water evaporates and then turns back to water.
- Supporting Details—1 – An important part of the experiment is adding the food color before putting the sealed plastic bag in a warm place.; 2 – You need a plastic bag, clear cup, water, red food color, and a marker before setting up the experiment

**10** Students should complete the chart with the following details:
- Emergency Supplies—first aid kit; pet food; canned food
- Other Items—paper cups; blanket; trash bags

**11** To receive full credit for the response, the following information should be included: The main idea of "Make a Model of the Water Cycle" is that water in the ocean evaporates, condenses, and then falls as rain and snow to make its way back to the ocean. The main idea of "Be Prepared!" is that natural disasters can occur anywhere so families must make a plan. Both articles relate to weather, the first to details about precipitation and the second to steps in preparation for violent storms.

**Read the article "The Terror of the Middle Ages" before answering Numbers 1 through 5.**

# The Terror of the Middle Ages

In 1347, a ship sailed into the port at Messina, Sicily. The sailors on board were very sick, and they staggered through the streets before quickly dying. The people of Messina were terrified, for they had no idea what disease the sailors carried. It was the first hint of what was to come. The bubonic plague had arrived in Europe.

The bubonic plague was one of the most horrific events in world history. It started in Mongolia and was caused by tiny bacteria. The bacteria infected fleas, and the fleas that carried the germ jumped onto rats and then quickly spread. From the first landing in Sicily, the plague spread throughout Italy and then moved all across Europe. People bitten by fleas developed high fevers and terrible, painful swellings on their bodies. Sufferers died quickly and in huge numbers. An even worse form of the plague was airborne, passing from person to person through their breath. This form of the disease killed even more people and killed them faster.

It is hard to know how many people actually died in the epidemic. The numbers are between 33 percent and 50 percent of the total population of Europe. The plague also spread to the Middle East, through much of Asia, and to parts of North Africa.

Scientists have studied the plague to learn what caused it. Historians have studied it to find out how it affected people and the course of history itself. They looked at several sources. Some cities kept burial records that told how many people had been buried in the years of the plague. Other cities developed public health departments during the plague years, and these departments kept records of illnesses and deaths. Their numbers were not exact, but they gave researchers a good idea of the impact of the disease.

**GO ON →**

Some small towns and villages were completely destroyed by the disease. Everyone died, leaving cottages and other abodes empty. Historians could look at these ghost villages to see the impact of the plague.

Many writers in the 1300s described what happened in the plague years. Their writings tell of the fear and despair that people felt as the disease raced through their towns. At that time, people did not understand that germs caused disease, so they had no idea why they were getting sick. There was no useful medicine to fight the plague. It took hundreds of years for scientists to discover the germ behind the plague, and even more time for them to find a way to treat it. In the Middle Ages, though, people thought that the plague was caused by bad air, bad water, or bad behavior. They tried a variety of things to prevent it, but none of their efforts helped.

The plague continued in Europe until 1351. It had reached almost every inch of Europe at that point, and there were few people left to get sick. Gradually the disease ended, though it reappeared over and over again. It never again had such severe effects, so the earlier epidemic was the most devastating. Today, people still get bubonic plague, and even in the United States, a few people die from it each year. Now, though, we have medicine that can cure it. The research that scientists and historians have done on the plague has made sure that the disease will never again threaten the world as it did in 1347.

**GO ON →**

Name: _____ Date: _____

**Now answer Numbers 1 through 5. Base your answers on "The Terror of the Middle Ages."**

**1** This question has two parts. First, answer part A. Then, answer part B.

**Part A:** Which statement **best** describes the author's point of view about the plague?

(A) People in the Middle Ages did not understand the disease.

(B) People in the Middle Ages did not take the disease seriously.

(C) People in the Middle Ages were not aware they had the disease.

(D) People in the Middle Ages were overly concerned about the disease.

**Part B:** Which detail from the text **best** supports your answer in part A?

(A) Some cities began to keep public health records that told how many people died and were buried.

(B) The plague was caused by bacteria that lived in fleas, and the fleas were carried by rats.

(C) People thought the plague was caused by bad air, bad water, or bad behavior.

(D) The disease spread quickly over Europe, Asia, and parts of North Africa.

**2** Underline the sentence that **best** states the main idea of the paragraph.

The bubonic plague was one of the most horrific events in world history. It started in Mongolia and was caused by tiny bacteria. The bacteria infected fleas, and the fleas that carried the germ jumped onto rats and then quickly spread. From the first landing in Sicily, the plague spread throughout Italy and then moved all across Europe. People bitten by fleas developed high fevers and terrible, painful swellings on their bodies. Sufferers died quickly and in huge numbers. An even worse form of the plague was airborne, passing from person to person through their breath. This form of the disease killed even more people and killed them faster.

**GO ON →**

**Name:** _____ **Date:** _____

**3** Read the sentence from the text.

Everyone died, leaving cottages and other <u>abodes</u> empty.

Based on the clues in the sentence, what does the word <u>abodes</u> mean?

(A) areas

(B) homes

(C) lawns

(D) towns

**4** Which evidence supports the author's point that huge numbers of people died from the plague? Select **two** options.

(A) records from the time

(B) interviews from the time

(C) research done about the time

(D) films about the bubonic plague

(E) the author's personal experiences

(F) scientific experiments with the plague

**GO ON →**

**5** This question has two parts. First, answer part A. Then, answer part B.

**Part A:** Read the sentence from the article.

It never again had such severe effects, so the earlier epidemic was the most devastating.

What does <u>devastating</u> mean in the sentence?

(A) destructive

(B) limited

(C) understood

(D) well-defined

**Part B:** Which phrase in the sentence **best** helps to show the meaning of <u>devastating</u>?

(A) "never again"

(B) "severe effects"

(C) "earlier epidemic"

(D) "the most"

**GO ON →**

**Read the article "The Cliff Palace" before answering Numbers 6 through 10.**

# The Cliff Palace

There was snow blowing across the Colorado mesa on December 18, 1888. Two cowboys were riding across the plains looking for stray cattle, and the snow made it hard for them to be sure of what they were seeing. As they described it, it looked like a magnificent city. The cowboys were probably the first people in six hundred years to set eyes on the Cliff Palace of Mesa Verde, deserted since its builders left.

The cowboys, Richard Wetherill and Charlie Mason, soon came back to look around some more. They found that the Cliff Palace was an enormous village. It included a series of rooms made of sandstone blocks, held together with a mixture of mud and water and built into the side of a canyon. The Cliff Palace was similar to pueblos, or cliff dwellings, that had been discovered before, but it was much larger. Soon, the cowboys began to bring tourists with them and people were amazed by the number of rooms. They camped out nearby and spent days walking through the village.

Archaeologists quickly came to study the ancient discovery. They knew it had been constructed by Native Americans, but they were not cognizant of when it was built. It wasn't until 1935 that they were able to learn that the village was built in the 1200s.

**GO ON →**

The Cliff Palace includes more than a hundred rooms. There are rooms called kivas that were used for religious events. There are walkways and towers. There are living rooms, storage rooms, and rooms for eating. Groups of rooms are organized around a central courtyard. Archaeologists assume that families lived in these rooms.

The Native Americans who lived in the Cliff Palace did not leave any written information. Archaeologists had to use the artifacts that had belonged to them to learn about them. These artifacts included pieces of jars, mugs, axes, pots, baskets, and sandals. The fragments, or pieces, of jars and pots tell them how food was stored. The remains of fireplaces tell them where the food was cooked and how people stayed warm. Archaeologists know that there was no source of water for the cliff dwellers. They had to go quite a distance to get water to bring to their village.

The Cliff Palace was unprotected for hundreds of years and a lot of valuable information about its people was lost. Most things made of wood and cloth were destroyed by weather. We do not know what clothing the people of the Cliff Palace wore and we cannot tell exactly what they ate. There is no furniture left in the Palace. Nobody knows how many artifacts were taken away by people who came to view the site. However, there is a slope in front of the village where the cliff dwellers threw their trash. Archaeologists look through this trash very carefully and find many clues about the people who lived there.

In 1906, the area around the Cliff Palace was made into a national park. It is called Mesa Verde National Park. It includes many other cliff dwellings, too. The highlight of the park is the Cliff Palace because of its vast size and different kinds of rooms. Visitors must keep to the paths around the village now. This helps to preserve its structure. Thousands of people visit it each year. They are lucky to get a glimpse of a culture that has been gone for hundreds of years.

**GO ON →**

Name: _____ Date: _____

**Now answer Numbers 6 through 10. Base your answers on "The Cliff Palace."**

**6** This question has two parts. First, answer part A. Then, answer part B.

**Part A:** Read the sentence from the article.

It included a series of rooms made of sandstone blocks, held together with a <u>mixture</u> of mud and water and built into the side of a canyon.

What does the sentence suggest about a <u>mixture</u>?

Ⓐ It is a simple recipe.

Ⓑ It is difficult to measure.

Ⓒ It has unknown ingredients.

Ⓓ It has more than one ingredient.

**Part B:** Which phrase in the sentence **best** helps to show what <u>mixture</u> means?

Ⓐ "a series of rooms"

Ⓑ "made of sandstone blocks"

Ⓒ "mud and water"

Ⓓ "the side of a canyon"

**GO ON →**

**7** This question has two parts. First, answer part A. Then, answer part B.

**Part A:** Which statement **best** describes the author's point of view about the Cliff Palace?

(A) Much about the Cliff Palace is unknown.

(B) The Cliff Palace is not a safe tourist destination.

(C) Archaeologists are not studying the Cliff Palace well enough.

(D) Archaeologists will discover many more things about Cliff Palace.

**Part B:** Which sentence from the text **best** supports your answer in part A?

(A) "It wasn't until 1935 that they were able to learn that the village was built in the 1200s."

(B) "The remains of fireplaces tell them where the food was cooked and how people stayed warm."

(C) "We do not know what clothing the people of the Cliff Palace wore and we cannot tell exactly what they ate."

(D) "In 1906, the area around the Cliff Palace was made into a national park."

**8** Read the sentence from the text.

These <u>artifacts</u> included pieces of jars, mugs, axes, pots, baskets, and sandals.

What does the word <u>artifacts</u> mean?

(A) art

(B) facts

(C) objects

(D) rooms

**GO ON →**

Name: _____ Date: _____

**9** The author has the point of view that the Cliff Palace is a popular site. Select **two** pieces of text evidence that support this viewpoint. Write the sentences in the chart.

| Author's Point of View | The Cliff Palace is a popular site. |
|---|---|
| **Text Evidence** | |
| | |

**Text Evidence:**

The Cliff Palace was similar to other pueblos.

People spent many days visiting the Cliff Palace.

The Cliff Palace is located on a mesa in Colorado.

A lot of information about the Cliff Palace was lost.

Thousands of people come to visit the Cliff Palace every year.

The people who lived at Cliff Palace left more than six hundred years ago.

**10** With which statements would the author **most likely** agree? Select **two** options.

(A) People in the Cliff Palace lived a very difficult life.

(B) The Cliff Palace should have never been discovered.

(C) The Cliff Palace should have been protected and preserved.

(D) People in the Cliff Palace did not leave behind many things.

(E) The Cliff Palace helps us understand how people lived in the past.

(F) People in the Cliff Palace did not understand how to build a safe home.

**Weekly Assessment · Unit 3, Week 5**

Name: _____ Date: _____

**Now answer Number 11. Base your answer on "The Terror of the Middle Ages" and "The Cliff Palace."**

**11** What details in "The Terror of the Middle Ages" and "The Cliff Palace" support the authors' views that historians and archaeologists use historical events to explain what happened in the past? Support your answer with details from both texts.

_____

_____

_____

_____

_____

_____

_____

_____

_____

_____

_____

_____

_____

_____

_____

_____

# Answer Key

Name: _____

| Question | Correct Answer | Content Focus | CCSS | Complexity |
|---|---|---|---|---|
| 1A | A | Author's Point of View | RI.6.6 | DOK 3 |
| 1B | C | Author's Point of View/ Text Evidence | RI.6.6/ RI.5.1 | DOK 3 |
| 2 | see below | Main Idea and Key Details | RI.5.2 | DOK 2 |
| 3 | B | Context Clues: Sentence Clues | L.5.4a | DOK 2 |
| 4 | A, C | Author's Point of View | RI.6.6 | DOK 3 |
| 5A | A | Context Clues: Sentence Clues | L.5.4a | DOK 2 |
| 5B | B | Context Clues: Sentence Clues/ Text Evidence | L.5.4a/ RI.5.1 | DOK 2 |
| 6A | D | Context Clues: Sentence Clues | L.5.4a | DOK 2 |
| 6B | C | Context Clues: Sentence Clues/ Text Evidence | L.5.4a/ RI.5.1 | DOK 2 |
| 7A | A | Author's Point of View | RI.6.6 | DOK 3 |
| 7B | C | Author's Point of View/ Text Evidence | RI.6.6/ RI.5.1 | DOK 3 |
| 8 | C | Context Clues: Sentence Clues | L.5.4a | DOK 2 |
| 9 | see below | Author's Point of View | RI.6.6 | DOK 2 |
| 10 | C, E | Author's Point of View | RI.6.6 | DOK 3 |
| 11 | see below | Writing About Text | W.5.9b | DOK 4 |

| | | |
|---|---|---|
| **Comprehension** 1A, 1B, 2, 4, 7A, 7B, 9, 10 | /12 | % |
| **Vocabulary** 3, 5A, 5B, 6A, 6B, 8 | /8 | % |
| **Total Weekly Assessment Score** | /20 | % |

**2** Students should underline the following sentence:
- The bubonic plague was one of the most horrific events in world history.

**9** Students should complete the chart with the following text evidence:
- People spent many days visiting the Cliff Palace.
- Thousands of people come to visit the Cliff Palace every year.

**11** To receive full credit for the response, the following information should be included: Each author explains that historians and archaeologists use sources from the historical time, such as artifacts and writings, to get information about the historical events.

**Read the passage "A Giant of a Man" before answering Numbers 1 through 5.**

# A Giant of a Man

Back in 1913, I worked on one of Paul Bunyan's famous crews. Let me tell you, there are many good tales about the legendary Paul Bunyan, but they don't tell half the story. He was a giant of a man who could pick up four horses with their load of logs and turn them around on the road. He led crews of us loggers to hew trees and chop them into logs during the days when this country was growing really fast. His helper was Babe, the big blue ox. Babe could pull any load, no matter how big. I saw Babe eat as much in one night as a crew could haul in a year.

Feeding Bunyan's crews of ravenous loggers was a big job. Paul had bad luck getting good cooks until he hired Big Joe. Big Joe wanted a griddle to cook pancakes. Big Ole, the blacksmith, made a griddle so immense a logger couldn't see across the steam made by a pancake that was cooking on it. The pancake batter was stirred in machines like concrete mixers and it was poured on the griddle with cranes. One day, a visitor at a camp saw a crew unloading sleds at the cook's shanty. It looked as if they were unloading logs, so I set him straight. "Those aren't logs, but rather sausages for the loggers' breakfast," I said.

**GO ON →**

Everything got buried in the Winter of the Deep Snow. It was a predicament. Paul dealt with the challenge by digging down to find the tops of the tall pine trees and lowering his loggers to chop logs. His blue ox, Babe, wore snowshoes to haul the wood to the surface of the snow. In another cold year, the year of the Two Winters, the Great Lakes that Paul had built froze all the way to the bottom. Paul had to chop the ice, and he put it on the shore to melt in the sun.

Paul had a cow named Lucy. She had the appetite of a wolf. In the winter of the Deep Snow, the loggers gave Lucy a pair of Babe's old snowshoes and green goggles. They turned her out to graze in the snow. She learned to run in the snowshoes and ran all over North America. Finally, Paul put a big bell on her.

Chris Crosshaul was careless. He took a load of logs down the Mississippi River for Paul. When the logs were delivered, they were the wrong logs. Paul had to get them back upstream. Driving logs upstream is impossible, but an impossible job never stopped Paul. He fed Babe salt and took him to the upper Mississippi to drink. Babe drank the river dry and the logs traveled up the river faster than they had gone down.

Paul could solve problems like no one else I ever knew or you ever heard of. In the Winter of the Blue Snow, Shot Gunderson was in charge of the Big Tadpole River area. He chopped his logs so that they landed in a lake. He planned to move them in the spring. To his surprise, when he tried to move the logs, he discovered the lake had no outlet to the river. He thought the whole winter's work was lost until Paul, who was always clever, came up with an ingenious idea. He called in Sourdough Sam, a cook who made everything out of sourdough except the coffee. Paul ordered him to mix enough sourdough to fill the big water tank. Then he hitched Babe the Blue Ox to the tank and dumped the sourdough into the lake. Dough rises. As Sam said, it "riz" and pushed the logs over the hills that surrounded the lake, all the way to the river. Today a lake in Minnesota is named "Sourdough Lake."

**GO ON →**

Name: _____ Date: _____

**Now answer Numbers 1 through 5. Base your answers on "A Giant of a Man."**

 1  Choose the narrator of the passage from the list and write it in the chart. Then choose **two** pieces of evidence that support your answer and write them in the chart.

| Narrator: |
| --- |
| **Text Evidence:** |
| |
| **Text Evidence:** |
| |

---

**Narrator:**

Babe            Paul Bunyan

a logger        Big Joe the cook

**Text Evidence:**

"Back in 1913, I worked on one of Paul Bunyan's famous crews."

"He was a giant of a man who could pick up four horses with their load of logs and turn them around on the road."

"He led crews of us loggers to hew trees and chop them into logs during the days when this country was growing really fast."

"Paul had bad luck getting good cooks until he hired Big Joe."

"In the winter of the Deep Snow, the loggers gave Lucy a pair of Babe's old snowshoes and green goggles."

**GO ON →**

**2** This question has two parts. First, answer part A. Then, answer part B.

**Part A:** Read the sentence from the text.

Let me tell you, there are many good tales about the <u>legendary</u> Paul Bunyan, but they don't tell half the story.

Which word has almost the same meaning as <u>legendary</u>?

(A) excited

(B) famous

(C) helpful

(D) wealthy

**Part B:** Which word means the **opposite** of <u>legendary</u>?

(A) broken

(B) careful

(C) unhappy

(D) unknown

**3** Which sentence from the text best supports the narrator's view of Paul as a giant of a man?

(A) "Feeding Bunyan's crews of ravenous loggers was a big job."

(B) "Paul dealt with the challenge by digging down to find the tops of the tall pine trees and lowering his loggers to chop logs."

(C) "Driving logs upstream is impossible, but an impossible job never stopped Paul."

(D) "To his surprise, when he tried to move the logs, he discovered the lake had no outlet to the river."

**GO ON →**

**4** This question has two parts. First, answer part A. Then, answer part B.

**Part A:** Which statement **best** summarizes a theme of the text?

(A) Lumberjacks are very resourceful.

(B) People should take good care of their pets.

(C) Legends are about larger-than-life characters.

(D) Size and strength are not important if you are determined.

**Part B:** Which sentence from the text **best** supports your answer in part A?

(A) "His blue ox, Babe, wore snowshoes to haul the wood to the surface of the snow."

(B) "Paul could solve problems like no one else I ever knew or you ever heard of."

(C) "He called in Sourdough Sam, a cook who made everything out of sourdough except the coffee."

(D) "Today a lake in Minnesota is named 'Sourdough Lake.'"

**5** Read the sentence from the text.

He thought the whole winter's work was lost until Paul, who was always clever, came up with an <u>ingenious</u> idea.

Which words mean the **opposite** of <u>ingenious</u>? Select **two** options.

(A) difficult

(B) dull

(C) hidden

(D) impossible

(E) unimaginative

(F) useless

**GO ON →**

**Read the passage "The Magpie's Nest" before answering Numbers 6 through 10.**

# The Magpie's Nest

Once, long, long ago, all the birds came to see the magpie. Now the magpie is known to be a chatty, noisy bird, but she is the cleverest of birds when it comes to building a nest, and that is why all the birds wanted her to teach them how.

Magpies are sleek and glossy with shiny black feathers. Their abdomens, or undersides, are white, and they have patches of white on their wings. Sometimes, depending on the way the light shines, a magpie looks blue, green, or purple. Magpies' relatives are the crows and jays. What distinguishes magpies, or sets them apart, from other birds is an unusually long tail.

So Madge, as she was named, called all the birds around her. First came the thrush with plump, soft feathers and one of the best singing voices of all the birds. Then came the blackbird. The female blackbird was actually dark brown in color, and all the birds knew she had a loud voice. The owl stood out from the others. What separates the owl from the other birds is her wide head, ruff of feathers, and hooked beak. The owl's sharp claws are called talons. Next, the small, brownish sparrow appeared. Although plain, the sparrow is popular because he sings pleasantly. Another songbird, the starling, came to learn about nest building. The starling's feathers are black with a greenish-purple shine. He has pointed wings, a short tail, and a sharp bill. Last of all, came the turtledove, a small, slender, graceful bird that makes soft, cooing sounds.

Once all the birds were assembled, Madge took some mud and formed it into a round cake. At that, the thrush said, "Oh, that's how it's done," and away she flew. Today that is how all thrushes build their nests.

Next Madge took some twigs and put them around in the cake of mud. With that, the blackbird exclaimed, "Now I know all about building a nest," and off she flew. That is how the blackbirds make their nests to this very day.

**GO ON →**

Then Madge put another layer of mud over the twigs, and the owl said, "Oh, that's quite apparent and obvious now." Away she flew, and since then owls have never made better nests. In fact, they usually just use the old nests of other birds, such as hawks and crows, or even holes in trees and ledges in caves.

After this Madge began to gather some more twigs and wind them around the outside of the nest. "The very thing!" called out the sparrow, and off she went. So sparrows collect twigs and make messy nests to this day.

Now Madge took some feathers and other stuff and lined the nest to make it very comfortable. "That suits me," cried the starling, and off he flew. You see, with starlings, the male starts the nest and decorates it with ornaments like flowers before the female comes along and helps finish it. Starlings have very comfortable nests even today.

So that is how the lesson went. Each bird learned a little bit about how to build a nest and left before Madge was finished.

Meanwhile, Madge worked and worked, and the only bird left was the turtledove. The problem was that the turtledove had not paid any attention but instead kept repeating a silly cry, "Take two, Taffy, take two-o-o-o."

Madge, the magpie, heard this just as she was putting a twig across the nest. She said, "One's enough."

The turtledove kept saying, "Take two, Taffy, take two-o-o-o."

Madge became angry and said, "One's enough I tell you," but still she cried, "Take two, Taffy, take two-o-o-o."

At last Madge looked up and saw nobody near but the silly turtledove. Then Madge became even angrier and flew away. She refused to tell the birds how to build nests again. And that is why different birds build their nests differently to this day.

**GO ON →**

**Now answer Numbers 6 through 10. Base your answers on "The Magpie's Nest."**

**6** This question has two parts. First, answer part A. Then, answer part B.

**Part A:** Read the sentences from the passage.

Magpies are <u>sleek</u> and glossy with shiny black feathers. Their abdomens, or undersides, are white, and they have patches of white on their wings.

Which word has almost the same meaning as the word <u>sleek</u> in the sentences above?

(A) dark

(B) glistening

(C) thin

(D) well-known

**Part B:** Which words in the sentence **best** show what <u>sleek</u> means? Select **two** options.

(A) glossy

(B) shiny

(C) black

(D) feathers

(E) undersides

(F) patches

**7** Which sentence from the text **best** shows the thrush's idea about making a nest?

(A) "First came the thrush with plump, soft feathers and one of the best singing voices of all the birds."

(B) "Once all the birds were assembled, Madge took some mud and formed it into a round cake."

(C) "At that, the thrush said, "Oh, that's how it's done," and away she flew."

(D) "With that, the blackbird exclaimed, "Now I know all about building a nest," and off she flew."

**GO ON →**

Name: _____ Date: _____

**8** Read the sentence from the text. Then, answer the question.

Then Madge put another layer of mud over the twigs, and the owl said, "Oh, that's quite <u>apparent</u> and obvious now."

Choose **two** synonyms of the word <u>apparent</u> from the list below. Then choose **two** antonyms. Write the synonyms and antonyms in the chart.

| Synonyms of "Apparent" | Antonyms of "Apparent" |
|---|---|
|  |  |

**Words:**
clear
crooked
dangerous
hidden
noticeable
strange
uncertain

**GO ON →**

**9** This question has two parts. First, answer part A. Then, answer part B.

**Part A:** What does the narrator think of the turtledove?

(A) It is a silly bird.

(B) It is always late.

(C) It is an angry bird.

(D) It has a very loud song.

**Part B:** Which sentence from the passage **best** supports your answer in part A?

(A) "Last of all, came the turtledove, a small, slender, graceful bird that makes soft, cooing sounds."

(B) "Meanwhile, Madge worked and worked, and the only bird left was the turtledove."

(C) "The turtledove kept saying, 'Take two, Taffy, take two-o-o-o.'"

(D) "At last Madge looked up and saw nobody near but the silly turtledove."

**10** Which detail would **most likely** be given if the passage were written from the turtledove's point of view?

(A) what Madge thinks of the turtledove

(B) what different birds feed the babies in their nests

(C) how Madge learned to build a superior kind of nest

(D) why the turtledove does not pay attention during the lesson

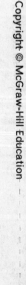

Name: _____ Date: _____

**Now answer Number 11. Base your answer on "A Giant of a Man" and "The Magpie's Nest."**

**11** How does the point of view used in each tale affect what you learn in the passages? Support your answer with details from both texts.

_____

_____

_____

_____

_____

_____

_____

_____

_____

_____

_____

_____

_____

# Answer Key

| Question | Correct Answer | Content Focus | CCSS | Complexity |
|---|---|---|---|---|
| 1 | see below | Point of View | RL.5.6 | DOK 3 |
| 2A | B | Synonyms and Antonyms | L.5.5c | DOK 2 |
| 2B | D | Synonyms and Antonyms | L.5.5c | DOK 2 |
| 3 | B | Point of View | RL.5.6 | DOK 2 |
| 4A | C | Theme | RL.5.2 | DOK 3 |
| 4B | B | Theme/Text Evidence | RL.5.2/ RL.5.1 | DOK 3 |
| 5 | B, E | Synonyms and Antonyms | L.5.5c | DOK 2 |
| 6A | B | Synonyms and Antonyms | L.5.5c | DOK 2 |
| 6B | A, B | Synonyms and Antonyms/ Text Evidence | L.5.5c/ RL.5.1 | DOK 2 |
| 7 | C | Point of View | RL.5.6 | DOK 2 |
| 8 | see below | Synonyms and Antonyms | L.5.5c | DOK 2 |
| 9A | A | Point of View | RL.5.6 | DOK 3 |
| 9B | D | Point of View/Text Evidence | RL.5.6/ RL.5.1 | DOK 3 |
| 10 | D | Point of View | RL.5.6 | DOK 3 |
| 11 | see below | Writing About Text | W.5.9a | DOK 4 |

| | | | |
|---|---|---|---|
| **Comprehension** 1, 3, 4A, 4B, 7, 9A, 9B, 10 | | /12 | % |
| **Vocabulary** 2A, 2B, 5, 6A, 6B, 8 | | /8 | % |
| **Total Weekly Assessment Score** | | /20 | % |

1 Students should complete the chart with the following information:
- Narrator—a logger
- Text Evidence—"Back in 1913, I worked on one of Paul Bunyan's famous crews."; "He led crews of us loggers to hew trees and chop them into logs during the days when this country was growing really fast."

8 Students should complete the chart with the following synonyms and antonyms:
- Synonyms for "Apparent"—clear, noticeable
- Antonyms for "Apparent"—hidden, uncertain

11 To receive full credit for the response, the following information should be included: "A Giant of a Man" is told in the first person, and 'the Magpie's Nest" is in the third person. "A Giant of a Man" gives the personal point of view of a logger who worked on one of Bunyan's crews. In contrast, the point of view in "The Magpie's Nest" is that of a detached outside observer of the action.

**Read the passage "The Case of the Missing Sandwiches" before answering Numbers 1 through 5.**

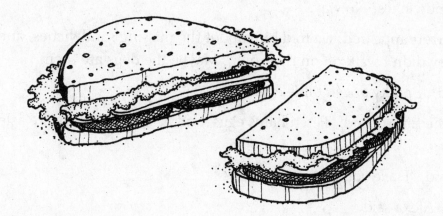

# The Case of the Missing Sandwiches

Hi, I'm Mikayla, and my best friend is Alexa. When Mom describes us, she says, "Birds of a feather flock together." She means we are alike, and she's right because we are both eleven, and we both like movies, popcorn, and baseball. We have been friends for a while, so we've had many adventures. Let me tell you about the latest one because it shows that we always should expect the unexpected.

Alexa and I went with our dogs, Sparky and Fetch, on a picnic, but my mom laid down one rule. Garrett, my brother, was going fishing, and we had to stay with him. I don't know if you have an older brother, but if you do, you know how bossy he can be. Garrett doesn't like for me to tag along with him either.

Alexa and I enjoy watching the ducks on the river, while Garrett fishes. As soon as we got to the picnic spot, Garrett told us not to leave there and went off with his tackle box and fishing pole.

Alexa and I played catch with the dogs, and then we watched some white ibis with orange, hooked beaks as they searched for insects in the grass. A blue heron flew over and landed not far away.

We were hungry, actually ravenous, so we opened the cooler and put the egg salad sandwiches on a plate, but before we could unwrap the ham and cheese sandwiches, we heard Garrett shout for us to come quickly.

We took off running, not knowing what to expect. At the riverbank, Garrett was trying to reel in a bass. We spent some time admiring the huge fish, and then we told Garrett we were ready to eat. He should come right away, or we would eat all of the lunch.

**GO ON →**

But when we got back to the picnic table, all of the sandwiches were gone! Where they had gone was a mystery. Alexa wondered if a squirrel took them, but I said, "Three sandwiches? No way."

When Garrett appeared, we told him about the missing sandwiches, and he said, "Girls, they didn't walk off on their own. Maybe the dogs ate them."

Alexa said, "Sparky doesn't like eggs."

At the same time, I said, "Fetch hates eggs, and besides the dogs are asleep in the sun."

Garrett said, "Have you seen anyone?"

"No one," Alexa said.

Garrett asked, "Did you see anything else?"

Alexa said, "We saw some ibis, but they were eating insects."

"We saw a blue heron, but it wouldn't eat a sandwich," I said.

Garrett said, "If you had left out shrimp, a heron would have taken your lunch, but, no, a heron would not go for egg salad."

"So what did happen?" I asked.

Garrett pointed to the tree. "Those ravens perched there are like big crows. See how they watch the table? They are scavengers, so I think that they swooped down and took the sandwiches."

Alexa said, "The mystery is solved, but what about lunch?"

Garrett said, "I would divide up the ham and cheese sandwiches. If we're still hungry, I'll get us sandwiches at the stand."

"That's a good solution, Garrett," said Alexa. I had to agree that older brothers are sometimes helpful. As Mom always says, "Two heads are better than one," but this time, it took three heads to solve the mystery of the missing sandwiches.

**GO ON →**

**Now answer Numbers 1 through 5. Base your answers on "The Case of the Missing Sandwiches."**

**1** Read the sentence from the text.

When Mom describes us, she says, "Birds of a feather flock together."

What does the phrase "Birds of a feather flock together" mean?

(A) Everyone should have as many friends as possible.

(B) Birds from northern areas migrate south in the winter.

(C) Birds live in flocks, unlike people who live in families.

(D) People, like birds, associate with those who are like themselves.

**2** This question has two parts. First, answer part A. Then, answer part B.

**Part A:** Who is the narrator of the passage?

(A) Alexa

(B) Garrett

(C) Mikayla

(D) an outside observer

**Part B:** Which evidence from the text **best** supports your answer in part A?

(A) "Hi, I'm Mikayla, and my best friend is Alexa."

(B) "Garrett, my brother, was going fishing, and we had to stay with him."

(C) "Alexa and I enjoy watching the ducks on the river, while Garrett fishes."

(D) "At the riverbank, Garrett was trying to reel in a bass."

**GO ON →**

Name: _____ Date: _____

**3** How does Mikayla's attitude about Garrett change from the beginning to the end of the passage? Complete the chart using the list below.

| | Mikayla's Attitude | Text Evidence |
|---|---|---|
| **Beginning** | | |
| **End** | | |

**Mikayla's Attitude:**

She is grateful for Garrett.

She points out Garrett's faults.

She wants to play with Garrett.

She is upset that Garrett is with her.

**Text Evidence:**

"Alexa and I went with our dogs, Sparky and Fetch, on a picnic, but my mom laid down one rule."

"I don't know if you have an older brother, but if you do, you know how bossy he can be."

"He should come right away, or we would eat all of the lunch."

"I had to agree that older brothers are sometimes helpful."

**GO ON →**

**4** Which sentences **best** show the point of view of the narrator? Select **two** options.

(A) "She means we are alike, and she's right because we are both eleven, and we both like movies, popcorn, and baseball."

(B) "Let me tell you about the latest one because it shows that we always should expect the unexpected."

(C) "As soon as we got to the picnic spot, Garrett told us not to leave there and went off with his tackle box and fishing pole."

(D) "We spent some time admiring the huge fish, and then we told Garrett we were ready to eat."

(E) "When Garrett appeared, we told him about the missing sandwiches, and he said, 'Girls, they didn't walk off on their own.'"

(F) "Garrett said, 'If you had left out shrimp, a heron would have taken your lunch, but, no, a heron would not go for egg salad.'"

**5** This question has two parts. First, answer part A. Then, answer part B.

**Part A:** Read the sentence from the passage.

As Mom always says, "Two heads are better than one," but this time, it took three heads to solve the mystery of the missing sandwiches.

What does the phrase "Two heads are better than one" mean?

(A) A mom always knows best.

(B) Sharing ideas can be helpful.

(C) Every group needs a leader to make decisions.

(D) One person cannot ever solve a problem without help.

**Part B:** Which phrase from the sentence **best** supports your answer in part A?

(A) "Mom always says"

(B) "but this time"

(C) "to solve the mystery"

(D) "missing sandwiches"

**GO ON →**

Read the passage "Who Were the Spiders?" before answering Numbers 6 through 10.

# Who Were the Spiders?

The Cooper family was about to move because Dad had a new job in Colorado. He had been out of work for a year, and Natalie and Mason knew he had been unhappy, but now a new job was making things look better. As Dad said, "Every cloud has a silver lining."

Dad was already in Colorado, but Mom stayed behind so that the twins Natalie and Mason could finish fifth grade at Oak School. Today, Natalie and Mason were helping to pack boxes, and they enjoyed looking at the old treasures, especially the photo albums.

Mason found many photos, and Natalie picked up one of a baseball team in which the men's uniforms had CLEVELAND printed on them. Someone had written 1895 on the photo, and Natalie asked, "Why is this photo here? The year is more than one hundred years ago."

Mason asked Mom, "Is there a famous baseball player in our family?"

"I don't know of anyone in my family, but maybe there was someone in your dad's family," she said, "so remember to ask about the photo when you talk to your dad tonight."

**GO ON →**

That night Dad called, and Mason was eager to talk to him. "Dad, we found a photo today of a baseball team that played in 1895. Did one of your relatives play on a team a long time ago?"

Dad said, "It's familiar, but I don't know the story. Some of the photos are my father's, so why don't you call him and see if he knows?"

Grandpa Ken recalled that a relative played for a Cleveland team, a cousin of his great-grandfather whose last name was Zimmer, so Grandpa suggested they look up early Cleveland teams.

Mason and Natalie headed for the computer and found a baseball encyclopedia, where they clicked on "Teams" and found links to "Active Franchises" and "Earlier Franchises." Mason knew that a franchise is a name for a professional sports team. Under "Earlier Franchises" they found three teams: Cleveland Blue, 1879–1884; Cleveland Infants, 1890–1890; and Cleveland Spiders, 1887–1899.

Mason shouted, "We found the answer! Our 1895 photo must show the Cleveland Spiders."

Natalie said, "You might be right, so let's find out about them."

They looked for Cleveland Spiders and found the headline, "Grand Opening. About Nine Thousand People See the First Game." A new Cleveland ballpark had opened on May 2, 1891. Cy Young was the starting pitcher, and Zimmer was listed as one of the players. "That's the cousin of our great-great-grandfather!" said Natalie.

Mom said, "That means he played on the same team as Cy Young, who was an exceptional pitcher that won more games than any other pitcher in history."

Mason wanted to know more, so they searched a baseball almanac. Natalie saw a list of players, and Zimmer was a catcher in 1895, a year in which the team came in second. She also read that in 1899, the Spiders were baseball's worst team. Natalie checked the 1899 team, and there was Zimmer again. "Oh, well, you can't win them all," she said.

Mom then said, "Early to bed and early to rise makes a man healthy, wealthy, and wise." They would have to find out more about the Cleveland Spiders tomorrow.

**GO ON →**

**Now answer Numbers 6 through 10. Base your answers on "Who Were the Spiders?"**

**6** This question has two parts. First, answer part A. Then, answer part B.

**Part A:** Read the paragraph from the text.

The Cooper family was about to move because Dad had a new job in Colorado. He had been out of work for a year, and Natalie and Mason knew he had been unhappy, but now a new job was making things look better. As Dad said, "Every cloud has a silver lining."

What does the phrase "Every cloud has a silver lining" mean?

Ⓐ Winning is not everything.

Ⓑ Every problem has some good effect as well.

Ⓒ Clouds that produce rain may be silver underneath.

Ⓓ There is never a right or wrong time to do something.

**Part B:** Which phrase from the paragraph **best** supports your answer in part A?

Ⓐ "about to move"

Ⓑ "out of work for a year"

Ⓒ "knew he had been unhappy"

Ⓓ "making things look better"

**GO ON →**

**7** Circle the paragraph that shows that Mason is excited after finding the baseball photo.

Mason asked Mom, "Is there a famous baseball player in our family?"

"I don't know of anyone in my family, but maybe there was someone in your dad's family," she said, "so remember to ask about the photo when you talk to your dad tonight."

That night Dad called, and Mason was eager to talk to him. "Dad, we found a photo today of a baseball team that played in 1895. Did one of your relatives play on a team a long time ago?"

Dad said, "It's familiar, but I don't know the story. Some of the photos are my father's, so why don't you call him and see if he knows?"

Grandpa Ken recalled that a relative played for a Cleveland team, a cousin of his great-grandfather whose last name was Zimmer, so Grandpa suggested they look up early Cleveland teams.

**8** What would the reader **most likely** learn if the passage were written from Mom's point of view? Select **all** that apply.

Ⓐ what Mason thought his new school would be like

Ⓑ how Cy Young felt about playing for the Spiders

Ⓒ what Natalie felt about moving from Cleveland

Ⓓ what Mom knew about the game of baseball

Ⓔ how Mom felt about the move to Colorado

Ⓕ how Grandpa Ken could remember so well

**GO ON →**

**9** This question has two parts. First, answer part A. Then, answer part B.

**Part A:** Which sentence states a theme of the passage?

(A) Not everyone will agree with you all the time.

(B) There is more than one way to solve a problem.

(C) You can find the answers you seek if you look hard enough.

(D) People with different opinions can still find a way to get along.

**Part B:** Which sentence **best** supports your answer in part A?

(A) "Dad was already in Colorado, but Mom stayed behind so that the twins Natalie and Mason could finish fifth grade at Oak School."

(B) "Today, Natalie and Mason were helping to pack boxes, and they enjoyed looking at the old treasures, especially the photo albums."

(C) "Mason wanted to know more, so they searched a baseball almanac."

(D) "'Oh, well, you can't win them all,' she said."

**10** Read the paragraph from the text. Then, answer the question.

Mom then said, "Early to bed and early to rise makes a man healthy, wealthy, and wise." They would have to find out more about the Cleveland Spiders tomorrow.

What is the meaning of "Early to bed and early to rise makes a man healthy, wealthy, and wise"?

(A) There is always another day to finish a task that is begun.

(B) It is good to both go to bed and get up early.

(C) Rich people get up at dawn to start working.

(D) Good health requires hard work.

Name: _____  Date: _____

**Now answer Number 11. Base your answer on "The Case of the Missing Sandwiches" and "Who Were the Spiders?"**

**11** Both passages involve solving mysteries. How does point of view affect the way that each passage is narrated? Support your answer with details from both texts.

_____

_____

_____

_____

_____

_____

_____

_____

_____

_____

_____

_____

_____

_____

# Answer Key

| Question | Correct Answer | Content Focus | CCSS | Complexity |
|---|---|---|---|---|
| 1 | D | Adages and Proverbs | L.5.5b | DOK 2 |
| 2A | C | Point of View | RL.5.6 | DOK 2 |
| 2B | A | Point of View/Text Evidence | RL.5.1 | DOK 2 |
| 3 | see below | Point of View | RL.5.6 | DOK 2 |
| 4 | A, B | Point of View | RL.5.6 | DOK 3 |
| 5A | B | Adages and Proverbs | L.5.5b | DOK 2 |
| 5B | C | Adages and Proverbs/Text Evidence | L.5.5b/ RL.5.1 | DOK 2 |
| 6A | B | Adages and Proverbs | L.5.5b | DOK 2 |
| 6B | D | Adages and Proverbs/Text Evidence | L.5.5b/ RL.5.1 | DOK 2 |
| 7 | see below | Point of View | RL.5.6 | DOK 2 |
| 8 | D, E | Point of View | RL.5.6 | DOK 2 |
| 9A | C | Theme | RL.5.2 | DOK 3 |
| 9B | C | Theme/Text Evidence | RL.5.1 | DOK 3 |
| 10 | B | Adages and Proverbs | L.5.5b | DOK 2 |
| 11 | see below | Writing About Text | W.5.9a | DOK 4 |

| | | | |
|---|---|---|---|
| **Comprehension** 2A, 2B, 3, 4, 7, 8, 9A, 9B | /12 | % |
| **Vocabulary** 1, 5A, 5B, 6A, 6B, 10 | /8 | % |
| **Total Weekly Assessment Score** | /20 | % |

**3** Students should complete the chart as follows:
- Beginning—Mikayla's Attitude: She points out Garrett's faults. Text Evidence: "I don't know if you have an older brother, but if you do, you know how bossy he can be."
- End—Mikayla's Attitude: She is grateful for Garrett. Text Evidence: "I had to agree that older brothers are sometimes helpful."

**7** Students should circle the following paragraph:
- That night Dad called, and Mason was eager to talk to him. "Dad, we found a photo today of a baseball team that played in 1895. Did one of your relatives play on a team a long time ago?"

**11** To receive full credit for the response, the following information should be included: "The Case of the Missing Sandwiches" is told from the first-person point of view. In contrast, "Who Were the Spiders?" is told from the third-person point of view. This means that in "The Case of the Missing Sandwiches" the reader learns about the events as Mikayla sees them, but in "Who Were the Spiders?" the reader sees events through the eyes of an outside observer who knows the thoughts of all the characters.

**Read the article "Small Loan, Big Effect" before answering Numbers 1 through 5.**

# Small Loan, Big Effect

In a small village in Nepal, a young woman wanted to start a tailor shop so that she could make clothes to sell. She did not have enough money, however, to get started, and it was impossible for her to obtain a loan from a big bank. She knew she could never get the money from them, so she applied for a microloan.

A microloan is a loan of a small amount of money to a person or group. Some microloans are made by banks or large organizations, while others are made by individuals. Microloans can go a long way in changing peoples' lives for the better. For example, a loan of as little as twenty-five dollars can allow the tailor in Nepal to buy the material needed to make several items of clothing. The tailor can then sell the clothes and make enough money to buy more material. If the tailor is careful, she can make enough to buy a sewing machine to make even more clothes. Then her business can really take off!

Microloans are made to people in developing countries in Africa, Asia, and South America. These people do not have access to banks. People in the United States can benefit from microloans too. The loans are becoming increasingly popular. The World Bank believes that 160 million people around the world are now benefiting from microloans. Not all of these loans are used to start businesses. Some help families send their children to school or allow them to take classes to learn new skills. Others help farmers pay for seed so that their harvests will be bigger and earn the farmers more money.

**GO ON →**

For some people, the loans have a great effect. A carpenter in Afghanistan named Behnam received a $465 microloan. He used it to expand his carpentry business. With his larger business, he is able to provide more and better food and clothing for his four children. Lucas, who lives in Mozambique, used microloans to buy chickens and to irrigate his farmland. Now he is able to employ four people and to send his children to school. Beatrice, who lives in Kenya, started with a microloan of less than forty dollars. She used the money to buy vegetables, which she sold at local markets. Now she has a much larger business and sells to other businesses. Asaed, who lives in Jordan, used a microloan to buy some old machines, which he repaired and sold. Now he builds and sells machines that make hummus, a local food. An American woman named Liliana received a $500 loan and was able to open a day-care center where she cares for young children near Boston, Massachusetts.

Microloans often help other people in a community as well as the person who receives the loan. When the person's business does well, it brings money into a community. This makes a noticeable difference and helps other businesses sell or do more. Groups involved in microloans find that what is good for one person is also good for those around that person. Often, people who get microloans will repeatedly apply for loans to improve their businesses, which may, in turn, help the community even more.

What about paying these loans back? After all, a loan is not a gift. The people who receive microloans are often very poor. Are they less likely to pay back the loan? The answer might be surprising. Over ninety-seven percent of microloans are paid back! So, microloans are a very good way of helping people help themselves, and doing it with little risk.

**GO ON →**

**Now answer Numbers 1 through 5. Base your answers on "Small Loan, Big Effect."**

**1** Draw a line to match each statement of the author's point of view on the left with the text evidence from the article that supports it.

| | |
|---|---|
| Microloans can help large groups. | "Some help families send their children to school or allow them to take classes to learn new skills." |
| Microloans are not very risky. | "When the person's business does well, it brings money into a community." |
| Microloans can help individuals. | "Over ninety-seven percent of microloans are paid back!" |

**2** Read the sentence from the article.

The loans are becoming <u>increasingly</u> popular.

If *increasing* means "growing," what does <u>increasingly</u> mean?

(A) quietly

(B) slowly

(C) less and less

(D) more and more

**GO ON →**

**3** Read the excerpt from the article.

For some people, the loans have a great effect. A carpenter in Afghanistan named Behnam received a $465 microloan. He used it to expand his carpentry business. With his larger business, he is able to provide more and better food and clothing for his four children. Lucas, who lives in Mozambique, used microloans to buy chickens and to irrigate his farmland. Now he is able to employ four people and to send his children to school. Beatrice, who lives in Kenya, started with a microloan of less than forty dollars. She used the money to buy vegetables, which she sold at local markets.

What do the details in the excerpt have in common? Select **two** options.

(A) They tell how microloans help the community.

(B) They tell how microloans can be very important.

(C) They tell how microloans are simpler than one thinks.

(D) They tell how difficult microloans can be to pay back.

(E) They tell how microloans have improved individual lives.

(F) They tell how hard it is to make a living in developing countries.

**GO ON →**

**4** Read the sentence from the text.

This makes a <u>noticeable</u> difference and helps other businesses sell or do more.

The suffix -*able* means "able to be." Which word uses the suffix in the same way as in <u>noticeable</u>?

(A) cable

(B) enjoyable

(C) stable

(D) table

**5** This question has two parts. First, answer part A. Then, answer part B.

**Part A:** Which sentence states the author's point of view of microloans?

(A) They help people, not communities.

(B) They can change people's lives for the better.

(C) They need to be changed in order to work correctly.

(D) They should be paid back quickly to make a difference.

**Part B:** Which sentence from the text **best** supports your answer in part A?

(A) "A microloan is a loan of a small amount of money to a person or group."

(B) "Microloans are made to people in developing countries in Africa, Asia, and South America."

(C) "Groups involved in microloans find that what is good for one person is also good for those around that person."

(D) "The people who receive microloans are often very poor."

**GO ON →**

**Read the article "The Courage of Mum Bett" before answering Numbers 6 through 10.**

# The Courage of Mum Bett

Around the year 1742, a woman named Elizabeth was born a slave. She had no last name. She and her younger sister Lizzie grew up in the household of Pieter Hogeboom, a Dutch landowner. He lived in the Hudson Valley of New York State. Elizabeth and Lizzie were either sold or given by the Hogeboom family to the Ashley family of Sheffield, Massachusetts.

Elizabeth lived in the Ashley household for about thirty years. There are not many documents that give information about her early life, and the facts are difficult to determine. Records state that she married and had a child. By that time, she was known as "Mum Bett," and her daughter was called "Little Bett." Her husband fought in the American Revolution and was probably killed in battle.

John Ashley, the head of the Ashley household, was an important man in eighteenth-century Massachusetts. He was a lawyer and a judge, and he was involved in writing the state constitution, which established the laws of the state. The constitution, adopted in 1780, included a statement called the Sheffield Declaration. It said, "Mankind in a State of Nature are equal, free, and independent of each other, and have a right to the undisturbed Enjoyment of their lives, their Liberty and Property."

No one knows just how Mum Bett learned about this statement. Some sources say she overheard a discussion about it when serving at the family table or working around the house. Others say she heard the Sheffield Declaration read aloud at the village meetinghouse. Either way, the statement made her think about the injustice of slavery.

**GO ON →**

No one is sure, either, what drove Mum Bett to act. One story claims that Mrs. Ashley discovered that Mum Bett's sister Lizzie had made a cake for herself. Furious, she tried to strike Lizzie with a hot shovel. Unafraid, Mum Bett pushed Lizzie aside. The shovel hit her own arm instead of Lizzie's, injuring and burning it.

Mum Bett left the Ashley house and refused to return. The Ashleys tried to use the law to bring her back. At that time, slavery was legal in Massachusetts. Mum Bett went to a lawyer named Theodore Sedgewick, who was known for his anti-slavery views. She asked him to help file a lawsuit for her freedom. Sedgewick agreed, and another slave, a man named Brom, joined in the lawsuit. Sedgewick sued for their freedom. Since the state constitution was now law, Sedgewick claimed that Ashley was acting unlawfully by enslaving Mum Bett.

The case was tried in 1781, and in August of that year, Sedgewick won the case. There is no record of what happened to Brom after the trial. The court fined Ashley, and Mum Bett was freed. Other similar cases were tried in Massachusetts, and finally, in 1783, slavery was outlawed in the state. Massachusetts was only the third state in the U.S. to ban slavery, and it did so more than eighty years before slavery was banned in the country as a whole.

Mum Bett took the last name Freeman and went to work as a paid servant for the Sedgewicks, staying with them until she was able to buy her own house. The family loved and relied on her, and in an uprising called Shays' Rebellion, she defended the Sedgewicks' house against rebels who tried to enter and loot it. Holding a shovel and using her wits, she convinced the rebels to leave. Mum Bett died in 1829 and is buried in the Sedgewick family burial plot.

Mum Bett Freeman could not read or write. She never had the opportunity to become educated, but she had strong beliefs, and she was courageous. Without Mum Bett's daring and inspiring efforts, the Massachusetts law allowing slavery would have remained unchanged. Thousands of men and women would have continued living in slavery for years more.

**GO ON →**

**Now answer Numbers 6 through 10. Base your answers on "The Courage of Mum Bett."**

**6** This question has two parts. First, answer part A. Then, answer part B.

**Part A:** Read the sentence from the article.

Either way, the statement made her think about the <u>injustice</u> of slavery.

What does the word <u>injustice</u> mean?

Ⓐ big argument

Ⓑ likely cause

Ⓒ unfair act

Ⓓ new law

**Part B:** The prefix -*in* can mean "in" or "not." Which word uses the prefix in the same way as in the word <u>injustice</u>?

Ⓐ income

Ⓑ independence

Ⓒ infield

Ⓓ inhabit

**GO ON →**

**7** This question has two parts. First, answer part A. Then, answer part B.

Part A: Which statement summarizes the author's point of view of Mum Bett?

(A) She put her family before anything else in her life.

(B) She was misunderstood by historians for many years.

(C) She would have accomplished more if she were educated.

(D) She was an intelligent woman who used the resources she had.

Part B: Which detail from the text **best** supports your answer in part A?

(A) Mum Bett got married and had a child.

(B) Mum Bett worked for the Sedgewicks for many years.

(C) Mum Bett used the law of the time to gain her freedom.

(D) Mum Bett took the name "Freeman" when she was freed.

**8** Read the sentence from the article.

She never had the opportunity to become educated, but she had strong beliefs, and she was <u>courageous</u>.

The word *courage* means "bravery." What does the word <u>courageous</u> mean?

(A) once brave

(B) never brave

(C) with bravery

(D) without bravery

**GO ON →**

**9** Read the author's point of view in the chart. Write **two** pieces of text evidence that the author uses to support it. Use the list below.

> **Point of View:** Mum Bett's actions changed many people's lives.
>
>
>
>
>
>

**Text Evidence:**

"Her husband fought in the American Revolution and was probably killed in battle."

"Since the state constitution was now law, Sedgewick claimed that Ashley was acting unlawfully by enslaving Mum Bett."

"Mum Bett died in 1829 and is buried in the Sedgewick family burial plot."

"Without Mum Bett's daring and inspiring efforts, the Massachusetts law allowing slavery would have remained unchanged."

"Thousands of men and women would have continued living in slavery for years more."

**10** With which statements would the author **most likely** agree? Select **two** choices.

- (A) Mum Bett had a good life.
- (B) Mum Bett was very determined.
- (C) Massachusetts was a good place to live in the past.
- (D) Mum Bett should be admired for what she achieved.
- (E) Massachusetts is the most important state in American history.
- (F) Massachusetts was slower to change its laws than most other states.

Name: _____ Date: _____

**Now answer Number 11. Base your answer on "Small Loan, Big Effect" and "The Courage of Mum Bett."**

**11** How do the authors have similar points of view about their subjects in both articles? Support your answer with text evidence from both articles.

_____

_____

_____

_____

_____

_____

_____

_____

_____

_____

_____

_____

_____

_____

_____

_____

# Answer Key

Name: _____

| Question | Correct Answer | Content Focus | CCSS | Complexity |
|----------|----------------|---------------|------|------------|
| 1 | see below | Author's Point of View | RI.5.8 | DOK 3 |
| 2 | D | Prefixes and Suffixes | L.3.4b | DOK 1 |
| 3 | B, E | Main Idea and Key Details | RI.5.2 | DOK 2 |
| 4 | B | Prefixes and Suffixes | L.3.4b | DOK 1 |
| 5A | B | Author's Point of View | RI.5.8 | DOK 3 |
| 5B | C | Author's Point of View/Text Evidence | RI.5.8/ RI.5.1 | DOK 3 |
| 6A | C | Prefixes and Suffixes | L.3.4b | DOK 1 |
| 6B | B | Prefixes and Suffixes | L.3.4b | DOK 1 |
| 7A | D | Author's Point of View | RI.5.8 | DOK 3 |
| 7B | C | Author's Point of View/Text Evidence | RI.5.8/ RI.5.1 | DOK 3 |
| 8 | C | Prefixes and Suffixes | L.3.4b | DOK 1 |
| 9 | see below | Author's Point of View | RI.5.8 | DOK 3 |
| 10 | B, D | Author's Point of View | RI.6.6 | DOK 3 |
| 11 | see below | Writing About Text | W.5.9b | DOK 4 |

| | | | |
|---|---|---|---|
| **Comprehension** 1, 3, 5A, 5B, 7A, 7B, 9, 10 | | /12 | % |
| **Vocabulary** 2, 4, 6A, 6B, 8 | | /8 | % |
| **Total Weekly Assessment Score** | | /20 | % |

**1** Students should draw lines to make the following matches:
- Microloans can help large groups.—"When the person's business does well, it brings money into a community."
- Microloans are not very risky.—"Over ninety-seven percent of microloans are paid back!"
- Microloans can help individuals.—"Some help families send their children to school or allow them to take classes to learn new skills."

**9** Students should complete the chart with the following sentences:
- "Without Mum Bett's daring and inspiring efforts, the Massachusetts law allowing slavery would have remained unchanged."
- "Thousands of men and women would have continued living in slavery for years more."

**11** To receive full credit for the response, the following information should be included: Both authors have a positive view of their subjects. The author of the first article believes microloans have changed many people's lives, and the author of the second sees Mum Bett's actions as helping to free thousands of people from slavery.

**Read the article "Food of the Future" before answering Numbers 1 through 5.**

# Food of the Future

Anyone who has gone swimming in the ocean knows the feeling of seaweed as it brushes against you. It is a little slimy, a little icky, but seaweed is not just a weed. It is also a vegetable, just like broccoli and green beans are. Millions of people eat it, and millions more might find it on their dining room tables in the future.

In much of the United States, people do not eat seaweed. It has become popular in Hawaii and California, though. But in many Asian countries, in the British Isles, in Canada, and in the Caribbean, it has been a part of people's diet for a long time. In Scotland, for example, people have eaten a kind of seaweed called dulse for more than a thousand years! In fact, people who live on the coast have probably been eating seaweed since the earliest days of humans.

Most people in the U.S. have probably eaten seaweed in one form or another too. You might not even know you have eaten it! Agar agar, a jelly-like substance, is made from seaweed. This material is used to thicken many different kinds of foods, such as pies and puddings, ice cream, yogurt, and salad dressings.

Seaweeds are amazing sources of vitamins, minerals, protein, and fiber. Some seaweeds can be eaten raw; others are better cooked, or dried and sprinkled over food. Some are made into tea or soup. One kind of seaweed looks like grapes, and people eat it scattered over salads or as a snack food.

**GO ON →**

Seaweed is available in profusion, or great amounts, in the ocean. Some of it is harvested from the sea with vacuum-like machines. This practice has led to a deficit of seaweed (that is, a shortage of it) in many places, though. Scientists have worked to persuade people to develop new ways to grow and harvest seaweed. Now, seaweed "farmers" grow different kinds of seaweeds in coastal waters. Some seaweeds are grown on ropes that rest in the water, and some are grown on nets. In Canada, farmers grow seaweed onshore, in tanks, but this does not work for every kind of seaweed. Some seaweeds require the active movement of seawater to grow well.

Seaweed harvesters wash the vegetables with seawater. Some plants are dried in the sun; others are packed and sold fresh. Because seawater is salty, most kinds of seaweeds are salty, too.

Seaweed has other uses besides providing nutrition for humans by giving them a healthful food. Some of it is dried and made into fertilizer, a material that improves soil. Because seaweed is so full of vitamins and minerals, it is great for soil, helping plants to grow faster and better. It can be added to animal feed to make it better for the animals. It can also be found in makeup, skin lotions, and bath products, and seaweed helps to give your toothpaste its gel-like smoothness.

Scientists have begun working on making seaweed into fuel. No one knows yet whether this experiment will work. If it does, seaweed could provide a great source of fuel. It grows more quickly than other plants used to make fuel and is less expensive.

Seaweed is easy to grow, and its cultivation—that is, the farming of it—does not take the place of other crops. Because of this, some people consider it the food of the future. Before too long, we could be seeing it on menus and supermarket shelves around the world.

**GO ON →**

Name: _____ Date: _____

**Now answer Numbers 1 through 5. Base your answers on "Food of the Future."**

**1** Read the sentence from the article.

Seaweed is available in <u>profusion</u>, or great amounts, in the ocean.

What does the word <u>profusion</u> mean in the sentence?

(A) less than enough

(B) a very large quantity

(C) just the right amount

(D) an amount that changes

**2** The author makes the point that seaweed can be more than a health food. Which evidence from the article supports this point? Select **three** options.

(A) Some seaweeds grow in coastal waters.

(B) Some seaweeds are added to animal feed.

(C) Some seaweeds are made into tea or soup.

(D) Some seaweeds grow on ropes resting in water.

(E) Some seaweeds are dried and made into fertilizer.

(F) Some seaweeds are used to make toothpaste feel smooth.

**GO ON →**

**3** Read the sentence.

Maybe someday our cars will be powered by seaweed.

Circle the paragraph that the detail above would **best** support.

Seaweed harvesters wash the vegetables with seawater. Some plants are dried in the sun; others are packed and sold fresh. Because seawater is salty, most kinds of seaweeds are salty, too.

Seaweed has other uses besides providing nutrition for humans by giving them a healthful food. Some of it is dried and made into fertilizer, a material that improves soil. Because seaweed is so full of vitamins and minerals, it is great for soil, helping plants to grow faster and better. It can be added to animal feed to make it better for the animals. It can also be found in makeup, skin lotions, and bath products, and seaweed helps to give your toothpaste its gel-like smoothness.

Scientists have begun working on making seaweed into fuel. No one knows yet whether this experiment will work. If it does, seaweed could provide a great source of fuel. It grows more quickly than other plants used to make fuel and is less expensive.

Seaweed is easy to grow, and its cultivation—that is, the farming of it—does not take the place of other crops. Because of this, some people consider it the food of the future. Before too long, we could be seeing it on menus and supermarket shelves around the world.

**GO ON →**

**4** This question has two parts. First, answer part A. Then, answer part B.

**Part A:** Which statement summarizes a point the author makes about seaweed and fuel?

(A) Seaweed could be a great source of fuel.

(B) Seaweed will soon replace gasoline as a fuel.

(C) Seaweed has been used as fuel for many years.

(D) Seaweed will never completely replace gasoline as fuel.

**Part B:** Which sentence from the article **best** supports this point of view?

(A) "In Canada, farmers grow seaweed onshore, in tanks, but this does not work for every kind of seaweed.

(B) "Some plants are dried in the sun; others are packed and sold fresh."

(C) "It grows more quickly than other plants used to make fuel and is less expensive."

(D) "Before too long, we could be seeing it on menus and supermarket shelves around the world."

**5** Read the sentence from the article.

Seaweed is easy to grow, and its cultivation—that is, the farming of it—does not take the place of other crops.

What does cultivation mean in the sentence above?

(A) act of eating

(B) act of growing

(C) expense or cost

(D) result of experiments

**GO ON →**

**Read the article "Desert Environments" before answering Numbers 6 through 10.**

# Desert Environments

Deserts cover about one fifth of Earth's surface. The terrain, or ground, of some deserts is sandy, while others have a rocky terrain. Yet all deserts have one major feature in common—lack of rainfall. Deserts are dry, desolate places, and the desert landscape is harsh. It seems cruel and unforgiving, and few large animals live in deserts. Few trees grow there, and the ones that do are not like most forest trees. Forest trees generally grow tall and straight, but desert trees are short, and they often have amazing shapes. The winds that buffet them twist the trees into these shapes. The cactus is one plant that has adapted to survive in the desert by storing water in its trunk. It has shallow roots that can take in any water that falls. Cactus leaves are often very thin, which gives them less exposure to the sun.

The temperature in deserts can be unbelievably hot or cold. The Sahara Desert in Africa gets very hot during the day, but at night the temperature goes down. Deserts like this are called "hot" deserts. In contrast, the Gobi Desert in Asia is always cold, as are the deserts at the South Pole. These are called "cold" deserts. They often get a lot of snow, and some get more rainfall than other kinds of deserts. There are also semidry deserts, such as the deserts in Utah and Montana and those in the Arctic. These have lower temperatures and more moisture. Finally, there are coastal deserts, which have warm days and cool nights. The soil is often salty, and there is more rainfall than in hot and semidry deserts.

Desert animals have special characteristics that allow them to adapt to their harsh settings. In hot deserts, some animals go on a quest for food early in the morning, the coolest time of the day. Early in the day, roadrunners chase rattlesnakes and coyotes hunt for ground squirrels. During the heat of the day, many animals are dormant, or motionless. Some hide under the ground, while others hide under rocks. At night, the temperature gets much cooler, and then the animals come out to find food. Scorpions and bats hunt for insects, and spiders as big as mice also hunt at night. In the driest deserts, animals might hibernate, or hide away, for months, only coming out when rain finally falls.

**GO ON →**

Animals in cold deserts have a different system. They hunt during the day when temperatures are slightly warmer, but the nights are very cold, and the animals take shelter.

Living conditions are harsh in a desert. Because food is never plentiful, most desert animals are small and skinny. How do desert animals survive with little or no food to eat? Some of them store fat in their bodies. For example, one type of desert lizard stores fat in its large tail; it uses this fat when food is scarce. This is similar to some types of forest bears who store fat in their bodies during the summer. In the winter, when they hibernate, they have a reduced need for food, but they still need some food, and they get it from their stored fat.

Deserts get very little rainfall. The driest deserts might get less than half an inch of moisture a year, and often this moisture is in the form of fog, not rain. When there is a rainstorm, pools of water form on the ground, and the animals drink as much as they can. Yet some desert animals do not drink at all, but rather they get all the water they need from the food they eat. Amazingly, deserts are second only to rainforests in the number of different plant and animal species that live there!

**GO ON →**

Name: _____ Date: _____

**Now answer Numbers 6 through 10. Base your answers on "Desert Environments."**

**6** Read the sentences from the text.

Deserts are dry, desolate places, and the desert landscape is <u>harsh</u>. It seems cruel and unforgiving, and few large animals live in deserts.

Which words from the sentences restate what <u>harsh</u> means? Select **all** that apply.

(A) dry

(B) desert

(C) cruel

(D) unforgiving

(E) few

(F) large

**7** This question has two parts. First, answer part A. Then, answer part B.

**Part A:** Which sentence summarizes the author's point about adaptation in the desert?

(A) Animals all adapt in the same way to survive in the desert.

(B) Adaptation is needed to survive in the desert environment.

(C) Animals are just beginning to adapt to the desert environment.

(D) Plants have adapted to the desert environment better than animals.

**Part B:** Which evidence from the text **best** supports the author's point?

(A) "The cactus is one plant that has adapted to survive in the desert by storing water in its trunk."

(B) "The temperature in deserts can be unbelievably hot or cold."

(C) "There are also semidry deserts, such as the deserts in Utah and Montana and those in the Arctic."

(D) "Because food is never plentiful, most animals are small and skinny."

**GO ON →**

Copyright © McGraw-Hill Education

**8** This question has two parts. First, answer part A. Then, answer part B.

**Part A:** Read the sentence from the text.

During the heat of the day, many animals are <u>dormant</u>, or motionless.

What does the word <u>dormant</u> mean in the sentence?

(A) alive

(B) fearful

(C) slow

(D) still

**Part B:** Which word from the sentence restates the meaning of <u>dormant</u>?

(A) heat

(B) day

(C) animals

(D) motionless

**9** Which statement **best** summarizes the author's point of view based on the evidence in the text?

(A) Deserts are growing larger all over the earth.

(B) Deserts can be great places for people to live.

(C) Living in a desert requires special characteristics.

(D) Without regular rainfall, animals and plants cannot live.

**GO ON →**

Name: _____  Date: _____

**10** Choose **one** sentence that states the author's point of view and write it in the chart. Then choose **two** sentences that support this point of view and write them in the chart.

| Author's Point of View | Supporting Details |
|---|---|
|  |  |
|  |  |

**Sentences:**

Most animals in the desert are skinny.

It is hard to find food in the desert.

It is very difficult to live in the desert.

Name: _____ Date: _____

**Now answer Number 11. Base your answer on "Food of the Future" and "Desert Environments."**

**11** What are the unusual and unique characteristics of the plants described in both articles? Use details from both texts to support your answer.

_____

_____

_____

_____

_____

_____

_____

_____

_____

_____

_____

_____

# Answer Key

| Question | Correct Answer | Content Focus | CCSS | Complexity |
|:---:|:---:|:---:|:---:|:---:|
| 1 | B | Context Clues: Definitions and Restatements | L.5.4a | DOK 2 |
| 2 | B, E, F, | Author's Point of View | RI.5.8 | DOK 3 |
| 3 | see below | Main Idea and Key Details | RI.5.2 | DOK 2 |
| 4A | A | Author's Point of View | RI.5.8 | DOK 3 |
| 4B | C | Author's Point of View/Text Evidence | RI.5.8/ RI.5.1 | DOK 3 |
| 5 | B | Context Clues: Definitions and Restatements | L.5.4a | DOK 2 |
| 6 | C, D | Context Clues: Definitions and Restatements | L.5.4a | DOK 2 |
| 7A | B | Author's Point of View | RI.5.8 | DOK 3 |
| 7B | A | Author's Point of View/Text Evidence | RI.5.8/ RI.5.1 | DOK 3 |
| 8A | D | Context Clues: Definitions and Restatements | L.5.4a | DOK 2 |
| 8B | D | Context Clues: Definitions and Restatements/Text Evidence | L.5.4a/ RI.5.1 | DOK 2 |
| 9 | C | Author's Point of View | RI.5.8 | DOK 3 |
| 10 | see below | Author's Point of View | RI.5.8 | DOK 3 |
| 11 | see below | Writing About Text | W.5.9b | DOK 4 |

| | | |
|:---|:---:|:---:|
| **Comprehension** 2, 3, 4A, 4B, 7A, 7B, 9, 10 | /12 | % |
| **Vocabulary** 1, 5, 6, 8A, 8B | /8 | % |
| **Total Weekly Assessment Score** | /20 | % |

**3** Students should circle the following paragraph:
- Scientists have begun working on making seaweed into fuel. No one knows yet whether this experiment will work. If it does, seaweed could provide a great source of fuel. It grows more quickly than other plants used to make fuel and is less expensive.

**10** Students should complete the chart with the following sentences:
- Author's Point of View—It is very difficult to live in the desert.
- Supporting Details—Most animals in the desert are skinny; It is hard to find food in the desert.

**11** To receive full credit for the response, the following information should be included:
Plants, like seaweed, in "Food of the Future" are an amazing source of vitamins, minerals, protein, and fiber. The plants and animals described in "Desert Environments" demonstrate characteristics that allow them to live in harsh desert environments.

**Read the passage "Marisa's Secret" before answering Numbers 1 through 5.**

# Marisa's Secret

"Do you want to go to my house this afternoon to hang out and make cookies?" Lisa asked her best friend Marisa.

"I can't today," Marisa said regretfully, "because I have to be somewhere."

Lisa frowned and said, "You had to be somewhere last Wednesday and the Wednesday before that, but you never say where you're going."

"I just have to do this thing," Marisa replied, "and we can hang out tomorrow, okay?" Lisa knew that Marisa was keeping a secret, and the secret hung between them like a dark cloud. She watched Marisa walk over to the bus stop, and when the bus pulled in, Marisa climbed on board. The bus pulled away with a groan, and almost without thinking, Lisa ran to the bus stop herself. After a few minutes another bus pulled up, and she climbed on board and paid her fare.

The bus headed downtown, and Lisa watched the sidewalk like a hawk. After about ten minutes she saw Marisa walking past a row of run-down buildings, dirty and neglected, and she pulled the bell and jumped off the bus. She watched as Marisa stopped at a small storefront with a sign out front, pushed open the door, and disappeared inside. Lisa walked up to the storefront and stared at the sign, which said, "Soup Kitchen." What on earth was Marisa doing there? Lisa took a deep breath and then pushed open the door. Inside, she saw a big room lined with long tables, and at each table were a dozen or more people—men, women, and children. The room was crowded but not very noisy; people spoke quietly, and the air was perfumed with the scents of baking bread and roasting vegetables.

"Can I help you, dear?" a woman asked Lisa. "The line for food starts over there," she said as she pointed to a line of people waiting patiently in front of a window.

"I am looking for a friend," Lisa explained, "Marisa Contes, do you know her?"

The woman smiled and said, "I am Amy Shu, and Marisa is one of my Wednesday regulars."

**GO ON →**

"But what does she do here?" Lisa asked.

"Come on back to the kitchen, and you can see for yourself," Mrs. Shu said. Lisa followed her through a set of swinging doors into a warm kitchen, where pots steamed on the stove and people worked cutting bread and ladling soup into bowls. There was Marisa, her hair in a net and a ladle in her hand, and when she saw Lisa, she looked like she had seen a ghost.

"I followed you," Lisa admitted. "I am sorry, but I was so curious—I know it was wrong. What are you doing here?"

Marisa wiped her hands on a towel and said, "I never told you about my uncle Tomas, did I?" When Lisa shook her head, she said, "Well, I did not really know about him until this year, because we never saw him, and we never saw him because he was homeless and had no address." Lisa was quiet, so Marisa went on, saying, "It took him a long time, but he finally found a good job and got an apartment, and then he contacted us. It was great to see him doing so well! He told us how hard it had been, living without a real home, and how he ate a lot of his meals at soup kitchens—that is how he managed to keep going—so I thought I would try to help other people like him by working in a soup kitchen myself. It makes me really happy to help people like my uncle."

Lisa reached out and hugged her friend. "I think it is awesome," she said. "Hey, if I help out here too, will you introduce me to your uncle?"

**GO ON →**

**Now answer Numbers 1 through 5. Base your answers on "Marisa's Secret."**

**1** Read the sentence from the passage.

Lisa knew that Marisa was keeping a secret, and the secret hung between them like a dark cloud.

Why does the author compare Marisa's secret to a dark cloud?

- Ⓐ to describe exactly what the secret is
- Ⓑ to show that the secret is something bad
- Ⓒ to show that secrets can interfere with friendships
- Ⓓ to show that the secret is something that happens at night

**2** This question has two parts. First, answer part A. Then, answer part B.

**Part A:** Which statement **best** summarizes the message in the text?

- Ⓐ Friends have many secrets.
- Ⓑ Everyone has a secret relative.
- Ⓒ Your closest friend can betray you.
- Ⓓ Doing good can be its own reward.

**Part B:** Which sentence from the text **best** supports your answer in part A?

- Ⓐ "The woman smiled and said, 'I am Amy Shu, and Marisa is one of my Wednesday regulars.'"
- Ⓑ "Marisa wiped her hands on a towel and said, 'I never told you about my uncle Tomas, did I?'"
- Ⓒ "'It makes me really happy to help people like my uncle.'"
- Ⓓ "'Hey, if I help out here too, will you introduce me to your uncle?'"

**GO ON →**

**3** This question has two parts. First, answer part A. Then, answer part B.

**Part A:** Read the sentence from the text.

There was Marisa, her hair in a net and a ladle in her hand, and when she saw Lisa, she looked <u>like she had seen a ghost</u>.

What does the phrase "like she had seen a ghost" mean?

(A) Marisa was not feeling well.

(B) Marisa did not expect to see her friend.

(C) Marisa was tired from working all afternoon.

(D) Marisa looked very white from working in the kitchen.

**Part B:** Which feeling in Marisa does the author communicate by using the simile above?

(A) anxiety

(B) fear

(C) joy

(D) shock

**4** Circle **one** way that **each** character contributes to the lesson of the passage.

| Lisa | Marisa |
|---|---|
| supports Marisa's actions | tells Lisa about her uncle |
| follows Marisa on the bus | works at the soup kitchen |
| walks into the soup kitchen | tells Lisa she cannot go over her house |

**GO ON →**

**5** Which excerpts from the passage **best** support the theme? Select **two** options.

Ⓐ "Inside, she saw a big room lined with long tables, and at each table were a dozen or more people—men, women, and children."

Ⓑ "Lisa followed her through a set of swinging doors into a warm kitchen, where pots steamed on the stove and people worked cutting bread and ladling soup into bowls."

Ⓒ "'I am sorry, but I was so curious—I know it was wrong.'"

Ⓓ "... 'It took him a long time, but he finally found a good job and got an apartment, and then he contacted us.'"

Ⓔ "'... I thought I would try to help other people like him by working in a soup kitchen myself.'"

Ⓕ "Lisa reached out and hugged her friend."

**GO ON →**

**Read the passage "To Honor a Hero" before answering Numbers 6 through 10.**

# To Honor a Hero

Martin sat quietly between his mother and his grandfather. The meeting hall was crowded with people who had come to pay their respects to a hero, but Martin was confused, for he had no idea who was being honored. He searched the smiling faces of many of the elderly people sitting around him. Some were as wrinkled as crumpled paper, but none of them looked much like a hero to him.

The speaker started his speech, saying, "Friends, we are here to honor a man who served the Navajo people and the United States of America. This was a man who enlisted in the Marines during World War II and signed up as a Navajo Code Talker." The speaker looked around the audience. "Some of our youngsters may not know that many Navajos fought with the Marines in every battle in the Pacific Corridor from 1942 to 1945. Our men served in more than one invasion, and they were a crucial part of these attacks."

Martin's eyes wandered over the faces of the older men. Did some of them really play such an important role in a war? It hardly seemed possible; these were people he saw every day—his friends' grandparents, shopkeepers, the owner of the local diner.

Martin's shoulders began to sag with boredom. He had heard about World War II in school, and it was part of the past, a closed book to Martin. What was so exciting about a war, anyway? People were always fighting. Even on reservation land where everyone lived and worked, people sometimes fought with each other.

**GO ON →**

Martin turned his attention again to the speaker. "The time has come," the man was saying, "to honor our Code Talkers, now that so many of them have passed on. These were the people who helped assure victory in the war by sending and receiving coded messages about troop actions and orders, by sending vital information about each battle location so the Allies could position themselves at the site of the action. No member of the enemy Axis forces could break the Navajo Code during the Battle of Iwo Jima, and six of our people worked without sleep until that battle was won."

The crowd murmured, and Martin leaned forward, paying attention. This was getting more interesting.

"A man we know only as a friend and neighbor was a Code Talker," said the speaker. "His valiant work in the war helped win it, and after the war, he came home to help his people on the reservation. He did not forget his home, and so he will not be forgotten."

The speaker closed his eyes and softly spoke the following poem in his native language.

> What is a hero, my brothers, my sisters?
> To find one, how long must you roam?
> Is it an eagle that soars for freedom?
> Is it the bear that defends its home?
>
> A hero is both the eagle and bear,
> One who will fight to protect.
> And then return to the Navajo land
> To show his love and respect.

Then a surprising thing happened: the speaker asked Martin's grandfather to rise, saying, "Let us honor one of our Code Talkers." Martin's grandfather slowly got up from his seat. He looked very serious, but his eyes were as bright as diamonds.

Martin glanced at his mom and saw that there were tears in her eyes, and he felt a wave of pride break over him as he looked up at the man he thought he knew so well. His own grandfather—a hero!

**GO ON →**

**Now answer Numbers 6 through 10. Base your answers on "To Honor a Hero."**

**6** This question has two parts. First, answer part A. Then, answer part B.

**Part A:** Read the sentences from the passage.

He searched the smiling faces of many of the elderly people sitting around him. Some were <u>as wrinkled as crumpled paper</u>, but none of them looked much like a hero to him.

What does the narrator suggest by saying the people's faces were "as wrinkled as crumpled paper"?

(A) The people in the crowd were very old.

(B) The people in the crowd were confused.

(C) The people in the crowd were very upset.

(D) The people in the crowd were reading a program.

**Part B:** Which word from the sentences **best** supports your answer in part A?

(A) smiling

(B) elderly

(C) around

(D) hero

**GO ON →**

**7** This question has two parts. First, answer part A. Then, answer part B.

**Part A:** Which sentence summarizes the message in the passage?

(A) We don't always know who has behaved heroically.

(B) Heroes should get prizes and honors.

(C) Grandparents are all heroes.

(D) Everybody is a hero.

**Part B:** Which action by a character **best** supports the message of the passage?

(A) The speaker describes the Navajo Code Talkers.

(B) Martin's grandfather keeps his heroism a secret.

(C) Martin is bored during the presentation.

(D) Martin's mother has tears in her eyes.

**8** Select **two** sentences from the text that support the theme.

(A) "'Some of our youngsters may not know that many Navajos fought with the Marines in every battle in the Pacific Corridor from 1942 to 1945.'"

(B) "Martin's eyes wandered over the faces of the older men."

(C) "Did some of them really play such an important role in a war?"

(D) "Even on reservation land where everyone lived and worked, people sometimes fought with each other."

(E) "The crowd murmured, and Martin leaned forward, paying attention."

(F) "The speaker closed his eyes and softly spoke the following poem in his native language."

**GO ON →**

**9** Read the sentence from the passage.

He had heard about World War II in school, and it was part of the past, a closed book to Martin.

Why does the author compare the past to a closed book?

(A) to show that Martin is not a very good reader

(B) to show that Martin has not learned any history

(C) to show that Martin does not care about the past

(D) to show that Martin has difficulty learning about the past

**10** Martin's point of view of the situation changes during the passage. Select **one** word from the list to describe Martin's point of view at **each** part of the story. Write the words in the chart.

| Beginning | Middle | End |
|-----------|--------|-----|
|           |        |     |
|           |        |     |
|           |        |     |
|           |        |     |
|           |        |     |

**Point of View:**

angry          bored          curious          nervous

proud          thrilled          worried

**Now answer Number 11. Base your answer on "Marisa's Secret" and "To Honor a Hero."**

**11** What is similar about the secrets that Marisa and Martin's grandfather keep? Support your answer with details from both texts.

_____

_____

_____

_____

_____

_____

_____

_____

_____

_____

_____

_____

| Question | Correct Answer | Content Focus | CCSS | Complexity |
|:---:|:---:|:---:|:---:|:---:|
| **1** | C | Simile | L.5.5a | DOK 2 |
| **2A** | D | Theme | RL.5.2 | DOK 3 |
| **2B** | C | Theme/Text Evidence | RL.5.2/ RL.5.1 | DOK 3 |
| **3A** | B | Simile | L.5.5a | DOK 2 |
| **3B** | D | Simile/Text Evidence | L.5.5a/ RL.5.1 | DOK 2 |
| **4** | see below | Theme | RL.5.2 | DOK 3 |
| **5** | E, F | Theme | RL.5.2 | DOK 3 |
| **6A** | A | Simile | L.5.5a | DOK 2 |
| **6B** | B | Simile/Text Evidence | L.5.5a/ RL.5.1 | DOK 2 |
| **7A** | A | Theme | RL.5.2 | DOK 3 |
| **7B** | B | Theme/Text Evidence | RL.5.2/ RL.5.1 | DOK 3 |
| **8** | A, C | Theme | RL.5.2 | DOK 3 |
| **9** | C | Metaphor | L.5.5a | DOK 2 |
| **10** | see below | Point of View | RL.5.6 | DOK 3 |
| **11** | see below | Writing About Text | W.5.9a | DOK 4 |

| | | | |
|:---|:---:|:---:|
| **Comprehension** 2A, 2B, 4, 5, 7A, 7B, 8, 10 | /12 | % |
| **Vocabulary** 1, 3A, 3B, 6A, 6B, 9 | /8 | % |
| **Total Weekly Assessment Score** | /20 | % |

**4** Students should circle the following phrases:
- Lisa—supports Marisa's actions
- Marisa—works at the soup kitchen

**10** Students should complete the chart with the following words:
- Beginning—bored
- Middle—curious
- End—proud

**11** To receive full credit for the response, the following information should be included: Marisa and Martin's grandfather both keep a secret about how they help or helped other people. Marisa helps by volunteering in a soup kitchen. Martin's grandfather helped by fighting heroically in World War II.

**Read the passage "Camp Pennacook" before answering Numbers 1 through 5.**

# Camp Pennacook

Eleven-year-old Henry lived in Manchester, New Hampshire, with his mom, two sisters, and grandmother. Their apartment was small for five people, and the building was on one of the busiest streets in the city. Henry didn't have a bedroom and slept on the couch. One day his teacher, Ms. Jeffers, asked him if he would like to go to a boys' camp in the summer. She had talked to Henry's mom, who said he could go to Camp Pennacook if he wanted. It was on an island in Lake Winnipesaukee. The camp would last a month, and there would be swimming, boating, hiking, and other activities. Henry knew about camps from his neighbor James and said yes.

On June 22, Henry met a group of other campers at a dock and got on a boat that would take them to the island. After a short trip, they reached their destination. Camp Pennacook was different from the city, with trees everywhere, even around the cabin where Henry would live with his teammates. At first Henry was shy. Then, Nathan, whose cot was next to his, offered to share his video game during leisure time, an hour in the evening that did not have anything scheduled for the campers. Henry had a new friend.

That night the boys had a chance to get acquainted at a hot dog and hamburger cookout. Henry sat with Nathan and Clark, another boy from his cabin, during the camp sing-along, and the boys went back to their cabins early because they had their first swimming lesson in the morning.

Henry did not know how to swim and was nervous about the lesson. When the boys got to the beach, he stepped slowly into the shallow water and found that it was cold but not icy. The instructor taught him how to float using a swim board, and when it was time to go to his work project, Henry did not want the swimming lesson to end.

**GO ON →**

Every boy in camp spent one hour a day working on a project. Henry's team was assigned the boathouse where they would scrub down boats and take out trash. Team members worked like busy bees except for Eric, who was not doing his share. Henry almost got into a fight with Eric because it was not fair for him not to help, but then he remembered the commitment he made when he was accepted at Camp Pennacook. He would live up to his responsibility and try hard to get along with his teammates, so he walked away to avoid trouble.

After the work hour, they went to see the ropes challenge course. The ropes were high and Henry could not imagine climbing to the top, but he remembered that he had agreed to try everything. He would climb a little way up the first time, and he could climb higher each day.

In the afternoon, Henry went to the arts and crafts room in the lodge. He had always liked to draw, so he chose the painting class. Later in the afternoon, the boys chose a sports team. It could be softball, basketball, or soccer. For Henry, the sport was not a difficult choice. He signed up for the softball team.

The boys followed a routine. Every day began with swimming, and then they worked on their projects. Later they practiced with their sports team. During the month, the cabin group went on a three-day hike in the mountains. First, they took a course in survival skills. The boys learned how to put out a campfire and tell direction from the sun's position. After three days sleeping in a tent, cooking over a fire, and hiking miles over a rough trail, Henry felt he could rely on his outdoor skills.

At the end of the month, Henry sadly said good-bye to all his new friends. He had pride in his skills and new self-respect for his own abilities. He hoped he could return next summer.

**GO ON →**

Name: _____ Date: _____

**Now answer Numbers 1 through 5. Base your answers on "Camp Pennacook."**

**1** This question has two parts. First, answer part A. Then, answer part B.

**Part A:** Which sentence **best** describes the two settings in the passage?

(A) Both are crowded, noisy places with a lot of kids.

(B) Both have no place for Henry to sleep at night.

(C) One is a busy city and the other is a natural setting.

(D) One is an apartment building and the other is a house.

**Part B:** Which detail from the passage **best** supports your answer in part A?

(A) "Henry knew about camps from his neighbor James . . ."

(B) "Camp Pennacook was different from the city, with trees everywhere, . . ."

(C) "Henry sat with Nathan and Clark, another boy from his cabin, . . ."

(D) "The ropes were high and Henry could not imagine climbing to the top, . . ."

**2** Read the sentence from the passage.

Then, Nathan, whose cot was next to his, offered to share his video game during leisure time, an hour in the evening that did not have anything scheduled for the campers.

What does the word leisure mean in the sentence?

(A) lesson

(B) meal

(C) relaxation

(D) visiting

**GO ON →**

Name: _____ Date: _____

**3** This question has two parts. First, answer part A. Then, answer part B.

**Part A:** Read the sentences from the passage.

Henry almost got into a fight with Eric because it was not fair for him not to help, but then he remembered the <u>commitment</u> he made when he was accepted at Camp Pennacook. He would live up to his responsibility and try hard to get along with his teammates, so he walked away to avoid trouble.

What does the word <u>commitment</u> mean in the sentences?

(A) mark

(B) problem

(C) promise

(D) speech

**Part B:** Which word from the sentences gives the **best** clue to the meaning of <u>commitment</u>?

(A) fight

(B) responsibility

(C) teammates

(D) trouble

**GO ON →**

**4** How are the first days at camp and the three-day hike different? Select **two** options.

Ⓐ On the hike, the boys sleep in tents.

Ⓑ There is a cookout on the first night in camp.

Ⓒ The boys take a course to prepare for the hike.

Ⓓ The boys have time to themselves only on the hike.

Ⓔ The first days at camp involve cooking over an open fire.

Ⓕ Henry does not have to try to get along with others on the hike.

**5** Underline the sentence in the paragraphs that **best** supports the overall theme of the passage.

The boys followed a routine. Every day began with swimming, and then they worked on their projects. Later they practiced with their sports team. During the month, the cabin group went on a three-day hike in the mountains. First, they took a course in survival skills. The boys learned how to put out a campfire and tell direction from the sun's position. After three days sleeping in a tent, cooking over a fire, and hiking miles over a rough trail, Henry felt he could rely on his outdoor skills.

At the end of the month, Henry sadly said good-bye to all his new friends. He had pride in his skills and new self-respect for his own abilities. He hoped he could return next summer.

**GO ON →**

**Read the passage "Books for Uganda" before answering Numbers 6 through 10.**

# Books for Uganda

Last year, Ms. Perry, who taught fifth grade in America, had read about the need for volunteers at a rural school in Africa. She applied and was accepted. Now it was summer break, and she was in Uganda, a country in Africa, a long way from her home in Minneapolis. She was staying with Mr. Omara, a teacher at the school, and his family.

When Mr. Omara showed her the school, she could not believe how many students were packed into the classroom. It was so overcrowded that students were seated on benches behind long tables and on the floor. She guessed there were ninety to a hundred students in one classroom! Mr. Omara asked a question, and the students responded from everywhere. Their voices came together and grew quickly louder like mushrooms sprouting up after a rain. Everyone paid close attention to Mr. Omara.

Mr. Omara explained that Ms. Perry could best help by working with a small group of students as they practiced writing and speaking English. From her conversations with them, she learned about their lives. Ritah, Joseph, and Winnie got up at 5 am and walked half a mile each way to collect water from the well before they walked to school. Before classes they had to do some cleanup in the room, and after classes, they had more chores to do at home. They did their homework by candlelight.

During her month in rural Uganda, Ms. Perry learned that not only did schools need pens and paper, but books. Five students in a class shared one textbook. Mr. Omara explained that textbooks had to match the curriculum and be bought in Uganda, yet many storybooks in English were needed for reading practice.

When Ms. Perry returned to Minneapolis, she met her new students as they got off the buses on the first day of school. Her class of 25 students looked small. She had much to tell them about the Ugandan school she had visited. After she finished, Jackson said, "The school needs supplies and books, so we should collect these and send them to the school."

**GO ON →**

"That's a great idea for a project," Victoria said. "How can we get started?"

Ms. Perry said, "Remember, we will need money for shipping expenses. If everyone lists their ideas for the project and funding them, we will talk about your ideas on Friday."

On Friday, everyone was eager to share ideas. Eva had found a Web site that listed books needed in Uganda. Ms. Perry suggested they focus on fiction, or storybooks about made-up people and events. It would help students practice their skills in reading English. Logan pointed out that drop-off boxes for books could be placed in the front hall of the school and in the cafeteria, where everyone would see them during lunchtime. Molly suggested publicity, saying they could make posters to get their information to the public. Ian said his parents had too many books on their bookshelves and were talking about giving some away. His idea was to collect books from families and neighbors and sell them in the shopping mall one weekend to make money.

Molly drew a poster decorated with some colorful books. It said, "Bring your books to Parkside School for our book drive. From November 1 through November 15, we are collecting books to send to a school in Uganda. We need picture books and especially the books listed below." She printed the titles of the recommended books.

At the very bottom, a line said, "We are selling used books for adult readers to pay for our shipping charges. Stop by Vernon Mall on November 13 or 14. You may see a book or two you want to buy, or you can donate a book in good condition for us to sell."

Everyone in Ms. Perry's class agreed that this was going to be a fun project!

**GO ON →**

Name: _____ Date: _____

**Now answer Numbers 6 through 10. Base your answers on "Books for Uganda."**

**6** Choose **two** details that tell how the school in Uganda is different from the school in Minneapolis. Write the details in the chart.

| How the School in Uganda Is Different From the School in Minneapolis |
|---|
|  |

**Details:**
Teachers are in the classroom in Uganda.
Students in Uganda use textbooks to learn.
There are a hundred students in one class in Uganda.
Students answer questions from their teacher in Uganda.
Students in Uganda need more books to help them learn English.

**7** How are the schools in Uganda and Minneapolis alike? Select **two** choices.

(A) Ms. Perry teaches in both.

(B) Neither has enough textbooks.

(C) Neither has a large enough room.

(D) Ms. Perry has a book sale in both.

(E) Both have desks for every student.

(F) Both are places where students learn.

**GO ON →**

**8** Read the sentence from the passage.

Ms. Perry suggested they focus on <u>fiction</u>, or storybooks about made-up people and events.

Which word from the sentence helps the reader understand what <u>fiction</u> means?

(A) focus

(B) storybooks

(C) people

(D) events

**9** This question has two parts. First, answer part A. Then, answer part B.

**Part A:** How is the setting for selling used books different from the setting for collecting children's books?

(A) One is in a school and the other is in a mall.

(B) One is in Minneapolis and the other is in Uganda.

(C) One takes place inside and the other takes place outside.

(D) One takes place in a home and the other takes place in a school.

**Part B:** Which sentence from the passage **best** supports your answer in part A?

(A) "'We need picture books and especially the books listed below.'"

(B) "She printed the titles of the recommended books."

(C) "At the very bottom, a line said, 'We are selling used books for adult readers to pay for our shipping charges.'"

(D) "'Stop by Vernon Mall on November 13 or 14.'"

**GO ON →**

Name: _____  Date: _____

**10**  This question has two parts. First, answer part A. Then, answer part B.

Part A: Read the sentence from the passage.

Molly suggested publicity, saying they could make posters to get their information to the public.

What does the word publicity mean in the sentence?

(A) advertising

(B) people

(C) readers

(D) support

Part B: Which word from the sentence **best** helps to show what publicity means?

(A) suggested

(B) saying

(C) posters

(D) information

Name: _____ Date: _____

**Now answer Number 11. Base your answer on "Camp Pennacook" and "Books for Uganda."**

**11** How are the settings in the passages alike? How are they different? Support your answer with details from both passages.

_____

_____

_____

_____

_____

_____

_____

_____

_____

_____

_____

_____

_____

_____

# Answer Key

Name: _____

| Question | Correct Answer | Content Focus | CCSS | Complexity |
|:---:|:---:|:---:|:---:|:---:|
| 1A | C | Character, Setting, Plot: Compare and Contrast | RL.5.3 | DOK 2 |
| 1B | B | Character, Setting, Plot: Compare and Contrast/Text Evidence | RL.5.3/RL.5.1 | DOK 2 |
| 2 | C | Context Clues: Comparison | L.5.4a | DOK 2 |
| 3A | C | Context Clues: Comparison | L.5.4a | DOK 2 |
| 3B | B | Context Clues: Comparison/Text Evidence | L.5.4a/RL.5.1 | DOK 2 |
| 4 | A, C | Character, Setting, Plot: Compare and Contrast | RL.5.3 | DOK 3 |
| 5 | see below | Theme | RL.5.2 | DOK 3 |
| 6 | see below | Character, Setting, Plot: Compare and Contrast | RL.5.3 | DOK 3 |
| 7 | A, F | Character, Setting, Plot: Compare and Contrast | RL.5.3 | DOK 3 |
| 8 | B | Context Clues: Comparison | L.5.4a | DOK 2 |
| 9A | A | Character, Setting, Plot: Compare and Contrast | RL.5.3 | DOK 3 |
| 9B | D | Character, Setting, Plot: Compare and Contrast/Text Evidence | RL.5.3/RL.5.1 | DOK 3 |
| 10A | A | Context Clues: Comparison | L.5.4a | DOK 2 |
| 10B | C | Context Clues: Comparison/Text Evidence | L.5.4a/RL.5.1 | DOK 2 |
| 11 | see below | Writing About Text | W.5.9a | DOK 4 |

| | | | |
|:---|:---:|:---:|:---:|
| **Comprehension** 1A, 1B, 4, 5, 6, 7, 9A, 9B | /12 | % |
| **Vocabulary** 2, 3A, 3B, 8, 10A, 10B | /8 | % |
| **Total Weekly Assessment Score** | /20 | % |

**5** Students should underline the following sentence in the paragraphs:
- He had pride in his skills and new self-respect for his own abilities.

**6** Students should write the following details in the chart:
- There are a hundred students in one class in Uganda.
- Students in Uganda need more books to help them learn English.

**11** To receive full credit for the response, the following information should be included: The settings of "Camp Pennacook" are an American city and a summer camp for boys in the state of New Hampshire, while the settings of "Books for Uganda" are a classroom in Uganda and an American classroom. The outdoor setting in "Camp Pennacook" is new to the boys at camp, and the school in rural Uganda is new to Ms. Perry and very different from her classroom in Minneapolis.

**Read the passage "The New Village" before answering Numbers 1 through 5.**

# The New Village

"I am going to the store, Uncle Moti," Mina said to her uncle. "Do you want to come along? You have not seen much of the neighborhood yet, and I could introduce you to some people."

Uncle Moti shook his head and said, "No thank you, Mina, it is just too loud and crowded for me out there. Everyone is always on the go, while I am used to the peace and quiet of our village. I have to admit the city frightens and confuses me, and I get panicky out there, like a frightened child."

Mina sat on the sofa next to her uncle and said, "Tell me about the village, Uncle Moti. Would I like it there?"

Uncle Moti laughed and said, "Without a doubt, you would find it dull at first—the loudest sound is usually birdsong, or sometimes a truck backfiring. You can hear the sound of the water in the canal and the bells that hang around the goats' necks. The people I meet on the street are all people I know, and we stop and talk or go to the tea shop and have tea. There are not many shops, but the shopkeepers know all their customers. Everyone is friendly and has a smile for everyone else."

"It sounds really nice," Mina said, "and really different—in some ways—but I think maybe it is not different in every way. I really wish you would come with me, and I could show you why I say that."

Uncle Moti sighed and got up, saying, "All right, Mina, I will go, and you can show me what you mean."

Out on the street, cars zoomed by, some of them honking, people shouted to each other, and kids ran up and down the street playing. Uncle Moti looked very nervous at all the noise and activity, and Mina took his hand.

**GO ON →**

"Look, Uncle," she said, "there is my friend Nate and his brother, and coming down the street is my teacher from last year, Ms. Sanchez." Mina waved to Nate, who waved back, and then she called hello to her teacher. Then Mina led her uncle down the street to the store, where she greeted the shopkeeper. "Hi, Ms. Franklin, this is my Uncle Moti, who has come here from India to live."

"Hello, Uncle Moti, and welcome to the United States!" the woman replied, smiling. "And what can I get for you today?" Mina handed Ms. Franklin her shopping list, and they went through the little store collecting the items.

When they left the little store, a horn honked, making Uncle Moti jump. Someone pushed by them, bumping into the grocery bag Uncle Moti carried. "Hey, Mr. Watkins, watch your step!" Mina cried.

The man called back, "Sorry, sorry!" as he hurried on.

"Look, Uncle Moti," Mina said, pointing ahead of them at a tree that grew up from the sidewalk, surrounded by a little iron fence. On the lowest branch of the tree was a little sparrow, and as they drew closer they could hear it chirp.

"Over here, Uncle," Mina instructed, taking her uncle's arm and leading him across the street. A sign over a door read "Navid's Tea Shop," and Uncle Moti broke into a big smile. He and Mina went in and took a seat at a table, setting down the grocery bag in an empty chair. They ordered tea, and Uncle Moti sighed happily.

"Well, I see what you were trying to show me, Mina," he said. "This neighborhood is your village, and now it will be mine, too. It has friends, kind shopkeepers, birds, and even a tea shop, and I think that once I get used to it, I could be very happy here."

GO ON →

**Now answer Numbers 1 through 5. Base your answers on "The New Village."**

**1** This question has two parts. First, answer part A. Then, answer part B.

**Part A:** Which statement about Mina and Uncle Moti is supported in the text?

Ⓐ Mina is calmer than Uncle Moti.

Ⓑ Mina is not as friendly as Uncle Moti.

Ⓒ Mina is more careful than Uncle Moti.

Ⓓ Mina is not as thoughtful as Uncle Moti.

**Part B:** Which sentence from the text **best** supports your answer in part A?

Ⓐ "Uncle Moti looked very nervous at all the noise and activity, and Mina took his hand."

Ⓑ "Mina waved to Nate, who waved back, and then she called hello to her teacher."

Ⓒ "On the lowest branch of the tree was a little sparrow, and as they drew closer they could hear it chirp."

Ⓓ "A sign over a door read "Navid's Tea Shop," and Uncle Moti broke into a big smile."

**2** Read the paragraph from the text.

When they left the little store, a horn honked, making Uncle Moti jump. Someone pushed by them, bumping into the grocery bag Uncle Moti carried. "Hey, Mr. Watkins, watch your step!" Mina cried.

Which phrases from the paragraph **best** show what the idiom "watch your step" means? Select **two** phrases.

Ⓐ "they left the little store"

Ⓑ "a horn honked"

Ⓒ "pushed by them"

Ⓓ "bumping into"

Ⓔ "the grocery bag"

Ⓕ "Mina cried"

**GO ON →**

**3** This question has two parts. First, answer part A. Then, answer part B.

**Part A:** Read the sentences in the text.

He and Mina went in and <u>took a seat</u> at a table, setting down the grocery bag in an empty chair. They ordered tea, and Uncle Moti sighed happily.

What does the idiom "took a seat" mean?

Ⓐ sat down

Ⓑ stood to leave

Ⓒ moved a chair

Ⓓ carried away a chair

**Part B:** Which detail from the text **best** supports your answer in part A?

Ⓐ Mina takes Uncle Moti across the street to the tea shop.

Ⓑ Uncle Moti smiles when he sees the tea shop.

Ⓒ Mina and Uncle Moti carry a grocery bag.

Ⓓ Mina and Uncle Moti stay to order tea.

**GO ON →**

**4** Sort the phrases to compare and contrast the settings in the passage. Write each word from the list in the correct place in the chart.

| Mina's Neighborhood | Both | Moti's Village |
|---|---|---|
|  |  |  |

| | | |
|---|---|---|
| kind shopkeepers | peaceful and quiet | honking cars |
| | rushing water | friends on street | |
| loud and crowded | tea shops | goats with bells |

**5** Read the paragraph and answer the question.

"Well, I see what you were trying to show me, Mina," he said. "This neighborhood is your village, and now it will be mine, too. It has friends, kind shopkeepers, birds, and even a tea shop, and I think that once I get used to it, I could be very happy here."

What does this paragraph suggest about how Uncle Moti will change?

(A) He will tell his family if he feels unhappy.

(B) He will become friends with Mina's friends.

(C) He will be willing to go out in the neighborhood.

(D) He will start to do the food shopping for the family.

**GO ON →**

**Read the passage "All in a Day's Work" before answering Numbers 6 through 10.**

# All in a Day's Work

Dr. Schwartz studied the elements of soil and plant life. Because of her work, she spent a great deal of time looking for specimens. She searched the woods, looking under rocks, on leaves, and in the soil for interesting plants to use in her experiments.

One day she found some algae, a slimy plantlike life form, in a dirty, murky pond and carefully placed it in a plastic bag before picking some mushrooms off a tree. Finally, before ending her search for that day, she scooped some soil from the ground. The soil contained bacteria that she needed to complete her research.

Back in her quiet, peaceful lab, Dr. Schwartz first performed tests on the soil she had collected. She cleaned up as she went along, leaving everything orderly and neat, and was just about to start her experiments on the algae when a co-worker, Dr. Rao, threw open the door to her lab. He shouted, "We need you to look at our latest experiment in my lab!"

"I don't think I can get away right now," Dr. Schwartz said, her hands full of tubes and dirt. "I will be happy to take a look at your experiment later today—or maybe tomorrow, when I am done with this."

"Just for a few moments," he pleaded wildly. "Something awful has occurred!"

"Not again!" said Dr. Schwartz, wiping the dirt off her hands and following Dr. Rao down the hall. "What is it this time?" she asked him.

"Our mixture was dormant, like a sleeping baby," Dr. Rao explained as they walked quickly down the hall. "It was inactive, but—" He paused as he opened the door, and Dr. Schwartz peered inside.

**GO ON →**

"Oh, my," said Dr. Schwartz, taken aback but speaking in a matter-of-fact tone. "It is definitely not inactive anymore." The mixture had erupted all over the lab! Thick slime was shooting out of beakers, like a volcano exploding all over. The slime hung from the ceiling and covered the floor. As they watched, the green goo seemed to spread, quickly moving over desks and blocking the sun that streamed in the windows.

"I am just an observer," Dr. Schwartz said, "and I am not conducting this experiment, but if worse comes to worst, we could be in danger and had better get out of here."

Dr. Schwartz, Dr. Rao, and the other people who had been working in his lab backed out of the room and slammed the door behind them. They stood in the hallway arguing, trying to decide what to do. Dr. Rao was hopping from one foot to the other. Only Dr. Schwartz, who was thinking hard, was quiet.

At last Dr. Schwartz spoke, saying, "We have to do something before it slimes the entire building. We are working against the clock here. I have an idea that I think may work, so let me handle this." She hurried to her lab and was back in a matter of seconds, clutching a bag. Then she opened the door to Dr. Rao's lab and threw in the contents of the bag, which was full of dirt.

She smiled as she observed the slime being scrubbed away. The soil seemed to clean the slime from the room, destroying the green stuff that had dirtied the walls and floor. Dr. Rao and the others watched in amazement as Dr. Schwartz explained, "The soil I'm studying appears to have anti-slime properties. I discovered the soil in an area that had no algae—not a single one was to be found. But I never expected that my discovery would come in handy so soon." Then she turned to leave and said, "Well, back to work for me."

**GO ON →**

**Now answer Numbers 6 through 10. Base your answers on "All in a Day's Work."**

**6** This question has two parts. First, answer part A. Then, answer part B.

**Part A:** Which sentence explains how Dr. Schwartz and Dr. Rao are different?

(A) Dr. Schwartz is not as creative as Dr. Rao.

(B) Dr. Schwartz does less research than Dr. Rao.

(C) Dr. Rao makes more decisions than Dr. Schwartz.

(D) Dr. Rao is more likely to panic than Dr. Schwartz.

**Part B:** Which sentences from the text **best** support your answer in part A? Select **all** that apply.

(A) "'Just for a few moments,' he pleaded wildly."

(B) "He paused as he opened the door, and Dr. Schwartz peered inside."

(C) "They stood in the hallway arguing, trying to decide what to do."

(D) "Dr. Rao was hopping from one foot to the other."

(E) "Only Dr. Schwartz, who was thinking hard, was quiet."

(F) "She smiled as she observed the slime being scrubbed away."

**GO ON →**

**7** Read the sentence from the text.

"We are <u>working against the clock here</u>."

Circle the sentence in the paragraph that **best** helps to explain what the idiom "working against the clock" means.

At last Dr. Schwartz spoke, saying, "We have to do something before it slimes the entire building. We are <u>working against the clock here</u>. I have an idea that I think may work, so let me handle this." She hurried to her lab and was back in a matter of seconds, clutching a bag. Then she opened the door to Dr. Rao's lab and threw in the contents of the bag, which was full of dirt.

**8** Which conclusion can be drawn about Dr. Schwartz and Dr. Rao?

(A) Dr. Schwartz is older than Dr. Rao.

(B) Dr. Schwartz is kinder than Dr. Rao.

(C) Dr. Schwartz is more careful than Dr. Rao.

(D) Dr. Schwartz is more successful than Dr. Rao.

**GO ON →**

**9**  This question has two parts. First, answer part A. Then, answer part B.

**Part A:** Which conclusion can be made about the two labs?

- Ⓐ  They both belong to Dr. Schwartz.
- Ⓑ  They both belong to Dr. Rao.
- Ⓒ  They look exactly the same.
- Ⓓ  They look very different.

**Part B:** Which evidence from the text **best** supports your answer in part A?

- Ⓐ  "Dr. Schwartz studied the elements of soil and plant life."
- Ⓑ  "Because of her work, she spent a great deal of time looking for specimens."
- Ⓒ  "She cleaned up as she went along, leaving everything orderly and neat, . . ."
- Ⓓ  "'Our mixture was dormant, like a sleeping baby,' Dr. Rao explained . . ."

**10**  Read the sentence from the text.

"But I never expected that my discovery would <u>come in handy</u> so soon."

What does the idiom "come in handy" mean in the sentence?

- Ⓐ  be useful
- Ⓑ  be held up
- Ⓒ  come inside
- Ⓓ  be handed around

Name: _____ Date: _____

**Now answer Number 11. Base your answer on "The New Village" and "All in a Day's Work."**

**11** How do Mina and Dr. Schwartz both help other people? Support your answer with details from both texts.

_____

_____

_____

_____

_____

_____

_____

_____

_____

_____

_____

_____

_____

_____

_____

| Question | Correct Answer | Content Focus | CCSS | Complexity |
|----------|----------------|---------------|------|------------|
| 1A | A | Character, Setting, Plot: Compare and Contrast | RL.5.3 | DOK 2 |
| 1B | A | Character, Setting, Plot: Compare and Contrast/Text Evidence | RL.5.3/ RL.5.1 | DOK 2 |
| 2 | C, D | Idioms | L.5.5b | DOK 2 |
| 3A | A | Idioms | L.5.5b | DOK 2 |
| 3B | D | Idioms/Text Evidence | L.5.5b/ RL.5.1 | DOK 2 |
| 4 | see below | Character, Setting, Plot: Compare and Contrast | RL.5.3 | DOK 3 |
| 5 | C | Character, Setting, Plot: Compare and Contrast | RL.5.3 | DOK 3 |
| 6A | D | Character, Setting, Plot: Compare and Contrast | RL.5.3 | DOK 3 |
| 6B | A, D, E | Character, Setting, Plot: Compare and Contrast/Text Evidence | RL.5.3/ RL.5.1 | DOK 3 |
| 7 | see below | Idioms | L.5.5b | DOK 2 |
| 8 | C | Character, Setting, Plot: Compare and Contrast | RL.5.3 | DOK 3 |
| 9A | D | Character, Setting, Plot: Compare and Contrast | RL.5.3 | DOK 2 |
| 9B | C | Character, Setting, Plot: Compare and Contrast/Text Evidence | RL.5.3/ RL.5.1 | DOK 2 |
| 10 | A | Idioms | L.5.5b | DOK 2 |
| 11 | see below | Writing About Text | W.5.9a | DOK 4 |

| | | | |
|---|---|---|---|
| **Comprehension** 1A, 1B, 4, 5, 6A, 6B, 8, 9A, 9B | | /12 | % |
| **Vocabulary** 2, 3A, 3B, 7, 10 | | /8 | % |
| **Total Weekly Assessment Score** | | /20 | % |

**4** Students should complete the chart as follows:
- Mina's Neighborhood—honking cars; loud and crowded
- Both—kind shopkeepers; friends on street; tea shops
- Moti's Village—peaceful and quiet; rushing water; goats with bells

**7** Students should circle the following sentence in the paragraph:
- At last Dr. Schwartz spoke, saying, "We have to do something before it slimes the entire building."

**11** To receive full credit for the response, the following information should be included: Mina and Dr. Schwartz both work calmly with others. Mina calms her uncle and shows him his new home has similarities to his old home. This makes him feel better about his situation. Dr. Schwartz calms Dr. Rao and the others in the lab by finding a solution to their problem and getting rid of the slime.

**Read the article "From Enemy to Friend" before answering Numbers 1 through 5.**

# From Enemy to Friend

Wolves and dogs are closely related. After all, most scientists believe that dogs' ancestors were wolves. Over time, wolves became tame enough to live with humans and help them. The change from wolf to dog was, it is believed, mostly a result of careful breeding. Early humans allowed only the friendliest wolf pups to remain near them. This ensured that, over time, the wolves that stayed with groups of humans became tamer and tamer.

As wolves were influenced by their relationship with humans, they slowly became what we know today as dogs. Eventually, they arrived at the point where they were useful in ways besides just warning people of danger. They became adept at protecting and herding sheep and other animals whereas their ancestors would have made a meal of them. This ability made dogs very useful. However, although they are quite similar, wolves and dogs are also quite different.

Wolves are wild animals that live in packs, or groups, and eat only meat. They find their food by hunting. The most common noise they make is a howl. They may also bark, growl, yelp, and whine, but these sounds are much less common than howling. All wolves look very much alike, although their colors vary. They are large, slender, powerful animals with long legs and tails.

Wolves are quite wary of people; they don't trust them. They prefer to keep their distance from humans and will make every effort to avoid them. They attack people only on rare occasions, usually when they are startled.

**GO ON →**

Dogs, on the other hand, are tame. They have been influenced by people for many, many years, which has made them quite different from wolves. For one thing, dogs eat vegetables and grains as well as meat products. They are much more likely to bark than to howl. Their sizes range from gigantic animals that are much larger than wolves to tiny animals that can sit comfortably in a cereal bowl. Large dogs are not only taller than wolves, but they are much heavier, and their appearances can vary as much as their sizes. Many look nothing like a wolf. However, the main difference is found in dogs' relationship with humans, whom they usually prefer to be near. The main effect of this is that most dogs are friendly to people. Some show hostility, but almost always only to strangers. This willingness to be friendly is especially true if they do not feel threatened or are not protecting their property. Although most dogs are no smarter than wolves, they can certainly be trained more easily. Dogs can be taught to do many more things than a wolf can be taught to do, including performing complicated tricks and obeying hand signals. They rarely hunt prey to eat and depend on their owners to supply them with food. This reliance on people just adds to the closeness of the relationship.

Wolves and dogs both pant to stay cool. They both can hear and smell very well, and they both can run silently. They even have the same number of teeth: 42. However, no matter how similar wolves and dogs may seem to be, a wolf can never be made into a pet. No one can tame a wolf so that it can be counted on to be gentle. Wolves are, by nature, suspicious, which makes them untrustworthy. They are also worthless as guard animals because they are shy. Domestic animals, such as cats and small dogs, are in more danger from wolves than humans are, but small children can also be in danger. The Big Bad Wolf may exist only in fairy tales, but real wolves can be as much of a threat, especially if they are not understood.

**GO ON →**

**Now answer Numbers 1 through 5. Base your answers on "From Enemy to Friend."**

**1** This question has two parts. First, answer part A. Then, answer part B.

**Part A:** How does the author show the relationship between wolves and dogs?

(A) by telling how their habitats are similar

(B) by describing how they find ways to survive

(C) by listing the ways they developed over time

(D) by comparing and contrasting their characteristics

**Part B:** Which detail from the text **best** supports your answer in part A?

(A) "Early humans allowed only the friendliest wolf pups to remain near them."

(B) "Large dogs are not only taller than wolves, but they are much heavier, . . ."

(C) "This reliance on people just adds to the closeness of the relationship."

(D) "The Big Bad Wolf may exist only in fairy tales, . . ."

**2** Read the sentences from the article.

They became adept at protecting and herding sheep and other animals whereas their ancestors would have made a meal of them. This ability made dogs very useful.

What does the word adept mean in the sentences?

(A) fast

(B) hungry

(C) skillful

(D) trusting

**GO ON →**

**3** Complete the chart to show how wolves and dogs are **different**. Choose from the sentences in the box. All of the sentences will not be used.

|  | Wolves | Dogs |
|---|---|---|
| **Description** |  |  |
| **Text Evidence** |  |  |

**Descriptions:**

They hear very well.

They get along with people.

They do not protect others well.

They pant to keep themselves cool.

**Text Evidence:**

"They find their food by hunting."

"Dogs, on the other hand, are tame."

"They both can hear and smell very well, and they both can run silently."

"They are also worthless as guard animals because they are shy."

**GO ON →**

**4** This question has two parts. First, answer part A. Then, answer part B.

**Part A:** Read the sentences from the article.

The main effect of this is that most dogs are friendly to people. Some show hostility, but almost always only to strangers.

What does the word hostility mean?

(A) affection

(B) fear

(C) gratitude

(D) unfriendliness

**Part B:** Which word from the sentences is the **best** clue to the meaning of hostility?

(A) main

(B) effect

(C) friendly

(D) people

**5** Which details **best** support the author's point of view that wolves are dangerous? Select **two** options.

(A) Wolves can be a threat if misunderstood.

(B) Wolves like to howl more than bark.

(C) Wolves are very large and slender.

(D) Wolves have suspicious natures.

(E) Wolves attack people rarely.

(F) Wolves look a lot like dogs.

**GO ON →**

**Read the article "Marvels of Engineering" before answering Numbers 6 through 10.**

# Marvels of Engineering

It's hard to imagine two more different structures than the Eiffel Tower and Hoover Dam.

For one thing, the Eiffel Tower is in Paris, France and Hoover Dam is on the border between Nevada and Arizona. The Eiffel Tower is elegant and delicate looking, but Hoover Dam looks like a huge slab of concrete. The Eiffel Tower was made of many individual parts and then put together, but the concrete for Hoover Dam was poured at the site, right where the dam would be. The Eiffel Tower was built for a fair and was not intended to remain in place for long. Hoover Dam was built to allow water to be used in desert country and to create electricity. Everyone expected it to remain in place for many, many years.

Even though these two structures are so different, there are similarities. Each required great effort to complete; each also necessitated the involvement of many workers. The workers on each faced many challenges and difficulties, and each was built in a series of steps. Each is huge but was built quickly, considering the amount of labor involved.

All of the Eiffel Tower's parts were made in a factory near Paris. Each piece had to be the right size and shape. Smaller parts were put together and then joined to form a larger piece. These large pieces were put together at the site of the tower. Bolts held together the pieces made at the factory. At the tower, these bolts were pulled out and replaced with hot rivets. When the rivets cooled, they shrank, which held the pieces firm. Teams of people worked to take out the bolts and put in the rivets.

**GO ON →**

Hoover Dam was built to replace one that had been washed away, but it was built in a new place. First the water that flowed through the Colorado River had to be diverted. Four tunnels were blasted through rock to cause the water to go in new directions. Then the river's canyon walls had to be cleared. From great heights, workers dangled from ropes. With only air below their feet, they prepared the area for great concrete walls. Far underneath them, the area for the foundation was cleared of mud and loose rock. When this was all finished, tons of wet concrete were poured into a gigantic form. For thirty months, concrete was poured until finally the work was done. Across the Colorado River stood a dam 700 feet tall. When the water was allowed to rush through tunnels, it passed through giant rotary engines, and as their parts whirled, they created electricity.

Making electricity and using water to irrigate dry land were both practical purposes for Hoover Dam, but the Eiffel Tower had no original purpose but to be beautiful. The man who designed it, Gustave Eiffel, did not want it to be torn down. He hated the idea of his great creation being destroyed, so he looked for a practical use for it. He thought it might be used to study the weather, or it might be used as a radio station. Given that it was more than a thousand feet tall, it was a perfect place for a radio antenna. This would allow the French army to keep in contact across the whole country. Soon, a radio station was built on the tower. A practical use for it had been found that helped the tower survive, and now no one can imagine Paris without it.

Both the Eiffel Tower and Hoover Dam are popular tourist attractions. They are majestic sights, and everyone who sees them is amazed. Each, to this day, is considered a marvelous example of engineering skill.

**GO ON →**

**Now answer Numbers 6 through 10. Base your answers on "Marvels of Engineering."**

**6** This question has two parts. First, answer part A. Then, answer part B.

**Part A:** What is the purpose of the first paragraph of the article?

Ⓐ to tell where the Eiffel Tower and Hoover Dam are located

Ⓑ to show just how different the Eiffel Tower and Hoover Dam are

Ⓒ to explain what is meant by the phrase "marvels of engineering"

Ⓓ to describe how one type of material was used to make different structures

**Part B:** Which detail from the text best supports your answer in part A?

Ⓐ "It's hard to imagine two more different structures . . ."

Ⓑ "Everyone expected it to remain in place for many, many years."

Ⓒ "Each piece had to be the right size and shape."

Ⓓ "Teams of people worked to take out the bolts and put in the rivets."

**7** What is a major similarity between the Eiffel Tower and Hoover Dam?

Ⓐ their height

Ⓑ how they were built

Ⓒ what they are made of

Ⓓ the effort needed to complete them

**GO ON →**

**8** This question has two parts. First, answer part A. Then, answer part B.

**Part A:** Read the sentences from the article.

From great heights, workers dangled from ropes. With only air below their feet, they prepared the area for great concrete walls.

What does the word dangled help to explain about the workers?

(A) They were hung from something.

(B) They were carried up to something.

(C) They were dropped from something.

(D) They jumped down from something.

**Part B:** Which phrase from the sentences **best** supports your answer in part A?

(A) "from great heights"

(B) "only air below their feet"

(C) "prepared the area"

(D) "great concrete walls"

**GO ON →**

**9** Which statements summarize what is different about the original purposes of each structure? Select **two** options.

(A) The tower was built to be decorative; the dam was built for practical uses.

(B) The tower was built by a single engineer; the dam was built by many workers.

(C) The tower was built to serve a purpose; the dam was built for people to admire.

(D) The tower was built for business reasons; the dam was built for personal reasons.

(E) The tower was built to increase tourism; the dam was built to discourage tourism.

(F) The tower was built to be temporary; the dam was built to last for a very long time.

**10** Circle the word in the sentences below that helps to show the meaning of the word <u>rotary</u>.

Across the Colorado River stood a dam 700 feet tall. When the water was allowed to rush through tunnels, it passed through giant <u>rotary</u> engines, and as their parts whirled, they created electricity.

**STOP**

Name: _____ Date: _____

**Now answer Number 11. Base your answer on "From Enemy to Friend" and "Marvels of Engineering."**

**11** Compare and contrast the text structures used in the articles. How are the articles organized to best suit the authors' purposes? Support your answer with details from both articles.

_____

_____

_____

_____

_____

_____

_____

_____

_____

_____

_____

_____

_____

_____

# Answer Key

Name: _____

| Question | Correct Answer | Content Focus | CCSS | Complexity |
|---|---|---|---|---|
| 1A | D | Text Structure: Compare and Contrast | RI.5.3 | DOK 3 |
| 1B | B | Text Structure: Compare and Contrast/ Text Evidence | RI.5.3/ RI.5.1 | DOK 3 |
| 2 | C | Context Clues: Paragraph Clues | L.5.4a | DOK 2 |
| 3 | see below | Compare and Contrast | RI.5.3 | DOK 3 |
| 4A | D | Context Clues: Paragraph Clues | L.5.4a | DOK 2 |
| 4B | C | Context Clues: Paragraph Clues/ Text Evidence | L.5.4a/ RI.5.1 | DOK 2 |
| 5 | A, D | Author's Point of View | RI.5.8 | DOK 2 |
| 6A | B | Compare and Contrast | RI.5.3 | DOK 3 |
| 6B | A | Compare and Contrast/ Text Evidence | RI.5.3/ RI.5.1 | DOK 3 |
| 7 | D | Compare and Contrast | RI.5.3 | DOK 3 |
| 8A | A | Context Clues: Paragraph Clues | L.5.4a | DOK 2 |
| 8B | B | Context Clues: Paragraph Clues/ Text Evidence | L.5.4a/ RI.5.1 | DOK 2 |
| 9 | A, F | Compare and Contrast | RI.5.3 | DOK 3 |
| 10 | see below | Context Clues: Paragraph Clues | L.5.4a | DOK 2 |
| 11 | see below | Writing About Text | W.5.9b | DOK 4 |

| | | |
|---|---|---|
| **Comprehension** 1A, 1B, 3, 5, 6A, 6B, 7, 9 | /12 | % |
| **Vocabulary** 2, 4A, 4B, 8A, 8B, 10 | /8 | % |
| **Total Weekly Assessment Score** | /20 | % |

**3** Students should complete the chart as follows:
- Wolves—Description: They do not protect others well; Text Evidence: "They are also worthless as guard animals because they are shy."
- Dogs—Description: The get along with people; Text Evidence: "Dogs, on the other hand, are tame."

**10** Students should circle the word "whirled" in the sentences.

**11** To receive full credit for the response, the following information should be included: Using these particular text structures allows the authors to tell how wolves and dogs are alike and different and how the Eiffel Tower and Hoover Dam are alike and different. The text structures suit the authors' purposes in that they present information that highlights the characteristics of each subject.

**Read the article "The Birth of the Movies" before answering Numbers 1 through 5.**

# The Birth of the Movies

Why do we love the movies? There is something magical about watching a story play out on a screen as we sit in the darkness. We love westerns, cartoons, horror films, action movies, and love stories. Many of the films we watch are filled with special effects. We might watch them in 3-D or admire their wild car chases or glorious landscapes, but when movies began, films were much simpler and more basic.

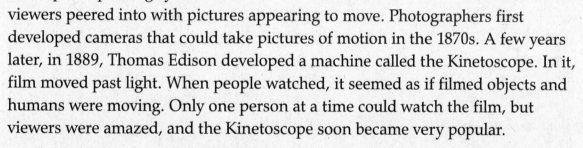

In the 1830s, inventors created machines that spun around like wheels and had pictures on them. Viewing the pictures as they cycled around made it look as if the images were moving. Next came the zoetrope, a spinning cylinder that viewers peered into with pictures appearing to move. Photographers first developed cameras that could take pictures of motion in the 1870s. A few years later, in 1889, Thomas Edison developed a machine called the Kinetoscope. In it, film moved past light. When people watched, it seemed as if filmed objects and humans were moving. Only one person at a time could watch the film, but viewers were amazed, and the Kinetoscope soon became very popular.

In France in 1895, the Lumiere brothers created a machine that could take movies and show them, too. Now groups of viewers could watch films at the same time. Thomas Edison and others soon realized that movies could tell stories. By the early 1900s, the first animated movie and the first western had been made. Comedies were especially popular, since people loved to laugh at the movies. By 1909, there were about 9,000 movie theaters in America.

Films were very short in the early 1900s, and there were no such things as movie stars. The performers were unknown, but that did not last long. Moving picture companies organized into film studios and began promoting actors and actresses, who quickly became stars. Audiences were thrilled by pictures of and articles about the theatrical people they saw up on the screen.

**GO ON →**

At that point, movies were silent, accompanied only with music and sometimes with written titles. Filmmakers had been trying to figure out how to use sound with film for years. The technology was complicated. Thomas Edison had produced a machine that included sound, but he was not able to get the sound to work correctly with the images on film. Finally, in 1927, Warner Brothers Studio produced the first film with sound, *The Jazz Singer*. Other films with sound quickly followed. In 1935, color films were first produced. Films began to look like the movies we know today.

In 1952, film studios introduced 3-D films, movies that, when viewed with special glasses, look as if they were three-dimensional. Eight years later studios brought viewers "Smell-O-Vision," which allowed audiences to smell the scents that were in the movies. Apparently people did not really want to smell their films, so Smell-O-Vision failed.

Since the 1960s, movies have gotten bigger, more full of stars, and more expensive to make. They can be watched on television sets and computers, tablets, and phones. The film industry has changed in many ways, but one thing remains the same. Since the very first days of the moving picture, audiences have been entranced by the ability to watch dramatic stories on the screen. With sound or without, in color or black and white, movies have created joy and amazement in viewers for more than a hundred years.

**GO ON →**

**Now answer Numbers 1 through 5. Base your answers on "The Birth of the Movies."**

 This question has two parts. First, answer part A. Then, answer part B.

**Part A:** What resulted from Thomas Edison's invention of film that moved past light?

(A) Sound was matched to film.

(B) Films became a social event.

(C) Filmed objects became visible.

(D) Things appeared to be moving.

**Part B:** Which sentence from the text **best** supports your answer in part A?

(A) "A few years later, in 1889, Thomas Edison developed a machine called the Kinetoscope."

(B) "When people watched, it seemed as if filmed objects and humans were moving."

(C) "Only one person at a time could watch the film, but viewers were amazed, and the Kinetoscope soon became very popular."

(D) "In France in 1895, the Lumiere brothers created a machine that could take movies and show them, too."

**GO ON →**

**2** Why did going to the movies become a social activity?

Ⓐ People enjoyed looking through the zoetrope.

Ⓑ People liked going to films with sound.

Ⓒ Movie theaters became very large.

Ⓓ People could view films in groups.

**3** Draw a line to match the underlined word in each sentence on the left with the meaning of its Greek root on the right.

| | |
|---|---|
| Viewing the pictures as they cycled around made it look as if the images were moving. | light |
| Photographers first developed cameras that could take pictures of motion in the 1870s. | skill |
| The technology was complicated. | wheel |

**GO ON →**

**4** What happened as a result of film studios promoting actors and actresses? Select **two** options.

(A) Producers made better movies.

(B) Actors and actresses became movie stars.

(C) Animated films started to become popular.

(D) People became more excited about movies.

(E) Movies started to be seen on television sets.

(F) Actors and actresses started to work on stage.

**5** Read the sentence from the article.

Since the very first days of the moving picture, audiences have been entranced by the ability to watch <u>dramatic</u> stories on the screen.

The origin of the word <u>dramatic</u> is the Greek word *dramatikos*, meaning "having to do with plays." What does this suggest about the stories that audiences watch on the screen?

(A) They include a performance of some kind.

(B) They give an opinion about something.

(C) They provide a history lesson.

(D) They were created on a stage.

**GO ON →**

Read the article "Up, Up, and Away!" before answering Numbers 6 through 10.

# Up, Up, and Away!

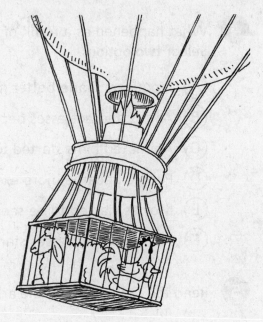

More than a century before the Wright brothers' famous plane flight took place, a different type of object rose into the sky. It was a balloon filled with heated air. The year was 1783, and the place was France. Two brothers named Montgolfier launched the very first hot-air balloon. It was made of four huge pieces of fabric and paper, held together by almost 2,000 buttons.

The balloon stayed in the air about ten minutes. There were no humans on board because that would have been too dangerous. Instead, the aerial passengers were a sheep, a duck, and a rooster. After this historic event, interest in balloons grew quickly, and inventors began competing to see who could make the safest balloon and take the longest flight. Some people continued to work on balloons filled with heated air, while others developed balloons filled with hydrogen, a gas lighter than air.

A few months after the flight of the Montgolfier balloon, another first in balloon history took place. A Frenchman named Jacques Charles launched a beautiful balloon made of silk and filled with hydrogen. Charles's balloon looked lovely as the gas lifted it in the air.

In November of that same year, the Montgolfier brothers again made history. A giant balloon they had constructed carried humans into the air for the first time. One of the aeronauts was a French science teacher who had helped with the Montgolfier flight of the animals, and his companion was a French nobleman. The two men sailed over Paris for 25 minutes. The mechanism that heated the air and inflated the balloon was a fire of burning straw. It was a wonderful flight until the balloon caught on fire, but luckily, no one was hurt.

The first balloon flight in the United States traveled from Philadelphia, Pennsylvania, to New Jersey in 1793. George Washington was one of the spectators who watched as the anchored balloon was released and soared into the air. Balloons had officially entered into United States history.

**GO ON →**

While the first hot-air balloons were used for adventure, people soon saw that they could be used for military purposes, such as delivering messages across long distances. During the Civil War and in World War I, balloons were used for communication and transportation. In World War II, they served another purpose as well. Wires were strung between balloons, forming a trap that military planners hoped would stop enemy airplanes.

Soon there was nearly an epidemic of hot-air balloonists trying to see how far up they could soar. In 1932, balloonists went into the stratosphere, more than 52,000 feet up. Their cabin had to be pressurized so they could endure the trip. Since then, balloonists have been going ever farther into the sky. In 1988, a record was set: 65,000 feet upward, more than 10 miles high!

More recently, balloons have been used to travel long distances. In 1978, a balloon called the Double Eagle crossed the Atlantic Ocean. The balloon was filled with helium and carried three passengers. In 1991, a hot-air balloon crossed the Pacific Ocean, reaching speeds of up to 245 miles an hour! Later in 1991, two men completed a balloon flight around the world. It was a thrilling feat. Another record was set the following year when two balloonists spent more than 144 hours in the air, flying from Bangor, Maine, to Morocco.

Today, many hot-air balloons are used for science and studying the weather. They often carry thermometers and other weather-measuring devices. So, while hot-air balloons often are used for fun, they still are used for serious purposes, as well.

**GO ON →**

Name: _____ Date: _____

**Now answer Numbers 6 through 10. Base your answers on "Up, Up, and Away!"**

**6** Complete the chart below to show causes and effects. Choose the correct causes and effects from the list below and write them in the chart. Not all causes and effects will be used.

| Cause | |
|---|---|
| **Effect/Cause** | |
| **Effect/Cause** | |
| **Effect** | |

**Causes and Effects:**
Public interest in balloons grows.
Inventors develop hydrogen balloons.
The very first hot-air balloon is launched.
A silk balloon filled with hydrogen is launched.
The first hot-air balloon is held together with buttons.

**7** Read the sentence from the text.

The <u>mechanism</u> that heated the air and inflated the balloon was a fire of burning straw.

The Greek root of <u>mechanism</u> is *mech,* which means "machine." What does this suggest about a <u>mechanism</u>?

(A) It relates to how the balloon works.

(B) It relates to what a hot-air balloon looks like.

(C) It relates to the people who invented the balloon.

(D) It relates to how it feels to be in a hot-air balloon.

**GO ON →**

**8** Besides adventure, for which reasons have hot-air balloons been used? Select **two** options.

(A) space exploration

(B) presidential travel

(C) geology experiments

(D) daily work commutes

(E) weather advancements

(F) wartime communication

**9** This question has two parts. First, answer part A. Then, answer part B.

**Part A:** Read the sentence from the text.

Soon there was nearly an <u>epidemic</u> of hot-air balloonists trying to see how far up they could soar.

The origin of <u>epidemic</u> includes the Greek root *dem*, meaning "people." What does this information suggest about an <u>epidemic</u>?

(A) It affects many.

(B) It is easily fixed.

(C) It is hard to locate.

(D) It does not affect anyone.

**Part B:** Which word has the same Greek root as <u>epidemic</u>?

(A) epic

(B) episode

(C) demand

(D) democracy

**GO ON →**

**10** This question has two parts. First, answer part A. Then, answer part B.

**Part A:** What was one effect of advances in ballooning?

(A) a balloon flight around the world

(B) a way to measure temperature

(C) the development of airplanes

(D) the end of World War II

**Part B:** Which sentence from the text **best** supports your answer in part A?

(A) "More recently, balloons have been used to travel long distances."

(B) "Later in 1991, two men completed a balloon flight around the world."

(C) "They often carry thermometers and other weather-measuring devices."

(D) "So, while hot-air balloons often are used for fun, they still are used for serious purposes, as well."

STOP

Name: _____ Date: _____

**11** What conclusion can be drawn about how technology has changed over time? Use details from both texts to support your answer.

_____

_____

_____

_____

_____

_____

_____

_____

_____

_____

_____

_____

_____

_____

# Answer Key

Name: _____

| Question | Correct Answer | Content Focus | CCSS | Complexity |
|---|---|---|---|---|
| 1A | D | Text Structure: Cause and Effect | RI.5.5 | DOK 2 |
| 1B | B | Text Structure: Cause and Effect/ Text Evidence | RI.5.5/ RI.5.1 | DOK 2 |
| 2 | D | Text Structure: Cause and Effect | RI.5.5 | DOK 2 |
| 3 | see below | Greek Roots | L.5.4b | DOK 1 |
| 4 | B, D | Text Structure: Cause and Effect | RI.5.5 | DOK 2 |
| 5 | A | Greek Roots | L.5.4b | DOK 1 |
| 6 | see below | Text Structure: Cause and Effect | RI.5.5 | DOK 3 |
| 7 | A | Greek Roots | L.5.4b | DOK 1 |
| 8 | E, F | Main Idea and Key Details | RI.5.2 | DOK 1 |
| 9A | A | Greek Roots | L.5.4b | DOK 1 |
| 9B | D | Greek Roots | L.5.4b | DOK 1 |
| 10A | A | Text Structure: Cause and Effect | RI.5.5 | DOK 2 |
| 10B | B | Text Structure: Cause and Effect/ Text Evidence | RI.5.5/ RI.5.1 | DOK 2 |
| 11 | see below | Writing About Text | W.5.9b | DOK 4 |

| | | | |
|---|---|---|---|
| **Comprehension** 1A, 1B, 2, 4, 6, 8, 10A, 10B | /12 | % |
| **Vocabulary** 3, 5, 7, 9A, 9B | /8 | % |
| **Total Weekly Assessment Score** | /20 | % |

**3** Students should draw lines to match the following words to their Greek roots:
- Viewing the pictures as they cycled around made it look as if the images were moving.—wheel
- Photographers first developed cameras that could take pictures of motion in the 1870s.—light
- The technology was complicated.—skill

**6** Students should complete the chart with the following sentences:
- Cause—The very first hot-air balloon is launched.
- Effect/Cause—Public interest in balloons grows.
- Effect/Cause—Inventors develop hydrogen balloons.
- Effect—A silk balloon filled with hydrogen is launched.

**11** To receive full credit for the response, the following information should be included: Like other technologies, both movies and hot-air balloons have become more advanced and complex in terms of how they look and what they can do.

**Read the article "The First Rock Star" before answering Numbers 1 through 5.**

# The First Rock Star

Florence Bascom was born in Massachusetts in 1862. She was the daughter of a professor and a suffragist (someone who worked for women's right to vote). Her parents supported both the life of the mind and women's rights, so it might not seem unlikely that she became the first female geologist, but the path she took to her life's work was not an easy one.

Florence Bascom's love of geology began during a car trip she took with her father and a geologist friend of his, Edward Orton. In 1877, Bascom enrolled at the University of Wisconsin. Her father had recently taken the position of university president. Women had only been allowed to enroll there since 1875, and she was not permitted to take many of the classes the university offered. Her hours in the library were limited, but still, Bascom graduated with first a bachelor's degree and then a master's degree from the university in 1887. Two geologists, Roland Irving and Charles Van Hise, helped her in her studies, and she learned new ways of analyzing rocks and earth from them.

Florence Bascom wanted to go on with her studies. Though she had faced difficulties at Wisconsin, her father was the school's president. She had it easier there than she might have had elsewhere. She wanted to go to Johns Hopkins University to study for her doctorate, an even more advanced degree. A geology professor named George H. Williams was pioneering the use of microscopes to study geology at Johns Hopkins, and she wanted to work with him. Johns Hopkins, however, had never allowed a woman in its Ph.D. program before. It took seven months for a committee to agree to allow Bascom to attend classes there. They would not permit her to enroll officially, and the university told her that she would have to sit behind a screen in her classes so she would not disturb the male students. That seems unbelievable now!

**GO ON →**

This announcement did not stop Bascom, though. In 1892 she was secretly entered into the Johns Hopkins Ph.D. program. The paper she wrote to get her degree was brilliant, and she received her Ph.D. in 1893. It was the first Ph.D. Johns Hopkins University ever gave to a woman. One other woman had previously finished her studies for a Ph.D. there, but the university refused to give her the degree. Bascom's was the second Ph.D. in geology ever awarded to a woman from an American university.

After accepting a teaching post at Bryn Mawr, a women's college, Bascom founded the Department of Geology there. At first, geology was not considered an important science at Bryn Mawr. Bascom had to work in a storage space in the building that housed the other sciences. She created a large collection of minerals and rocks. She also focused on teaching numerous young women who wanted, like her, to become geologists. Under her influence, many Bryn Mawr graduates went on to work as mineralogists.

Bascom's specialty was the rock formations that created mountains. The studies she did and the papers she wrote were a vital contribution to understanding the geology of the Piedmont area. Florence Bascom was elected the first female Fellow of the Geological Society of America, and eventually she became the vice president of the organization. She worked for the United States Geological Survey, the first woman ever to do so. Her successes were astonishing at the time, and she deserves much credit for opening the door for generations of female scientists.

**GO ON →**

Name: _____ Date: _____

**Now answer Numbers 1 through 5. Base your answers on "The First Rock Star."**

**1** Read the sentence from the text.

Her parents supported both the life of the mind and women's rights, so it might not seem unlikely that she became the first female <u>geologist</u>, but the path she took to her life's work was not an easy one.

The word <u>geologist</u> comes from the root *geo,* which meanings "earth." What does this suggest that a <u>geologist</u> studies?

(A) animal life

(B) outer space

(C) the ocean currents

(D) rocks and minerals

**2** This question has two parts. First, answer part A. Then, answer part B.

**Part A:** Which statement **best** explains the author's point of view about women's roles in history?

(A) The author believes that it was once easier to become a geologist than it is now.

(B) The author believes that women were not treated equally in Bascom's time.

(C) The author thinks that people respected female scientists more in the past.

(D) The author thinks that women had no career choices in Bascom's time.

**Part B:** Which sentence from the text **best** supports your answer in part A?

(A) "Florence Bascom wanted to go on with her studies."

(B) "She had it easier there than she might have had elsewhere."

(C) "That seems unbelievable now!"

(D) "This announcement did not stop Bascom, though."

**GO ON →**

**3** Which conclusions can be drawn about the author's point of view of Florence Bascom? Select **all** that apply.

(A) Bascom did not give up in achieving her goals.

(B) Bascom faced challenges that male students did not.

(C) Bascom is one of the most important women in history.

(D) Bascom was more intelligent than all of her classmates.

(E) Bascom deserved the many achievements she was awarded.

(F) Bascom often questioned whether she should be a geologist.

**4** Read the sentence from the text.

The studies she did and the papers she wrote were a <u>vital</u> contribution to understanding the geology of the Piedmont area.

The word <u>vital</u> comes from a Latin root, *vit*, which means "life." What does this suggest about the papers Bascom wrote?

(A) They were upsetting.

(B) They were full of energy.

(C) They were very important.

(D) They were constantly changing.

**GO ON →**

**5** The author believes that Bascom had an influence on others in her field of study. Underline the sentence in the paragraph that **best** supports this view.

Bascom's specialty was the rock formations that created mountains. The studies she did and the papers she wrote were a vital contribution to understanding the geology of the Piedmont area. Florence Bascom was elected the first female Fellow of the Geological Society of America, and eventually she became the vice president of the organization. She worked for the United States Geological Survey, the first woman ever to do so. Her successes were astonishing at the time, and she deserves much credit for opening the door for generations of female scientists.

**GO ON →**

Read the article "Roald Amundsen, Polar Explorer" before answering
Numbers 6 through 10.

# Roald Amundsen, Polar Explorer

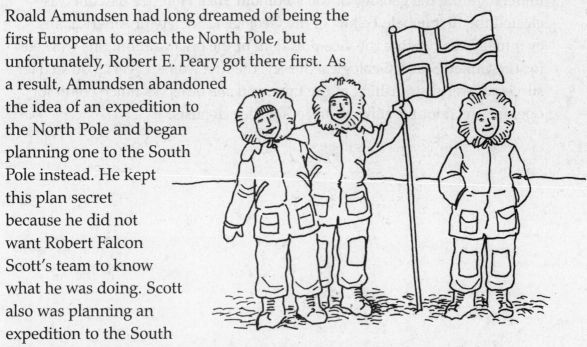

Roald Amundsen had long dreamed of being the
first European to reach the North Pole, but
unfortunately, Robert E. Peary got there first. As
a result, Amundsen abandoned
the idea of an expedition to
the North Pole and began
planning one to the South
Pole instead. He kept
this plan secret
because he did not
want Robert Falcon
Scott's team to know
what he was doing. Scott
also was planning an
expedition to the South
Pole, and Amundsen did not want him to know that he had competition.
Amundsen did not even tell the men on his own ship where they were going until
the night before they left.

The South Pole is a much more extreme environment than the North Pole. The
average year-round temperature there is minus fifty-six degrees, but at the North
Pole, the average temperature is zero degrees. There are mountains located at the
South Pole that rise far above sea level, while the North Pole does not have
mountains. There are no native human groups at the South Pole, and very few
animals live there.

Amundsen's ship, the *Fram*, left Norway on August 9, 1910. It was eight weeks
after the departure of Robert Scott's team. Amundsen's expedition was already
behind, but the team was incredibly well organized. On board were 97 Greenland
sled dogs. Amundsen believed that sled dogs would be more effective than the
ponies and tractors with motors that Scott used to pull his sledges. The *Fram* also
carried a hut and various supplies, and there was enough food to last the crew for
two years. The supplies included lamps, tools, and medicines for the treatment of
injuries and illnesses.

**GO ON →**

Four months later, the *Fram* reached the Ross Ice Shelf in Antarctica. The men built their base camp at the Bay of Whales. The team members would need supplies and shelter along the route to the South Pole. They set up depots, or storage places for supplies, along the way. The labor was difficult and demanding. The men had to finish their tasks as fast as they could. Amundsen put them on a strict schedule, regulating their work hours. He even instructed them on what to eat to ensure they stayed healthy. They were in a race against time. The long, dark nights of winter would begin in April, and then the sun would not rise at all. Amundsen also worried about Scott's team reaching the South Pole before him.

On September 8, the team of eight men started off over the dangerous ice. They rode in sledges that were pulled by 86 dogs. One man stayed behind to watch over their base camp. Frigid weather set in, so the team made a run for the nearest depot. The weather was so cold that the team could not proceed and had to return to the base camp. As soon as the weather improved, a smaller group started out again. Amundsen and four other men struggled through blizzards and over glaciers. They were determined to beat Scott's expedition, despite the delay that the terrible weather had caused.

Finally, on December 14, 1911, Amundsen and his men reached the South Pole. Many of the men had frostbite on their hands and faces, but all were alive. The team members planted the Norwegian flag in the frozen ground to claim their victory over Scott. Without Amundsen's organization and leadership skills, the team probably would have suffered loss of life and possibly failed entirely.

**GO ON →**

**Now answer Numbers 6 through 10. Base your answers on "Roald Amundsen, Polar Explorer."**

**6** Circle **one** sentence that states the author's point of view about the South Pole. Then circle **two** pieces of text evidence that support the author's point of view.

| Author's Point of View | Text Evidence |
|---|---|
| The South Pole was a dangerous place to explore. | "Amundsen did not even tell the men on his own ship where they were going until the night before they left." |
| The South Pole was an unnecessary place to explore. | "The South Pole is a much more extreme environment than the North Pole." |
| Amundsen could have reached the South Pole faster if he did things differently. | "The average year-round temperature there is minus fifty-six degrees, . . ." |
| Amundsen did not realize the risk he took in attempting to explore the South Pole. | "Many of the men had frostbite on their hands and faces, . . ." |

**7** Read the sentence from the text.

The *Fram* also carried a hut and <u>various</u> supplies, and there was enough food to last the crew for two years.

The Latin root of <u>various</u> is *var*, which means "different." What does this suggest about the <u>various</u> supplies?

(A) They were new.

(B) They were heavy.

(C) They were a mixture of things.

(D) They were previously used things.

**GO ON →**

**8** Read the sentence from the text.

Amundsen put them on a strict schedule, regulating their work hours.

Which points from the text does the evidence **best** support? Select **two** choices.

(A) Amundsen's men were lazy.

(B) Amundsen liked to keep busy.

(C) Amundsen's men needed to lose weight.

(D) Amundsen was well-organized and precise.

(E) Amundsen followed a plan to get what he wanted.

(F) Amundsen was very well-liked by all of the crew members.

**9** This question has two parts. First, answer part A. Then, answer part B.

**Part A:** Read the sentence from the text.

The weather was so cold that the team could not <u>proceed</u> and had to return to the base camp.

The origin of <u>proceed</u> is the Latin root *ceed*, meaning "go." What happened when the team could not <u>proceed</u>?

(A) They could not see ahead.

(B) They could not move forward.

(C) They could not hear each other.

(D) They could not remember the route.

**Part B:** Which word from the sentence **best** helps to explain what <u>proceed</u> means?

(A) weather

(B) team

(C) return

(D) base

**GO ON →**

**10** This question has two parts. First, answer part A. Then, answer part B.

**Part A:** What **most likely** does the author think about Roald Amundsen?

(A) His actions almost ruined the expedition.

(B) His leadership helped the group succeed.

(C) He had much better weather than Scott's men.

(D) He chose men who were braver than Scott's men.

**Part B:** Which sentence from the text **best** supports your answer in part A?

(A) "As soon as the weather improved, a smaller group started out again."

(B) "They were determined to beat Scott's expedition, despite the delay that the terrible weather had caused."

(C) "The team members planted the Norwegian flag in the frozen ground to claim their victory over Scott."

(D) "Without Amundsen's organization and leadership skills, the team probably would have suffered loss of life and possibly failed entirely."

STOP

Name: _____ Date: _____

**Now answer Number 11. Base your answer on "The First Rock Star" and "Roald Amundsen, Polar Explorer."**

**11** Compare and contrast the accomplishments of Florence Bascom and Roald Amundsen. Explain how the authors of both articles view their subjects. Support your answer with details from both texts.

_____

_____

_____

_____

_____

_____

_____

_____

_____

_____

_____

_____

_____

# Answer Key

| Question | Correct Answer | Content Focus | CCSS | Complexity |
|:---:|:---:|:---:|:---:|:---:|
| **1** | D | Root Words | L.5.4b | DOK 1 |
| **2A** | B | Author's Point of View | RI.5.8 | DOK 2 |
| **2B** | C | Author's Point of View/Text Evidence | RI.5.8/ RI.5.1 | DOK 2 |
| **3** | A, B, E | Author's Point of View | RI.5.8 | DOK 3 |
| **4** | C | Root Words | L.5.4b | DOK 1 |
| **5** | see below | Author's Point of View | RI.5.8 | DOK 2 |
| **6** | see below | Author's Point of View | RI.5.8 | DOK 2 |
| **7** | C | Root Words | L.5.4b | DOK 1 |
| **8** | D, E | Author's Point of View | RI.5.8 | DOK 2 |
| **9A** | B | Root Words | L.5.4b | DOK 1 |
| **9B** | C | Root Words | L.5.4b/ RI.5.1 | DOK 1 |
| **10A** | B | Author's Point of View | RI.5.8 | DOK 3 |
| **10B** | D | Author's Point of View/Text Evidence | RI.5.8/ RI.5.1 | DOK 3 |
| **11** | see below | Writing About Text | W.5.9b | DOK 4 |

| | | |
|:---|:---:|:---:|
| **Comprehension** 2A, 2B, 3, 5, 6, 8, 10A, 10B | /12 | % |
| **Vocabulary** 1, 4, 7, 9A, 9B | /8 | % |
| **Total Weekly Assessment Score** | /20 | % |

**5** Students should underline the following sentence in the paragraph:
- Her successes were astonishing at the time, and she deserves much credit for opening the door for generations of female scientists.

**6** Students should circle the following sentences in the chart:
- Author's Point of View—The South Pole was a dangerous place to explore.
- Text Evidence—"The South Pole is a much more extreme environment than the North Pole"; "The average year-round temperature there is minus fifty-six degrees, . . ."

**11** To receive full credit for the response, the following information should be included: Both authors admire their respective subjects and provide details that point to the determination and abilities of Bascom and Amundsen.

**Read the passage "Joining Forces for Freedom" before answering Numbers 1 through 5.**

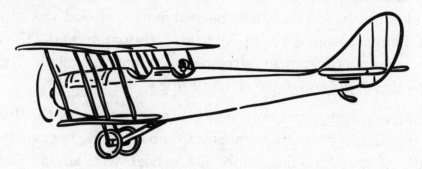

# Joining Forces for Freedom

The year was 1918, and Emma lived in Buffalo, New York. One day in April almost a year before, her dad came home from work with a newspaper under his arm. The headline said, "PRESIDENT CALLS FOR WAR DECLARATION." Dad explained that Germany was trying to take over other countries and attacking ships, including American ships, so President Wilson had asked Congress to declare war and join forces with Germany's enemies. America had a duty to fight for freedom.

Along with many of the men where he worked, Dad joined the U.S. Army to fight in World War I. He went to training camp and then was sent to France. Emma knew Mom missed him and was sad, even though her mother did not say it aloud, but Emma was proud her dad was helping the cause of freedom.

Mom missed Aunt Edith, too, who was Mom's younger sister and had lived with them as long as Emma could remember. When Aunt Edith was eighteen, she got a job as a switchboard operator for the telephone company. Then, for the first time in American history, women were allowed to join the U.S. Navy because of the Naval Act of 1916. It said "all persons" who were able to provide "useful service" could be in the Navy. When America entered the war, telephone operators, chauffeurs, and truck drivers were needed. Aunt Edith wanted to serve her country, so she signed up and moved to Washington, D.C., where she shared an apartment with other young women.

Aunt Edith wrote home often. She was proud of her uniform, a navy blue jacket with gold buttons and navy blue skirt. She said that the bottom of the skirt had to be exactly eight inches from the floor. Her blouse was called a waist, and she wore a scarf called a neckerchief around the open collar. The photo she sent to the family was displayed on the table in the living room.

**GO ON →**

With so many men joining the armed forces, many jobs at home needed to be filled. Companies were hiring women for jobs that men usually held. Some of Mom's friends had jobs and the family needed money, so Dad's mom agreed to help care for Emma if Mom got a job. Mom saw ads for jobs at the Curtiss Company, a corporation that made airplanes at a plant outside the city of Buffalo. The company was at the end of the streetcar line.

Mom applied for and got a job, and when she came home after the first day at the factory, she told Emma about the company. Company workers made two kinds of aircraft: flying boats and training planes. Flying boats were aircraft that could land on water, and training planes were light aircraft not closed-in at the top.

To manufacture the aircraft, different departments carried out the various steps. One department worked with machines, another with the wood used for the frames of airplanes, and other departments assembled the craft and finished it. Mom was an inspector. Each part had to be carefully checked with tools that measured very short lengths and small diameters. Every bolt and screw had to match exactly the length and width shown on the plans. The job was important because lives of pilots who flew the planes depended on careful attention to detail. Mom enjoyed her work at the factory.

In August, 1918, the family received a letter from Dad. He had fought in a battle but was fine. Then, in November of 1918, the German Kaiser, or emperor, gave up his rule. The fighting stopped on November 11, and Dad wrote that he was coming home. The family was so happy and ready to see him. Mom wanted to keep working but was not sure it would be possible because the men returning from war would want their old jobs back.

**GO ON →**

**Now answer Numbers 1 through 5. Base your answers on "Joining Forces for Freedom."**

**1** This question has two parts. First, answer part A. Then, answer part B.

**Part A:** Which statement **best** summarizes the theme of the text?

(A) Attention to details is an important habit.

(B) People working together can accomplish much.

(C) Working hard is considered to be its own reward.

(D) The actions of the past affect the events of the future.

**Part B:** Which sentence from the text **best** supports your answer in part A?

(A) "The year was 1918, and Emma lived in Buffalo, New York."

(B) "Emma knew Mom missed him and was sad, even though her mother did not say it aloud, but Emma was proud her dad was helping the cause of freedom."

(C) "With so many men joining the armed forces, many jobs at home needed to be filled."

(D) "Mom wanted to keep working but was not sure it would be possible because the men returning from war would want their old jobs back."

**GO ON →**

**2** The author uses a word that is a homophone for a word that means "useless spending" or "something worthless." Underline the homophone in the paragraph.

Aunt Edith wrote home often. She was proud of her uniform, a navy blue jacket with gold buttons and navy blue skirt. She said that the bottom of the skirt had to be exactly eight inches from the floor. Her blouse was called a waist, and she wore a scarf called a neckerchief around the open collar. The photo she sent to the family was displayed on the table in the living room.

**3** What does the passage suggest about freedom? Select **two** options.

(A) Freedom should be protected.

(B) Not everyone believes in freedom.

(C) The American flag stands for freedom.

(D) People should never take their freedom for granted.

(E) Freedom means different things to different people.

(F) Young people do not have the same freedom as adults.

**GO ON →**

Name: _____ Date: _____

**4** Read the sentences from the text.

Every bolt and screw had to match exactly the length and width shown on the plans. The job was important because lives of pilots who flew the planes depended on careful attention to detail. Mom enjoyed her work at the factory.

Which word from the sentences is a homophone for a word that means "a disease that can be like a very bad cold"?

(A) bolt

(B) plans

(C) flew

(D) work

**5** Read the quotation.

The cost of freedom is always high, but Americans have always paid it.
–John F. Kennedy

Which idea from the text does the quote support?

(A) Americans are willing to fight to be free.

(B) Aunt Edith was proud of her Navy uniform.

(C) Women who worked during the war often enjoyed their jobs.

(D) Emma's mom knew that Dad needed to do what he was doing.

**GO ON →**

**Read the passage "Voices for Change" before answering Numbers 6 through 10.**

# Voices for Change

Anna Johnson was born in 1884 in Chicago, Illinois. She had always wanted to be a teacher, so she went to school for training. After graduating, she got a job as a teacher in the city. Anna loved teaching fifth grade, and she felt her job was important because her students were learning skills in reading and mathematics that would lead to success.

Sometimes students asked to stay after class for help or to talk, and George was one of these students. He told Anna that he liked school. At home, there were ten children in the family, and they lived in five rooms. It was a noisy and crowded place. One day George stopped coming to class. As she walked to school a few days later, Anna saw him at a street corner selling newspapers. He had a stack of newspapers under his arm and was holding one up to show the headline. Anna had seen young boys selling newspapers throughout the city, but she had never before seen one of her students working. George told her that he had to work to help his family. He went to the newspaper press in the middle of the night to wait for the papers, and then he had to be on the street in the early morning to sell papers to people on their way to work. George did not think he could come to school any more.

Anna realized this job was much harder than a paper route. She deeply worried about George and the brevity of his education, and she wondered how many other children had to work. She had read that Illinois had passed a law in 1897 that stated no one under fourteen years old could work for wages, but people must be ignoring the law if students as young as George were working to make money. Anna believed that anyone who was not yet sixteen should be in school. It was a right they should have in America in 1909, and she wanted to do something to help.

**GO ON →**

A friend gave Anna a photo essay by Lewis W. Hine. Like Anna, Hine had trained to be a teacher. He noticed that children were employed in dangerous and unhealthy jobs, and he wanted to show the need for change. He left teaching to become a photographer for the National Child Labor Committee.

His photographs of working children were taken across America, from the coal mines of Pennsylvania to fishing docks in Mississippi and cotton mills in Massachusetts. In the coal mines, children as young as eight years old separated coal from clay, soil, and slate. Sometimes they worked twelve hours a day in a room thick with coal dust. In a cotton mill in Georgia, boys and girls had to climb onto a frame in order to reach and replace empty bobbins. A bobbin is a kind of reel for holding thread. Other photos pictured boys tending furnaces in factories and children as young as five picking cotton in Texas. In Colorado, children worked in beet fields. Accidents happened because the children had to use a sharp knife to cut off the top of a beet. Seeing the photos made Anna's head throb and her heart beat in pain and sadness. She wanted to find a way to make a difference.

A teacher at her school told Anna about Jane Addams, who, along with Ellen Star, had started a settlement house to help immigrants. Other reformers had joined Addams and Star. They worked to improve conditions for working people. The site, or location, of Hull House was not far from Anna's school in Chicago. Anna wrote Jane Addams saying she would like to volunteer at Hull House, and she offered to tutor children or adult immigrants in reading. Anna hoped she could contribute to helping people get the education they needed for better jobs and lives.

**GO ON →**

**Now answer Numbers 6 through 10. Base your answers on "Voices for Change."**

**6** This question has two parts. First, answer part A. Then, answer part B.

**Part A:** Which of these messages about life is supported in the text?

(A) People need to work to make money.

(B) If something seems wrong, work to make it better.

(C) A person who wants to help children is a good person.

(D) Even young children are expected to work to help their family.

**Part B:** Which sentence from the text **best** supports your answer in part A?

(A) "After graduating, she got a job as a teacher in the city."

(B) "George did not think he could come to school any more."

(C) "It was a right they should have in America in 1909, and she wanted to do something to help."

(D) "In the coal mines, children as young as eight years old separated coal from clay, soil, and slate."

**7** Read the sentences from the text.

In a cotton mill in Georgia, boys and girls had to climb onto a frame in order to reach and replace empty bobbins. A bobbin is a kind of reel for holding thread.

Which word from the sentences is a homophone for a word that means "not imagined or made up; actual"?

(A) mill

(B) frame

(C) empty

(D) reel

**GO ON →**

**8** Compare and contrast the characters in the text. Select words from the list to describe the characters and write them in the chart. Then select the numbers for the sentences from the text that support your answers. Write the numbers in the chart. Not all words and numbers will be used.

|  | **Anna Johnson** | **Lewis Hine** | **Both** |
|---|---|---|---|
| Word to Describe |  |  |  |
| Text Evidence |  |  |  |

**Words:**

educator          parent          reporter

employer          photographer          volunteer

**Text Evidence:**

1 – "A friend gave Anna a photo essay by Lewis W. Hine."

2 – "Like Anna, Hine had trained to be a teacher."

3 – "He left teaching to become a photographer for the National Child Labor Committee."

4 – "Sometimes they worked twelve hours a day in a room thick with coal dust."

5 – "The site, or location, of Hull House was not far from Anna's school in Chicago."

6 – "Anna hoped she could contribute to helping people get the education they needed for better jobs and lives."

**GO ON →**

**9** Read the sentences from the text.

Other reformers had joined Addams and Star. They worked to improve conditions for working people. The site, or location, of Hull House was not far from Anna's school in Chicago.

Which word from the sentences is a homophone for a word that means "vision"?

(A) reformers

(B) joined

(C) improve

(D) site

**10** Which sentences summarize the theme of the passage? Select **three** options.

(A) People can make a difference.

(B) Working together brings change.

(C) It takes courage to be a reformer.

(D) Everyone should be paid a fair wage.

(E) You should act to correct an injustice.

(F) Look to your friends in a time of trouble.

**STOP**

**Now answer Number 11. Base your answer on "Joining Forces for Freedom" and "Voices for Change."**

**11** How do Emma's mom in "Joining Forces for Freedom" and Anna Johnson in "Voices for Change" respond to the challenges of their times? Support your answer with details from both texts.

_____

_____

_____

_____

_____

_____

_____

_____

_____

_____

_____

_____

# Answer Key

Name: _____

| Question | Correct Answer | Content Focus | CCSS | Complexity |
|:---:|:---:|:---:|:---:|:---:|
| **1A** | B | Theme | RL.5.2 | DOK 3 |
| **1B** | B | Theme/Text Evidence | RL.5.2/ RL.5.1 | DOK 3 |
| **2** | see below | Homophones | L.5.4a | DOK 1 |
| **3** | A, D | Theme | RL.5.2 | DOK 3 |
| **4** | C | Homophones | L.5.4a | DOK 1 |
| **5** | A | Theme | RL.5.2 | DOK 3 |
| **6A** | B | Theme | RL.5.2 | DOK 3 |
| **6B** | C | Theme/Text Evidence | RL.5.2/ RL.5.1 | DOK 3 |
| **7** | D | Homophones | L.5.4a | DOK 1 |
| **8** | see below | Character, Setting, Plot: Compare and Contrast | RL.5.3 | DOK 3 |
| **9** | D | Homophones | L.5.4a | DOK 1 |
| **10** | A, B, E | Theme | RL.5.2 | DOK 3 |
| **11** | see below | Writing About Text | W.5.9a | DOK 4 |

| | | |
|:---|:---:|:---:|
| **Comprehension** 1A, 1B, 3, 5, 6A, 6B, 8, 10 | /12 | % |
| **Vocabulary** 2, 4, 7, 9 | /8 | % |
| **Total Weekly Assessment Score** | /20 | % |

**2** Students should underline the word "waist" in the paragraph.

**8** Students should write the following details in the chart:
- Word to Describe—Anna Johnson: volunteer; Lewis Hine: photographer; Both: educator.
- Text Evidence—Anna Johnson: 6 – "Anna hoped she could contribute to helping people get the education they needed for better jobs and lives."; Lewis Hine: 3 – "He left teaching to become a photographer for the National Child Labor Committee."; Both: 2 – "Like Anna, Hine had trained to be a teacher."

**11** To receive full credit for the response, the following information should be included: In "Joining Forces for Freedom," Emma's mom takes a job in a factory to help her country when workers are needed during World War I. In "Voices for Change," Anna Johnson becomes concerned about child labor when she learns some children have to work to help support their families, and so she volunteers at Hull House. Both women take action because of their beliefs.

**Read the passage "New Country, New School" before answering Numbers 1 through 5.**

# New Country, New School

Vlad lived in Moscow, a big city in Russia, until he was ten years old. Then his father received a letter from Uncle Igor, who was living in Alexandria, Virginia. Like his father, Uncle Igor was a chemist. He wrote that there were jobs for trained chemists in the Washington, D.C. area where he lived, and he wanted Vlad's father to move to America. He said that life was good in his adopted country.

Vlad's mother was hardworking and ambitious, and she said, "If we don't make this move now, we never will do it, so now is the time to make a change."

Vlad didn't want to leave his chess players club, Saturday gymnastics classes, and friends, but the decision was made and his parents packed for the move.

Uncle Igor and Aunt Irina, who were friendly and not at all cold, met them at the airport. Vlad and his parents would stay with them until they found a place of their own. In Russia, Vlad and his parents shared a tiny apartment in a high-rise building with Vlad's grandparents because it was customary to live with relatives.

Uncle Igor and Aunt Irina lived in a townhouse where Vlad had his own room on the lower level. When Vlad saw the room, he was enthusiastic and said, "Wow! This is big. It's great!"

Vlad's parents enrolled him at Jefferson School nearby so that he wouldn't miss any time. They hoped to find a place in the area so Vlad wouldn't have to change schools again. Vlad was nervous on his first day, but the teacher, Ms. Chin, made him feel very welcome and introduced him to the class. She said they were studying Russia, and Vlad could give them firsthand information. Vlad did not understand all of her words, but she smiled and seemed kind.

**GO ON →**

At lunch, Anthony motioned for him to sit at his table in the cafeteria. Even though Anthony and the others spoke no Russian, and Vlad knew only a few English words, they communicated by signaling with their hands. Vlad would point to a food on someone's tray, and Anthony would say the English word. Vlad repeated the word, and by the end of the lunch break, he had a few new words in his vocabulary and new friends as well.

Vlad's parents took a class to learn to speak better English. His father got a job as a chemist, and his mother took a position on the staff of a hospital. After a few months, all three were becoming familiar with their new life in America. Mother thought they had taken advantage of Uncle Igor and Aunt Irina's generosity long enough and needed to get a place of their own, so on a Saturday, they went looking for an apartment. The typical apartments in Alexandria were larger than apartments in Moscow, and they found a nice one that day.

Vlad was happy to be able to stay at Jefferson School, and his parents said he could join a gymnastics club where he could continue improving his skills. He was enjoying his new friends and learning the language, and he also liked sharing information about Russia. During class, he showed photographs of Moscow. His mother made *blinis*, which are thin pancakes, and filled them with the traditional smoked salmon and sour cream. He took them to share with classmates.

Vlad's favorite activity was the chess club that met after school. He was teaching interested classmates how to play chess. They said it was a good game and that they never would have learned if Vlad hadn't taught them. Vlad realized that he could make new friends by expressing his interest in American customs and sharing his Russian culture with his new friends.

**GO ON →**

**Now answer Numbers 1 through 5. Base your answers on "New Country, New School."**

**1** Select the statement that **best** explains the message of the passage.

(A) Vlad is a typical ten-year-old Russian boy.

(B) Americans always welcome people from other countries.

(C) Gymnastics is an important sport in Russia and in America.

(D) People adjust to change by learning new things and making new friends.

**2** This question has two parts. First, answer part A. Then, answer part B.

**Part A:** Read the sentence from the passage.

Vlad's mother was hardworking and <u>ambitious</u>, and she said, "If we don't make this move now, we never will do it, so now is the time to make a change."

What does the use of the word <u>ambitious</u> suggest about Vlad's mother?

(A) She is famous.

(B) She is very wealthy.

(C) She is a forceful person.

(D) She is unconcerned about the future.

**Part B:** Which other word has the same connotation as the word <u>ambitious</u>?

(A) assertive

(B) angry

(C) pushy

(D) rude

**GO ON →**

**3** Sort the words from the passage in the list below. Write each word in the chart to show if it has a positive connotation or a negative connotation.

| | |
|---|---|
| **Positive Connotation** | |
| | |
| | |
| **Negative Connotation** | |
| | |
| | |

**Words:**
cold
enthusiastic
generosity
nervous
sharing
tiny

**GO ON →**

**4** This question has two parts. First, answer part A. Then, answer part B.

**Part A:** Which sentence **best** summarizes the theme of the passage?

(A) Every culture has special foods that others may enjoy.

(B) Reaching out helps us get along with others.

(C) School is the same anywhere you go.

(D) Food is the universal language.

**Part B:** Which sentence from the passage **best** supports your answer in part A?

(A) "Like his father, Uncle Igor was a chemist."

(B) "He said that life was good in his adopted country."

(C) "The typical apartments in Alexandria were larger than apartments in Moscow, and they found a nice one that day."

(D) "Vlad realized that he could make new friends by expressing his interest in American customs and sharing his Russian culture with his new friends."

**5** Which actions by the characters **best** describe the lesson of the passage? Select **three** options.

(A) Vlad's new friends help him learn English.

(B) Vlad's mother encourages the family to move.

(C) Vlad brings *blinis* to class to teach about his culture.

(D) Vlad teaches some of his classmates how to play chess.

(E) Uncle Igor and Aunt Irina meet the family at the airport.

(F) Vlad's mother accepts a position on the staff of a hospital.

**GO ON →**

**Read the passage "Getting Along with Grandma" before answering Numbers 6 through 10.**

# Getting Along with Grandma

Sam and his friends Robert and Scott had formed a jazz band and were practicing at Sam's house. Robert played the keyboard, Scott the drums, and Sam the bass guitar. Sam's young brother, Guy, pestered them and asked silly questions because he wanted attention.

Finally, Sam said, "Guy, just go to your own room because you are annoying us."

Guy's expression turned into a pout, and Sam was hoping he would not cry when Mom came into the room. She said, "I have some great news. Guy and Sam, your grandmother is coming from Thailand to live with us."

A few days later, Mom said to the boys, "Guy will have to share Sam's room because we must make your grandmother feel welcome by giving her a room. You boys can get along if you try."

The boys each agreed to try, and that weekend, Guy moved into Sam's room. Guy had enough toys and games to fill the room, and Sam wondered if the arrangement would work, but he was determined to try. Sam told Guy which of his things he could use, but Guy paid no attention. First, he took Sam's baseball and left it at the park, and then he carelessly knocked Sam's soccer trophy off its base. Sam asked his dad to talk to Guy, and Dad suggested that they put tape down the middle of the room to separate it into two parts. Each boy would have his half and could not touch anything on the other side. The system worked.

Mom, Dad, and the boys went to the airport to meet Grandma, who had a nice smile and gave them many hugs. At home, May, the boys' older sister, had prepared a special Thai dinner in Grandma's honor. It was pad thai, a family favorite made with rice noodles and shrimp. Grandma spoke English well and enjoyed telling them about her life in Thailand. She explained that she had loved the dinner but would like to try some American food soon and learn some American customs.

**GO ON →**

A few days later, Robert and Scott came over to practice and started tuning their instruments. When Mom came from the kitchen and asked them not to play because Grandma was taking a nap, the boys were disappointed.

On Saturday afternoon, Dad was working, Mom was taking Guy to the dentist, and Sam had soccer practice, so Mom asked May to please stay home to keep Grandma company. May had planned on a long bike ride with friends but agreed to stay home instead. It was not going to be as easy to stay home, but she knew it was important to spend time with Grandma.

The next time Robert and Scott came to practice, Grandma came into the room and asked if she could listen. The boys looked at each other, and then Sam said, "Grandma, we don't mind, but you may not like our music because it's loud, and it has a strong beat."

Grandma explained that she wanted to hear some American music and would like to hear them play. She stayed through the practice session, and afterwards she clapped and said they had real talent. She wanted to be invited to their first performance on a stage.

Mom asked May and Sam to stay with Guy and Grandma on Saturday night. Immediately, Grandma spoke up, "May and Sam don't need to stay home because Guy and I will watch out for each other. He will take care of me, and I will take care of him."

Mom asked, "Are you sure, Mother? You didn't come here to work."

Grandma said, "I'm sure. You are helping me, and I want to help you, and besides, being with Guy is fun, not work."

**GO ON →**

Name: _____ Date: _____

**Now answer Numbers 6 through 10. Base your answers on "Getting Along with Grandma."**

 This question has two parts. First, answer part A. Then, answer part B.

**Part A:** Read the sentence from the passage.

Sam's young brother, Guy, <u>pestered</u> them and asked silly questions because he wanted attention.

What does the word <u>pestered</u> suggest about Guy?

(A) He is very intelligent.

(B) He bothers his brother.

(C) He does not remember things.

(D) He wants to be like his brother.

**Part B:** Which other words have a connotation that is similar to the word <u>pestered</u>? Select **two** words.

(A) annoy

(B) enjoy

(C) laugh

(D) poke

(E) practice

(F) sleep

**GO ON →**

**7** This question has two parts. First, answer part A. Then, answer part B.

**Part A:** Which sentence summarizes the problems between Sam and Guy when they start to share a room?

(A) Sam is selfish about his belongings.

(B) Guy is not responsible about Sam's belongings.

(C) The room is not large enough for the two brothers.

(D) The brothers do not stay out of each other's side of the room.

**Part B:** Which sentence from the passage **best** supports your answer in part A?

(A) "The boys each agreed to try, and that weekend, Guy moved into Sam's room."

(B) "Guy had enough toys and games to fill the room, and Sam wondered if the arrangement would work, but he was determined to try."

(C) "First, he took Sam's baseball and left it at the park, and then he carelessly knocked Sam's soccer trophy off its base."

(D) "Sam asked his dad to talk to Guy, and Dad suggested that they put tape down the middle of the room to separate it into two parts."

**8** Which sentence explains what the reader learns from the passage about getting along with people?

(A) It is very difficult to change one's ways.

(B) Children must respect older family members.

(C) People who help others receive help in return.

(D) The only way to share a space is to divide it in two.

**GO ON →**

**9** Read the sentences from the passage.

Grandma explained that she wanted to hear some American music and would like to hear them play. She stayed through the practice session, and afterwards she clapped and said they had real talent.

Which words from the sentence have a positive connotation? Select **two** words.

(A) hear

(B) music

(C) session

(D) afterwards

(E) clapped

(F) talent

**10** Circle the theme of the passage. Then circle **one** piece of text evidence that **best** supports the theme.

| Theme | Text Evidence |
|---|---|
| Grandparents should live with their families. | "'Guy and Sam, your grandmother is coming from Thailand to live with us.'" |
| Getting along means meeting others halfway. | "A few days later, Robert and Scott came over to practice and started tuning their instruments." |
| It is easy for members of a family to get along. | "'You didn't come here to work.'" |
| Practicing something will help you improve at it. | "'May and Sam don't need to stay home because Guy and I will watch out for each other.'" |

**Now answer Number 11. Base your answer on "New Country, New School" and
"Getting Along with Grandma."**

**11** How do Vlad in "New Country, New School" and Sam in "Getting Along with
Grandma" meet the challenge of getting along with new people? Support your
answer with details from both texts.

_____

_____

_____

_____

_____

_____

_____

_____

_____

_____

_____

_____

_____

# Answer Key

| Question | Correct Answer | Content Focus | CCSS | Complexity |
|---|---|---|---|---|
| 1 | D | Theme | RL.5.2 | DOK 3 |
| 2A | C | Connotation and Denotation | L.5.5 | DOK 2 |
| 2B | A | Connotation and Denotation | L.5.5 | DOK 2 |
| 3 | see below | Connotation and Denotation | L.5.5 | DOK 2 |
| 4A | B | Theme | RL.5.2 | DOK 3 |
| 4B | D | Theme/Text Evidence | RL.5.2/ RL.5.1 | DOK 3 |
| 5 | A, C, D | Theme | RL.5.2 | DOK 3 |
| 6A | B | Connotation and Denotation | L.5.5 | DOK 2 |
| 6B | A, D | Connotation and Denotation | L.5.5 | DOK 2 |
| 7A | B | Character, Setting, Plot: Problem and Solution | RL.4.3 | DOK 2 |
| 7B | C | Character, Setting, Plot: Problem and Solution/Text Evidence | RL.4.3/ RL.5.1 | DOK 2 |
| 8 | C | Theme | RL.5.2 | DOK 3 |
| 9 | E, F | Connotation and Denotation | L.5.5 | DOK 2 |
| 10 | see below | Theme | RL.5.2 | DOK 3 |
| 11 | see below | Writing About Text | W.5.9a | DOK 4 |

| | | | |
|---|---|---|---|
| **Comprehension** 1, 4A, 4B, 5, 7A, 7B, 8, 10 | | /12 | % |
| **Vocabulary** 2A, 2B, 3, 6A, 6B, 9 | | /8 | % |
| **Total Weekly Assessment Score** | | /20 | % |

**3** Students should sort the words in the chart as follows:
- Positive Connotation—enthusiastic, generosity, sharing
- Negative Connotation—cold, nervous, tiny

**10** Students should circle the following sentences:
- Theme—Getting along means meeting others halfway.
- Text Evidence—"'May and Sam don't need to stay home because Guy and I will watch out for each other.'"

**11** To receive full credit for the response, the following information should be included: In "New Country, New School," Vlad joins Anthony's table in the cafeteria and begins to learn a new language in order to communicate with his classmates. In "Getting Along with Grandma," Sam works to get along with Guy for his family's sake. Both Vlad and Guy share something from their own culture. Vlad shows photos of Moscow and brings *blinis* to school. Sam and his friends play jazz for Grandma.

**Read the article "Watch Out for the Octopus!" before answering Numbers 1 through 5.**

# Watch Out for the Octopus!

There are a lot of deadly animals in the world. Some are poisonous, meaning they use poison as a defense. If you touch them, you might absorb the poison through your skin. Others are venomous, meaning they use their poison to attack. What are some of the deadliest animals out there?

One truly deadly animal is the puffer fish, which does not look dangerous, but its skin and organs are poisonous to humans. Oddly, people like to eat the puffer fish. Cooks who work with it have to have a special license. It is supposed to be delicious—as long as you don't take a bite of those parts of it that might be fatal! Puffer fish could be the last meal you ever have. The stonefish is a poisonous fish covered with sharp spines where it stores its poison. If you step on it—watch out! It uses its spines to keep away predators.

The exotic poison dart frog is found in the jungles of South and Central America. These tiny frogs are unusually colorful, but their beauty is sinister. Their skin is so poisonous that if enemies touch it or try to eat it, they will quickly die.

Snakes, of course, are known for being venomous. The taipan, which lives in Australia, is considered the world's most venomous snake. Its venom is said to be four hundred times stronger than that of the next most venomous snake. Luckily, the taipan is very shy and secretive, and it is rarely seen by humans. King cobras are the longest venomous snakes, growing to more than eighteen feet in length. They live in East and Southeast Asia and have been known to kill full-grown elephants. The faint-banded sea snake, found in the Indian Ocean, is another deadly snake, though it rarely bites. When it does bite, it does not always release its poison.

**GO ON →**

Some animals have very venomous stings. Scorpions, with their sharp tails, are among them. The death starker scorpion, found in North Africa and the Middle East, has a strong, painful poison. Many spiders are venomous, too, including the Brazilian wandering spider. It is especially dangerous because it moves around a lot and might be found in someone's shoe or under a bed. In the United States, black widow spiders and brown recluse spiders are the most common venomous spiders, but they do not match the danger of the Brazilian wandering spider or the funnel-web spider of Australia. Like scorpions, venomous spiders use their poison to get food.

You might not think of an octopus as being venomous, but the blue-ringed octopus certainly is. It is small and brightly colored, and it can move very quickly. It lives in the waters around Asia and Australia, and its sting is both painful and dangerous. The waters off Japan, the Philippines, Australia, and Hawaii are home to the animal that is considered the world's most venomous— the box jelly, a fearsome creature with long tentacles that are full of poison. Like the blue-ringed octopus, the box jelly uses its poison to stun and kill other animals, which it then eats.

There are poisonous and venomous animals almost everywhere in the world. That is why it is usually a good idea to be careful if you see an unfamiliar animal— especially an unfamiliar snake, spider, jellyfish, scorpion, fish, or octopus!

**GO ON →**

Name: _____ Date: _____

**1** Which sentence **best** explains what the article is about?

(A) People should be afraid of all animals.

(B) Animals can be deadly to other animals.

(C) Brightly-colored animals are often poisonous.

(D) Animals use poison to defend themselves and to get food.

**2** This question has two parts. First, answer part A. Then, answer part B.

**Part A:** Read the sentences from the text.

Oddly, people like to eat the puffer fish. Cooks who work with it have to have a special license. It is supposed to be delicious—as long as you don't take a bite of those parts of it that might be <u>fatal</u>! Puffer fish could be the last meal you ever have.

What does the word <u>fatal</u> **most likely** mean?

(A) deadly

(B) fragile

(C) physical

(D) tasty

**Part B:** Which phrase from the sentences **best** shows what <u>fatal</u> means?

(A) "like to eat"

(B) "a special license"

(C) "take a bit of those parts"

(D) "the last meal you ever have"

**GO ON →**

**3** The author uses clues in the text to help the reader understand what the word sinister means. Circle **two** words in the paragraph that give clues to the meaning of sinister.

The exotic poison dart frog is found in the jungles of South and Central America. These tiny frogs are unusually colorful, but their beauty is <u>sinister</u>. Their skin is so poisonous that if enemies touch it or try to eat it, they will quickly die.

**4** This question has two parts. First, answer part A. Then, answer part B.

**Part A:** What is the main reason scorpions are poisonous?

(A) to scare people

(B) to kill their prey

(C) to chase off spiders

(D) to protect themselves

**Part B:** Which sentence from the text **best** supports your answer in part A?

(A) "Some animals have very venomous stings."

(B) "Scorpions, with their sharp tails, are among them."

(C) "The death starker scorpion, found in North Africa and the Middle East, has a strong, painful poison."

(D) "Like scorpions, venomous spiders use their poison to get food."

**GO ON →**

**5** Select **two** ways that the author shows the relationship between certain kinds of animals and humans.

(A) People must be careful around animals.

(B) Poisonous animals do not harm people.

(C) Some animals can be dangerous to people.

(D) People work with animals to help sustain nature.

(E) Animal bites must be treated promptly with medicine.

(F) People find some animals more interesting than others.

**GO ON →**

**Read the article "Animal Communities" before answering Numbers 6 through 10.**

# Animal Communities

In human communities, people work together to obtain food and shelter, raise children, and enjoy a better quality of life. When each person contributes to a community, the community functions better. A society needs many different kinds of workers in order to do well. Animals also live in varied communities. In fact, nature gives most creatures a social instinct that serves a number of purposes.

Many lions work together in well-organized groups. The females do the hunting, working in teams to trap their prey. Because of this, the lions can surround an animal and cut off its escape. Wolves also hunt in teams, and they have a strong social order in which they follow a leader and obey rules for the good of the pack.

Naturalist Dr. Regis Ferriere notes that some insect species exist cooperatively, as well. An example is the relationship between ants and aphids, or tiny plant insects. The ants protect the aphids from predators, watching over groups of aphids on grasses as if they were herds of cattle. In return, from time to time, the ants "milk" the aphids of sugar droplets in their bodies.

Bees, ants, and wasps have special jobs in their communities. For example, a queen bee lives with worker bees and other bees in a beehive. The worker bees serve the queen so the queen can lay eggs. If the queen did not lay enough eggs, the busy hive would become vacant. In an ant community, soldier ants are protectors for the colony, and in bee and wasp communities, females take on the job of providing defense.

**GO ON →**

Baboons and antelopes often eat together to protect one another. Baboons have excellent eyesight and antelopes have a keen sense of smell, so together they function as a warning system. Cattle and birds work in much the same way. The birds eat the insects that the cattle stir up when they move, and in turn, the birds make a lot of warning noises and fly off when they sense danger. Thus, their combined efforts benefit both the birds and the cattle.

Crocodiles and birds called plovers help each other in a unique way. Crocodiles have very sharp teeth. They often have tiny, harmful animals attached to their teeth that the plover will pick out, getting food for itself while helping to clean the crocodile's teeth.

On the African plains, the honeyguide bird looks for honey, but when it finds a beehive, it cannot open it. The ratel, or honey badger, comes to the rescue, tearing open the beehive that the honeyguide has found for it and exposing the honey so that both can eat.

In the desert, mongooses and hornbills (a type of bird) help each other out. There are few trees or other shelters available, and both mongooses and hornbills are very exposed to predators. The groups take turns guarding, using warning cries to tell when predators sneak up. A predator's ambush is difficult when so many are watching and warning.

Another example of two very different animals helping each other can be found in warm oceans. The remora is a fish that cannot swim well, but the form of its head allows it to attach itself to large sharks. It gets from one place to another in the ocean by getting rides from sharks. In turn, the remora eats small animals that attach themselves to the shark and can hurt it.

As you can see, there are certain basic similarities between human and animal societies. We have many of the same needs, after all. We must depend on one another to help all survive.

**GO ON →**

**Now answer Numbers 6 through 10. Base your answers on "Animal Communities."**

**6** This question has two parts. First, answer part A. Then, answer part B.

**Part A:** Which sentence **best** summarizes the way the author shows the relationship between human and animal communities?

Ⓐ Animals first inhabit an area; then humans follow.

Ⓑ Humans and animals form communities for different reasons.

Ⓒ Living in communities helps both humans and animals to survive.

Ⓓ Humans can learn to settle disputes by observing animal behavior.

**Part B:** Which detail from the text **best** supports your answer in part A?

Ⓐ Birds often fly away when they sense that danger is near.

Ⓑ Lions hunt together to improve their chances of success.

Ⓒ Wolves live in a group that is called a pack.

Ⓓ Antelopes have an excellent sense of smell.

**7** Read the sentences from the text.

The worker bees serve the queen so the queen can lay eggs. If the queen did not lay enough eggs, the busy hive would become vacant.

What does the word vacant **most likely** mean?

Ⓐ complete

Ⓑ dead

Ⓒ empty

Ⓓ full

**GO ON →**

**8** Which of the following are effects of the relationship between crocodiles and plovers? Select **all** that apply.

(A) clean skin

(B) clean teeth

(C) food to eat

(D) ability to move

(E) a warning system

(F) safety from attack

**9** This question has two parts. First, answer part A. Then, answer part B.

**Part A:** Read the sentences from the text.

The groups take turns guarding, using warning cries to tell when predators sneak up. A predator's <u>ambush</u> is difficult when so many are watching and warning."

What does the word <u>ambush</u> suggest about the predator?

(A) It is very large and powerful.

(B) It is trying to surprise its prey.

(C) It has not eaten for a long time.

(D) It has been running for a long time.

**Part B:** Which phrase from the sentences gives the **best** clue about the meaning of <u>ambush</u>?

(A) "take turns"

(B) "warning cries"

(C) "sneak up"

(D) "is difficult"

**GO ON →**

**10** The author mentions several reasons why animals cooperate with each other. Use the list to write these reasons in the chart. Not all of the possible reasons will be used.

| Reasons Why Animals Cooperate with Each Other |
|---|
|  |

**Possible Reasons:**

to travel

to have fun

to find food

for company

for protection

for cleanliness

Name: _____ Date: _____

**Now answer Number 11. Base your answer on "Watch Out for the Octopus!"
and "Animal Communities."**

**11** How have venomous animals and those that cooperate with other animals
adapted to survive? Support your answer with details from both texts.

_____

_____

_____

_____

_____

_____

_____

_____

_____

_____

_____

_____

_____

_____

_____

_____

# Answer Key

Name: _____

| Question | Correct Answer | Content Focus | CCSS | Complexity |
|---|---|---|---|---|
| 1 | D | Main Idea and Key Details | RI.5.2 | DOK 2 |
| 2A | A | Context Clues: Paragraph Clues | L.5.4a | DOK 2 |
| 2B | D | Context Clues: Paragraph Clues/ Text Evidence | L.5.4a/ RI.5.1 | DOK 2 |
| 3 | see below | Context Clues: Paragraph Clues | L.5.4a | DOK 2 |
| 4A | B | Cause and Effect | RI.5.3 | DOK 2 |
| 4B | D | Cause and Effect/Text Evidence | RI.5.3/ RI.5.1 | DOK 2 |
| 5 | A, C | Text Structure: Cause and Effect | RI.5.3 | DOK 2 |
| 6A | C | Text Structure: Cause and Effect | RI.5.3 | DOK 2 |
| 6B | B | Text Structure: Cause and Effect/ Text Evidence | RI.5.3/ RI.5.1 | DOK 2 |
| 7 | C | Context Clues: Paragraph Clues | L.5.4a | DOK 2 |
| 8 | B, C | Cause and Effect | RI.5.3 | DOK 2 |
| 9A | B | Context Clues: Paragraph Clues | L.5.4a | DOK 2 |
| 9B | C | Context Clues: Paragraph Clues/ Text Evidence | L.5.4a/ RI.5.1 | DOK 2 |
| 10 | see below | Text Structure: Cause and Effect | RI.5.3 | DOK 2 |
| 11 | see below | Writing About Text | W.5.9b | DOK 4 |

| | | |
|---|---|---|
| **Comprehension** 1, 4A, 4B, 5, 6A, 6B, 8, 10 | /12 | % |
| **Vocabulary** 2A, 2B, 3, 7 9A, 9B | /8 | % |
| **Total Weekly Assessment Score** | /20 | % |

**3** Students should circle the words "poisonous" and "die" in the paragraph.

**10** Students should write the following reasons why animals cooperate with each other:
- to travel
- to find food
- for protection
- for cleanliness

**11** To receive full credit for the response, the following information should be included: Both venomous animals and animals that cooperate have developed ways to defend themselves and to find food.

**Read the article "Reducing Our Lunch Waste" before answering Numbers 1 through 5.**

# Reducing Our Lunch Waste

At lunchtime, you walk to the cafeteria with your classmates, and you open your brown paper lunch bag and pull out the contents. Today's lunch consists of a sandwich wrapped in a plastic baggie, a disposable bottle of water, and pre-packaged bags of apples and carrots. The lunch might not sound bad to you, but what about the materials used to package it? At the end of lunch, a lot of waste will be left. If many students pack similar lunches, imagine how much waste will be created. Many people are trying to eat zero-waste lunches. Here are other options that will reduce the amount of lunch waste.

One option is to carry a reusable lunch bag instead of a brown paper bag. A reusable lunch bag may cost more than brown paper bags at first, but using one eventually saves money because it can last for years, while a brown paper bag lasts for one day.

Instead of throwing out your water bottle each day, carry a stainless steel water bottle. Plastic water bottles that are thrown in the trash can sit in landfills for as many as 1,000 years! Reusing your stainless steel bottle will keep plastic bottles out of the landfill.

The containers holding your food can easily be replaced, for there are reusable plastic containers that come in many sizes. These containers can be used for years, keeping baggies out of the landfill. Another option is to use reusable baggies, which are similar to the plastic baggie that you throw away. The difference is that they are more durable and washable.

This takes care of the containers holding your lunch, but what about any uneaten food? A lot of food ends up in landfills each year. What can be done with something as worthless as uneaten food?

**GO ON →**

Some schools turn uneaten food into compost, an organic matter used to make soil richer and to help plants grow bigger. Compost bins are not hard to assemble. Four supplies are used to construct the bins, including a container, newspaper, food scraps, and redworms.

The bins do not take up much space as they are usually 2 feet wide and 2–3 feet long. They are only 18 inches deep because the worms live near the top of the bin. The plastic or wooden container is lined with thin strips of newspaper to hold moisture in the bin so it does not dry out.

Now it is time to add the food waste. Redworms will eat almost anything, but some foods should not be put in a compost bin. Meat and bones start to smell as they decay, so they are better left out, and dairy products should not go in the compost bin, either. Other than these exceptions, redworms eat the same foods as people. Regular garbage, such as plastic bags, cannot be placed in the compost bin.

After a few months' time, there will be a rich supply of compost left behind by the worms that can be spread in gardens or around trees and provide many nutrients for these plants.

With some planning, it is possible to achieve a zero-waste lunch. The same lunch mentioned earlier could be easily converted. It could be packed in a reusable lunch bag. The disposable water bottle could be replaced with a stainless steel water bottle. The sandwich, apples, and carrots could be packed in reusable containers or baggies. Composting the leftover food would complete the effort to obtain a zero-waste lunch.

**GO ON →**

Name: _____ Date: _____

**Now answer Numbers 1 through 5. Base your answers on "Reducing Our Lunch Waste."**

**1** This question has two parts. First, answer part A. Then, answer part B.

**Part A:** Which sentence **best** states the main problem caused by lunches packed in brown paper bags?

Ⓐ Brown paper bags are expensive.

Ⓑ Brown paper bags do not keep lunches fresh.

Ⓒ The materials used to pack this lunch are unsafe.

Ⓓ The materials used to pack this lunch create a lot of garbage.

**Part B:** Which sentence from the text **best** supports your answer in part A?

Ⓐ "At lunchtime, you walk to the cafeteria with your classmates, and you open your brown paper lunch bag and pull out the contents."

Ⓑ "The lunch might not sound bad to you, but what about the materials used to package it?"

Ⓒ "At the end of lunch, a lot of waste will be left."

Ⓓ "Many people are trying to eat zero-waste lunches."

**2** Read the sentence from the text.

What can be done with something as <u>worthless</u> as uneaten food?

Which words have the **opposite** meaning of <u>worthless</u>? Select **two** options.

Ⓐ hopeless

Ⓑ important

Ⓒ sparkling

Ⓓ useless

Ⓔ valuable

Ⓕ worldly

**GO ON →**

**3** Read the detail related to the information in the text.

It does not take long to fill a bottle with water from home.

Circle the paragraph that the detail above **best** supports.

One option is to carry a reusable lunch bag instead of a brown paper bag. A reusable lunch bag may cost more than brown paper bags at first, but using one eventually saves money because it can last for years, while a brown paper bag lasts for one day.

Instead of throwing out your water bottle each day, carry a stainless steel water bottle. Plastic water bottles that are thrown in the trash can sit in landfills for as many as 1,000 years! Reusing your stainless steel bottle will keep plastic bottles out of the landfill.

The containers holding your food can easily be replaced, for there are reusable plastic containers that come in many sizes. These containers can be used for years, keeping baggies out of the landfill. Another option is to use reusable baggies, which are similar to the plastic baggie that you throw away. The difference is that they are more durable and washable.

This takes care of the containers holding your lunch, but what about any uneaten food? A lot of food ends up in landfills each year. What can be done with something as worthless as uneaten food?

**GO ON →**

**4** Which sentence summarizes what the author says can be done with uneaten food?

Ⓐ Uneaten food can be thrown in landfills.

Ⓑ Uneaten food may be composted with worms.

Ⓒ The students can take all the uneaten food home.

Ⓓ The students should be told to eat all of their food.

**5** Read the sentence from the text.

Meat and bones start to smell as they <u>decay</u>, so they are better left out, and dairy products should not go in the compost bin, either.

Which word has almost the **same** meaning as <u>decay</u>?

Ⓐ boil

Ⓑ develop

Ⓒ rest

Ⓓ rot

**GO ON →**

**Read the article "Kind Actions" before answering Numbers 6 through 10.**

# Kind Actions

We are all affected by the actions of those around us. Your class would most likely have a positive reaction if your teacher announced a delightful surprise, such as ice cream, as a treat for all students. You may think that only adults are able to influence others, but this is not true. Anyone can improve another person's life with his or her actions, and we all can take time to help others in need.

A simple way to help others is to spend time with them. Some residents of nursing homes may be lonely and in need of a friend. You could get permission to visit a nursing home. If your parents give their consent, you could talk with some residents. They might like to hear about your life and what you like to do, or they might like to have someone listen to their stories. Talking and listening are gifts that do not cost any money and can make a big difference in the life of someone who is lonely.

Some people need help doing tasks that they are unable to do for themselves. You may know someone who could use help with chores around the house. A great gesture is offering to help without expecting any money in return. Performing the tasks in a dependable way will be a big help.

**GO ON →**

There might be opportunities to help people in your community that you may not know personally. You can donate your time by helping out at a soup kitchen, which is a place that provides free meals for those in need. These are staffed by volunteers, so any help is welcome, and there are many tasks that need to be done. Do not be discouraged by the smallness of tasks such as serving food, washing dishes, and cleaning up tables. They are of great importance to those who run the soup kitchens. Without help, soup kitchens are unable to provide meals for those who need them.

Sometimes, people are in need of things instead of time. When the weather turns colder, some people in your community may be in need of extra blankets or coats. The solution to this problem does not have to be expensive. With the help of others, you could organize a collection of an assortment of coats and blankets that are no longer needed. If you hold this drive at your school or in your neighborhood, you should get a variety of coat sizes and blanket types. Collections like this can be held at any time of the year. Many people like to clean out closets in the spring time, so this might be a good time to gather coats that have been outgrown.

While cleaning out closets or looking for coats and blankets, you may want also to look for toys or books that are no longer used. If they are in good shape, you could consider donating them. Thrift shops sell these items, and the profits benefit the organization, or you could donate them to a homeless shelter. Non-profit organizations that care for children may also be able to use these items. There are many places that would gladly accept things in good condition that you no longer need.

Sharing time and unused items with others in need are actions that can have a positive effect on those around us. These are just a few ways that you could impact your community, but many other opportunities exist. Gather a group of your friends and see if you can find a way to make a difference in your school or community. You will be glad that you took action.

**GO ON →**

**Now answer Numbers 6 through 10. Base your answers on "Kind Actions."**

**6** This question has two parts. First, answer part A. Then, answer part B.

**Part A:** Which **best** explains the author's solution for helping people who are lonely?

Ⓐ visiting with them

Ⓑ helping them with chores

Ⓒ giving them warm blankets

Ⓓ volunteering at a soup kitchen

**Part B:** Which sentence from the text **best** supports your answer in part A?

Ⓐ "We are all affected by the actions of those around us."

Ⓑ "You may think that only adults are able to influence others, but this is not true."

Ⓒ "A simple way to help others is to spend time with them."

Ⓓ "Some residents of nursing homes may be lonely and in need of a friend."

**7** Read the sentence from the text.

If your parents give their <u>consent</u>, you could talk with some residents.

Which word has almost the same meaning as <u>consent</u>?

Ⓐ denial

Ⓑ permission

Ⓒ question

Ⓓ understanding

**GO ON →**

**8** Which of the following is a problem that is solved by soup kitchens?

(A) Some people do not know how to cook.

(B) Some people want to try different foods.

(C) Some people are allergic to certain foods.

(D) Some people are not able to afford a meal.

**9** Select **two** ways that cleaning out closets can help others.

(A) It comforts a lonely person.

(B) It raises money to help people.

(C) It can be a way to locate unused coats.

(D) It provides people with a needed meal.

(E) It can result in finding toys to give away.

(F) It gives people something to do to pass the time.

**GO ON →**

**10** Fill in the chart by writing the correct synonym and antonym for each word given. Choose from the list below. Not all of the words in the list will be used.

|  | **Synonym** | **Antonym** |
|---|---|---|
| delightful |  |  |
| dependable |  |  |
| donated |  |  |

| | | | |
|---|---|---|---|
| generous | given | horrible | received |
| simple | trustworthy | unreliable | wonderful |

STOP

Name: _____ Date: _____

**Now answer Number 11. Base your answer on "Reducing Our Lunch Waste" and "Kind Actions."**

**11** How can our actions affect our environment and the people in our communities? Support your answer with details from both texts.

_____

_____

_____

_____

_____

_____

_____

_____

_____

_____

_____

_____

_____

_____

_____

_____

# Answer Key

Name: _____

| Question | Correct Answer | Content Focus | CCSS | Complexity |
|:---:|:---:|:---:|:---:|:---:|
| 1A | D | Problem and Solution | RI.5.3 | DOK 2 |
| 1B | C | Problem and Solution/Text Evidence | RI.5.3/ RI.5.1 | DOK 2 |
| 2 | B, E | Synonyms and Antonyms | L.5.5c | DOK 1 |
| 3 | see below | Main Idea and Key Details | RI.5.2 | DOK 2 |
| 4 | B | Problem and Solution | RI.5.3 | DOK 2 |
| 5 | D | Synonyms and Antonyms | L.5.5c | DOK 1 |
| 6A | A | Problem and Solution | RI.5.3 | DOK 2 |
| 6B | C | Problem and Solution/Text Evidence | RI.5.3/ RI.5.1 | DOK 2 |
| 7 | B | Synonyms and Antonyms | L.5.5c | DOK 1 |
| 8 | D | Problem and Solution | RI.5.3 | DOK 2 |
| 9 | C, E | Problem and Solution | RI.5.3 | DOK 2 |
| 10 | see below | Synonyms and Antonyms | L.5.5c | DOK 1 |
| 11 | see below | Writing About Text | W.5.9b | DOK 4 |

| | | |
|:---|:---:|:---:|
| **Comprehension** 1A, 1B, 3, 4, 6A, 6B, 8, 9 | /12 | % |
| **Vocabulary** 2, 5, 7, 10 | /8 | % |
| **Total Weekly Assessment Score** | /20 | % |

**3** Students should circle the following paragraph:

- Instead of throwing out your water bottle each day, carry a stainless steel water bottle. Plastic water bottles that are thrown in the trash can sit in landfills for as many as 1,000 years! Reusing your stainless steel bottle will keep plastic bottles out of the landfill.

**10** Students should complete the chart with the following synonyms and antonyms:

- delightful—Synonym: wonderful; Antonym: horrible
- dependable— Synonym: trustworthy; Antonym: unreliable
- donated— Synonym: given; Antonym: received

**11** To receive full credit for the response, the following information should be included: We can choose to use reusable packaging for our lunches and compost uneaten food. We can clean out our closets and donate unwanted blankets to those who need them.

**Weekly Assessment** · Unit 6, Week 4

**Read the passage "Becoming a Musician" before answering Numbers 1 through 5.**

# Becoming a Musician

With frustration, I stared at the open pages of the piano music book. The musical notes mocked me as I tried to read them and play at the same time, and my brain seemed unable to tell my fingers which keys to play next. The resulting song sounded nothing like the familiar tune I was supposedly playing, so I closed the book and ended my practice session.

I started taking piano lessons because of my Uncle Sahil. He is a wonderful pianist, and any piano he touches welcomes his attention. Before I began taking lessons, I dreamed of a day when I would be able to play like Uncle Sahil, and I begged my parents until they agreed to let me take lessons. The first few months of lessons with my piano teacher, Ms. Wong, were fun and I practiced every day to learn the basics, but the trouble began once I was ready to progress to more complicated music.

I could not play the more advanced music as well as I wanted to. At the end of each lesson, I would leave Ms. Wong's house with a new song to learn for the week. The melody would be fresh in my head, because Ms. Wong would play the song for me before I left, but when I tried to play the same song at home, it sounded nothing like it was supposed to. I would practice for a while, but I felt as though I never made any improvement. The piano was no longer my friend, and I dreaded practicing.

My parents talked with me about my piano lessons. My mother explained that the lessons were very expensive and that I would not be allowed to continue them if I did not practice daily. The thought of not taking lessons saddened me, and I frowned at the idea. My father saw my frown and suggested that I talk with Uncle Sahil about his experiences learning how to play the piano.

**GO ON →**

"Kalinda, you will find that many things in life take hard work to accomplish," my father said. "If you give up when things are difficult, you will not succeed at much."

I thought about my father's words later that night as I lay in bed. I knew that working hard was important, but working hard took a lot of effort, so I decided to call Uncle Sahil in the morning and ask for his advice.

When I called Uncle Sahil, I explained my difficulty with piano lessons and asked if he had any advice. Uncle Sahil paused before answering, and then replied, "Kalinda, do you know that I almost quit playing the piano when I was young? Then I decided that I loved music so much that I wanted to keep playing. I practiced before and after school, and I still spend at least an hour every day playing the piano. You have to dedicate yourself in order to do well. If you commit to the music, you will learn to play like me."

This shocked me because I did not know that Uncle Sahil almost quit playing and that he still spent so much time practicing. The beautiful music did not happen by accident and was the result of hard work. I decided that I would spend more time practicing because I wanted to be able to play well, and for the next six months, I worked as hard as I could on my music. I was pleased to find out that the harder I worked, the better I became.

Finally, I was ready to do something that I had dreamed about. Uncle Sahil and I were going to play a duet together at my piano recital. As we drove to the auditorium on the night of the recital, the stars winked encouragingly at me. I smiled back at them and felt proud of what I had accomplished.

**GO ON →**

**Now answer Numbers 1 through 5. Base your answers on "Becoming a Musician."**

**1** Who is the narrator of the passage?

(A) Kalinda

(B) Uncle Sahil

(C) Kalinda's father

(D) someone outside the story

**2** This question has two parts. First, answer part A. Then, answer part B.

**Part A:** Read the sentence from the passage.

The musical notes mocked me as I tried to read them and play at the same time, and my brain seemed unable to tell my fingers which keys to play next.

Which sentence **best** describes the meaning of the phrase "the musical notes mocked me"?

(A) The notes copy exactly what Kalinda does as she plays them.

(B) Kalinda's family laughs at her when she makes mistakes.

(C) The music sounds like laughter when Kalinda plays it.

(D) Kalinda has a difficult time playing the notes.

**Part B:** What does the phrase "the musical notes mocked me" suggest about Kalinda?

(A) She is in a silly mood because of the music.

(B) She is frustrated because the music is too hard.

(C) She is angry because she does not like the music.

(D) She is happy about playing a new piece of music.

**GO ON →**

**3** Select **two** words that describe how Kalinda feels when she learns about Uncle Sahil's experiences when he was younger.

(A) angry

(B) confused

(C) encouraged

(D) surprised

(E) thrilled

(F) worried

**4** Read the sentence from the text.

As we drove to the auditorium on the night of the recital, the stars winked encouragingly at me.

Why does the author make the stars seem human in the sentence?

(A) to compare the stars to blinking lights

(B) to suggest the stars can communicate with people

(C) to show that Kalinda feels positively about herself

(D) to explain why the light coming from stars seems to flash

**GO ON →**

**5** Read the sentence.

Hard work has its rewards.

The events in the passage help to send the message in the sentence above. Underline **one** sentence in the paragraphs below that **best** states this message.

This shocked me because I did not know that Uncle Sahil almost quit playing and that he still spent so much time practicing. The beautiful music did not happen by accident and was the result of hard work. I decided that I would spend more time practicing because I wanted to be able to play well, and for the next six months, I worked as hard as I could on my music. I was pleased to find out that the harder I worked, the better I became.

Finally, I was ready to do something that I had dreamed about. Uncle Sahil and I were going to play a duet together at my piano recital. As we drove to the auditorium on the night of the recital, the stars winked encouragingly at me. I smiled back at them and felt proud of what I had accomplished.

**GO ON →**

**Read the three poems before answering Numbers 6 through 10.**

# Morning

Canoes are dancing near the shore.

The sun is smiling down.

The morning is a gentle hand

That wipes away my frown.

# The Wind

The wind is cold and strong and cruel

It tells me just what I must do.

I wear my mittens and my hat.

Well, I ask, now, wouldn't you?

Unsatisfied, it gives a roar

Of great displeasure and demands

I put on more and more and more

By grabbing me with ice-cold hands.

And so I turn and back I go

To find a scarf and warmer socks.

It claims it must come in with me.

I keep it out with chains and locks.

**GO ON →**

# Autumn

The breezes kiss the treetops as they pass

And make the leaves fall softly to the ground.

The branches tremble slightly but no more;

A gentle sighing is their only sound.


The leaves invite me then to romp and play

Among their red and yellow colors bright.

I rake them all into a pile and jump,

Until the day is chased away by night.


I find it odd that autumn comes so late,

For one finds so much freshness every day.

The air is crisp and clear and full of hope.

"A new beginning now!" the breezes say.

**GO ON →**

**Now answer Numbers 6 through 11. Base your answers on the three poems.**

**6** In the poem "Morning," how does the speaker feel about the day ahead? Select **all** that apply.

(A) bored

(B) eager

(C) impatient

(D) nervous

(E) uncaring

(F) welcoming

**7** This question has two parts. First, answer part A. Then, answer part B.

**Part A:** Read the lines from the poem "The Wind."

The wind is cold and strong and cruel
It tells me just what I must do.
I wear my mittens and my hat.
Well, I ask, now, wouldn't you?

What comparison does the speaker make in these lines?

(A) The speaker compares the wind to himself.

(B) The speaker compares the wind to cold air.

(C) The speaker compares the wind to a person.

(D) The speaker compares the wind to mittens and a hat.

**Part B:** What does the description of the wind suggest about it?

(A) It is usually very helpful.

(B) It has the ability to react.

(C) It changes quickly and often.

(D) It can be tricked into doing something.

**GO ON →**

**8** This question has two parts. First, answer part A. Then, answer part B.

**Part A:** Which sentence **best** summarizes the speaker's point of view in the poem "The Wind"?

Ⓐ The wind is misunderstood.

Ⓑ The wind is a cruel bully.

Ⓒ The wind is mysterious.

Ⓓ The wind is full of life.

**Part B:** Which detail from the poem **best** supports your answer in part A?

Ⓐ The wind has ice-cold hands.

Ⓑ The wind makes a loud noise.

Ⓒ The wind tells the speaker what to do.

Ⓓ The wind tries to go inside with the speaker.

**9** Why does the speaker in the poem "Autumn" find it unusual that autumn comes so late?

Ⓐ It is a windy time of the year.

Ⓑ It is a time for staying outside.

Ⓒ It is a colorful time of the year.

Ⓓ It is a time for making a fresh start.

**GO ON →**

**10** Underline each line that includes an example of personification in the poem "Autumn."

**Autumn**

The breezes kiss the treetops as they pass
And make the leaves fall softly to the ground.
The branches tremble slightly but no more;
A gentle sighing is their only sound.

The leaves invite me then to romp and play
Among their red and yellow colors bright.
I rake them all into a pile and jump,
Until the day is chased away by night.

I find it odd that autumn comes so late,
For one finds so much freshness every day.
The air is crisp and clear and full of hope.
"A new beginning now!" the breezes say.

STOP

Name: _____ Date: _____

**Now answer Number 11. Base your answer on "Becoming a Musician" and the poems "Morning," "The Wind," and "Autumn."**

**11** Compare the points of view in the three poems. What is similar about them? What is different? Support your answer with details from all three poems.

_____

_____

_____

_____

_____

_____

_____

_____

_____

_____

_____

_____

_____

_____

_____

# Answer Key

| Question | Correct Answer | Content Focus | CCSS | Complexity |
|----------|---------------|---------------|------|------------|
| 1 | A | Point of View | RL.5.6 | DOK 2 |
| 2A | D | Personification | RL.5.4 | DOK 2 |
| 2B | B | Personification | RL.5.4 | DOK 2 |
| 3 | C, D | Point of View | RL.5.6 | DOK 2 |
| 4 | C | Personification | RL.5.4 | DOK 2 |
| 5 | see below | Theme | RL.5.2 | DOK 3 |
| 6 | B, F | Point of View | RL.5.6 | DOK 2 |
| 7A | C | Personification | RL.5.4 | DOK 2 |
| 7B | B | Personification | RL.5.4 | DOK 2 |
| 8A | B | Point of View | RL.5.6 | DOK 2 |
| 8B | C | Point of View/Text Evidence | RL.5.6/ RL.5.1 | DOK 2 |
| 9 | D | Point of View | RL.5.6 | DOK 2 |
| 10 | see below | Personification | RL.5.4 | DOK 2 |
| 11 | see below | Writing About Text | W.5.9a | DOK 4 |

| | | | |
|---|---|---|---|
| **Comprehension** 1, 3, 5, 6, 8A, 8B, 9 | | /12 | % |
| **Vocabulary** 2A, 2B, 4, 7A, 7B, 10 | | /8 | % |
| **Total Weekly Assessment Score** | | /20 | % |

**5** Students should underline the following sentence in the paragraphs:
  - I was pleased to find out that the harder I worked, the better I became.

**10** Students should underline the following lines in the poem "Autumn":
  - The breezes kiss the treetops as they pass
  - A gentle sighing is their only sound.
  - The leaves invite me then to romp and play
  - Until the day is chased away by night.
  - "A new beginning now!" the breezes say.

**11** To receive full credit for the response, the following information should be included: The points of view are alike in that all the speakers view elements of nature as if they were human, using personification throughout. For example, the sun smiles; the wind grabs; the breezes speak. The points of view are different in that the speakers have different feelings about their subjects. In the first and third poems, the speakers' points of view are positive and appreciative. The speaker says the morning wipes away his or her frown in the first poem. The speaker says that everything is fresh in the third poem. In the second poem, the speaker's point of view is that the wind is cold and cruel.